SOFTWARE ENGINEERING
NEW APPROACH

(Traditional and Agile Methodologies)

SOFTWARE ENGINEERING NEW APPROACH

(*Traditional and Agile Methodologies*)

Ramisetty Rajeswara Rao

Professor & HOD

Department of Computer Science & Engineering (CSE),

JNTUK-UCEV, Vizianagaram.

V. S. Narayana.Tinnaluri

Professor & HOD

School of Engineering,

Department of Computer Science and Engineering (CSE),

SANDIP University, Nashik.

and

Dabbu Murali

Professor & HOD

Department of Computer Science and Engineering (CSE)

Vemu Institute of Technology,

Tirupati, Andhra Pradesh.

BSP **BS Publications**

A unit of **BSP Books Pvt., Ltd.**

4-4-309/316, Giriraj Lane,

Sultan Bazar, Hyderabad - 500 095.

Software Engineering New Approach (Traditional and Agile Methodologies)

by Ramisetty Rajeswara Rao, V. S. Narayana Tinnaluri, Dabbu Murali

© 2018, by Publisher,

Published by:

BSP BS Publications

A unit of **BSP Books Pvt., Ltd.**
4-4-309/316, Giriraj Lane, Sultan Bazar,
Hyderabad - 500 095.
Phone : 040 - 23445688, 23445600
e-mail : info@bspbooks.net

ISBN: 978-93-8830-504-4 (Hardbound)

CONTENTS

Chapter 1

Introduction to Software Engineering

Chapter 2

Software Process and Life Cycle Models

Chapter 3

Software Life-Cycle Model-2

Chapter 4

Software Requirements

Chapter 5

Software Requirement Engineering Process

Chapter 6

Software Reliability

Chapter 7

Software Design

Chapter 8

Object Oriented Design

Chapter 9

Software Implementation

Chapter 10

Software Maintenance

Chapter 11

Software Testing Strategies

Chapter 12

Software Metrics

Chapter 13

Quality Management

Chapter 14

Software Project Management

Chapter 15

Agile Programming

Chapter 16

Extreme Programming

Chapter 17

Extreme Programming Practices

Chapter 18

XP Events

Chapter 19

Extreme Programming Artifacts

Chapter 20

Roles in Extreme Programming

Chapter 21

Coding XP Style

Chapter 22

Adopting XP

Chapter 23

Agile Modeling with XP

Chapter 24

Dynamic Systems Development Methodology (DSDM)

Chapter 25

XP Tools

PREFACE

This book explores the concepts of software engineering, as its importance grows in software community attempts to develop technologies that will make it easier, faster and less expensive to build high quality software products. Software Engineering is essential for understanding how to build good error free software at lesser price, in time and for evaluating the risks and opportunities that software presents in our everyday lives. Today, every sector of the economy depends on computers to a greater extent. Software is a key element of any computer-based system. Development of even a piece of software requires many activities to be performed and it is regarded as a project. Development of software requires a systematic approach. All the engineering aspects relating to software development have combined to evolve as a discipline called software engineering. After studying this subject, you will become familiar with the terminologies used in software engineering. You should be able to describe project life cycle models and analyze software development models. You should be able to define Agile programming and explain refactoring techniques. You should also be able to provide an overview of Extreme Programming (XP), XP events, and XP practices.

This book has been split into 25 chapters to cover the New Approach of Software Engineering.

- Authors

About the Authors

Dr. Ramisetty Rajeswara Rao is presently working as Professor & HOD in the Department of Computer Science & Engineering (CSE), JNTUK-UCEV, Vizianagaram. He completed his B.Tech in CSE in the year 1999 from V. R. Siddartha Engineering College, Vijayawada. M.Tech in CSE from JNTUH-Hyderabad in the year 2003, PhD in CSE from JNTUH-Hyderabad in the year 2010. Prior to joining in JNTUK-UCEV, he worked as Professor and HOD in Mahatma Gandhi Institute of Technology (MGIT), Hyderabad. He authored one monograph titled with "Automatic Text Independent Speaker Recognition using Source Feature" (Lap LABERT Publishing GmbH Co. KG, Germany) in the year 2012 and one Text-Book with titled "Cloud Computing and virtualization" (BS Publications) in the year 2014. Under his guidance, one student was awarded Ph.D from JNTUH, Hyderabad in the year 2015. After joining in JNTU service he has co-ordinated one 2-day National workshop and one week Faculty Development Program. He is resource person to UGC Academic Staff College to JNTUH, Hyderabad. To his credit he had published papers in ACM, ELSEVIER Springer and other reputed journals. 47 Journals, 27 conferences, 13 sessions chairs and gave 13 invited talks in various reputed colleges in Andhra Pradesh. He received VIDYA RATAN award from T.E.H.E.G, New Delhi for the year 2011. He is a Member of CSI and Sr. Member in IEEE. His Areas of Interest are Speech Processing, Pattern Recognition, NLP and Cloud Computing.

Dr. V. S. Narayana.Tinnaluri is presently working as Professor and HOD, in School of Engineering, Department of Computer Science and Engineering (CSE), SANDIP UNIVERSITY, Nashik. He has more than 18 years of rich Academic and Research experience. He was previously associated with other prestigious organizations, Professor and Director, School of Computer science and Engineering, Malla Reddy Engineering College for Women (MRECW), Hyderabad, Sikkim Manipal University as Professor & In-charge Academics (SPOC-DDE) and KL University as Associate Professor. He is also holding other vital positions like Academic Counselor for IGNOU and Paper Setter & Examiner for IPE, Osmania University, Hyderabad. He received Dr. TMA Pai Award "SPIRIT OF MANIPAL" 2015-16. He was awarded with MaGEX Certificate of Excellence in Academics, from Manipal Group of Educational Universities. He is also Board of Studies, Academic Council member in SANDIP UNIVERSITY, Nashik. He authored his credit; he had published papers in IEEE, Springer and other reputed journals. 34 International Journal publications, 16 conferences. He is a Member of IACSIT and ISTE, IAENG and, he is working as Editorial and Review Board member in several international Journals. His Areas of Interest are Software Engineering, Software Quality Testing, Data Structures, Relational Database Management, Cloud Computing, C Programming, Operating System, Compiler Designing, Object Oriented Programming through C plus plus and Java, Computer Networks and Wireless Sensor Networks.

D. Murali is presently working as Professor & HOD (CSE),Vemu Institute of Technology, Tirupati in Andhra Pradesh. He completed his B.Tech (CSE) in the year 2002 from Jawaharlal Nehuru Technological University, Hyderabad. M.Tech (CSE) from JNTU - Hyderabad in the year 2006, Ph.D in CSE from JNTU - Hyderabad in the year 2016. Prior to joining in Vemu

Institute of Technology, he worked as Professor in CSE in Malla Reddy Engineering College For Women, Hyderabad. He authored his credit he had published papers in Springer and other reputed journals. 14 Journals, 08 conferences. He is a Member of CSI and ISTE, IAENG. His Areas of Interest are Formal Language and Automata Theory, Digital Logic Design, C Programming and Data Structures, Operating System, Software Engineering, Compiler Designing, Data Mining and Data Warehousing.

Introduction to Software Engineering

Structure

1.1 INTRODUCTION

Software Engineering is essential for understanding how to build good error free software at lesser price, in time and for evaluating the risks and opportunities that software presents in our everyday lives. Today, every sector of the economy depends on computers to a greater extent. Software is a key element of any computer-based system. Development of even a piece of software requires many activities to be performed and it is regarded as a project. Development of software requires a systematic approach. All the engineering aspects relating to software development have combined together to evolve as a discipline called software engineering.

In this unit, we are going to study about what is software engineering, software engineering principles, their characteristics and applications. We will also learn about objectives of software engineering and phases of software engineering.

Objectives

After studying this unit, you should be able to:

- Define software engineering
- Discuss software engineering principles
- List software characteristics
- Discuss various kinds of software applications
- List the objectives of software engineering
- Explain phases of software engineering

1.2   BASICS OF SOFTWARE ENGINEERING

The term software engineering was first introduced in 1968 North Atlantic Treaty Organization (NATO) conference held in Germany. Software Engineering is an engineering discipline whose focus is the cost-effective development of high-quality software systems. It is a sub discipline of Computer Science that attempts to apply engineering principles to the creation, operation, modification and maintenance of the software components of various systems.

Software engineering is concerned with the practicalities of developing and delivering useful software. The cost of software engineering includes roughly 60% of development costs and 40% of testing costs. Structured approaches to software development include system models, notations, rules, design advice and process guidelines. Coping with increasing diversity, demands for reduced delivery times and developing trustworthy software are the key challenges facing Software Engineering.

What is an engineering?

Engineering is an application of well-understood scientific methods to the construction, operation, modification and maintenance of useful devices and systems.

What is software?

Software is not just the programs but also all associated documentation and configuration data that is needed to make the programs to operate correctly. A software system usually consists of a number of separate programs, configuration files which are used to set up the programs, system documentation which describe the structure of the system and user documentation which explains how to use the system and websites for users to download the information.

Systems

A system is a grouping of components that interact in some manner among themselves and possibly, with the world outside the system boundary.

We understand systems by decomposing them into:

Subsystems

System components

It is very difficult to separate the software components of a system from the other components of a system.

1.3   PRINCIPLES OF SOFTWARE ENGINEERING

Alan Davis (1994) is one of the earlier authorities to bring forward a set of principles that underlie software engineering. Below are some principles of software engineering:

- **Give products to customers early**: In this principle, it is very difficult to completely understand and capture the user's needs during the requirement phase; thus it is more effective to give the users a prototype of the product, then gather the feedback and then go into full-scale development of the product.

- **Determine the problem before writing the requirements**: In this principle, before the software engineering rush to offer the solution, ensure that the problem is well understood. Then explore the potential solution and various alternatives.
- **Evaluate design alternatives**: In this principle, after the requirements are understood and agreed upon, explore a variety of design architecture and related algorithms. Ensure that the selected design and algorithms are the best match to satisfy the goals of the requirement.
- **Use an appropriate process model**: In this principle, since there is no universal process model that applies to all projects, each project must select a process that best fits the project based on parameters such as corporate culture, project circumstances, user expectations, requirements volatility and resource experiences.
- **Put technique before tools**: In this principle, before using the tools, the technique needs to be well understood. Otherwise, the tool just rushes us into performing the wrong thing faster.
- **Get it right before you make it faster**: In this principle, it is essential to make the software execute correctly first and then work on improving it. Don't worry about optimization for either execution speed or code during initial coding.
- **Inspect code**: In this principle, inspection as first proposed by IBM's Mike Fagan is a much better way to find errors. Some early data in inspection showed a reduction of 50% to 90% of the time-to-test.
- **Good management is more important than good technology**: In this principle, a good manager can produce extraordinary results even with limited resources.
- **People are the key to success**: In this principle, software is a labor-intensive profession and people with experience, talent and appropriate drive are the key. The right people can overcome many of the shortcomings in process, methodology or tools. There is no substitute for quality people.
- **Follow with care**: In this principle, be careful in adopting tools, process, methodology and so on. Do not follow just because someone else is doing it or using it. Run some experiments before making a major commitment.
- **Take responsibility**: In this principle, if you developed the system, then you should take responsibility to do it right. Blaming the failure or the problem on others, on the schedule or on the process is irresponsible.

1.4 SOFTWARE CHARACTERISTICS

Software is logical rather than a physical system element. Hence software has different characteristics than that of hardware:

(a) Software is not manufactured as in the traditional sense rather it engineered and developed.
(b) Software don't "wear down".
(c) Although the industry is moving toward component-based assembly, most software continues to be custom built.

1.5 SOFTWARE APPLICATIONS

Software may be applied in any situation for which a prespecified set of procedural steps that has been defined. Content and determinacy are important factors in determining the nature of a software application. Content refers to the information. Software that controls an automated machine accepts discrete data items with limited structure and produces individual machine commands in rapid succession.

Information determinacy refers to the predictability of the order and timing of information. An engineering analysis program accepts data that have a predefined order, executes the analysis algorithm without interruption and produces resultant data in report or graphical format. Such applications are determinate.

A multi-user operating system, accepts inputs that have varied content and arbitrary timing, executes algorithms that can be interrupted by external conditions, and produces output that varies as a function of environment and time. Applications with these characteristics are indeterminate.

Software applications can be compartmentalized into different categories:

System software: System software is a collection of programs written to service other programs. Some system software process complex information structures. Other systems applications process largely indeterminate data. It is characterized by heavy interaction with hardware, heavy usage by multiple users, concurrent operation that requires scheduling, resource sharing, and sophisticated process management, complex data structures and multiple external interfaces.

Real time software: Software that checks, evaluates, and manages real time events in the world as and when they occur.

Business Software: Business information processing is one of the major application area. Distinct applications like payroll, accounts accept/dispatch have transformed into Management Information Systems (MIS) software gets the business information by connecting few to many databases. Software helps to streamline existing data, such that it assists business development and decision making in an organization.

Engineering and scientific software: This software involves typically large number of arithmetic and floating point operations. Applications range from automotive stress analysis to automated manufacturing, Artificial intelligence to Data mining, whether forecast to critical applications like where human intervention is impossible.

Embedded software: This software is loaded merely into primary memory and used to manage systems and products for industrial and consumer markets. This software can provide partial control and capability with necessary functions.

Personal computer software: Day to day useful applications like word processing, spreadsheets, multimedia, database management, personal and business financial applications are some of the common examples for personal computer software.

Web-Based Software: This is the innovative approach of commercial software which can be accessed by a web browser through web pages. In core the internet becomes a huge computer system providing an unlimited software resource that can be accessed by anybody with their modem connected to the internet or wireless connection to the internet.

Artificial intelligence software: Artificial Intelligence software makes use of non-numerical algorithms to solve complex problems that are not amenable to computation or straightforward analysis. Knowledge based expert systems, robotics, optical character recognition, automatic speech recognition and personal identification systems are the various examples of applications within this category.

Software crisis: The set of problems that are encountered in the development of computer software is not limited to software that does not function properly rather the affliction encompasses problems associated with how we develop software, how we support a growing volume of existing software, and how we can expect to keep pace with a growing demand for more software.

1.6   OBJECTIVES OF SOFTWARE ENGINEERING

The software engineering is to develop high quality software, timely, within the budget and under the software production constraints. Below are some of the basic objectives of software engineering:

- **Maintainability** – The ease with which changes in a functional unit can be performed in order to meet prescribed requirements.
- **Correctness** – The extent to which software meets its specified requirements
- **Reuseability** - The extent to which a module can be used in multiple applications.
- **Testability** – The extent to which software facilities both the establishment of test criteria and the evaluation of the software with respect to those criteria.
- **Reliability** – An attribute of software quality. The extent to which a program can be expected to perform its intended function, over an arbitrary time period.
- **Portability** - The ease with which software can be transferred from one computer system or environment to another.
- **Adaptability** – The ease with which the software allows differing system constraints and user needs to be satisfied by making changes to the software.

1.7   PHASES OF SOFTWARE ENGINEERING

In the engineering domain, developing a solution to a given problem involves a sequence of interconnected steps, whether building a bridge or making an electronic component. These steps or phases occur in software development as well. The series of steps involved in developing the product is called the Software Development Life Cycle (SDLC). There are seven phases or stages in SDLC, which are discussed below:

- Analysis phase
- Design phase

- Development phase
- Testing phase
- Implementation phase
- Maintenance phase
- End-of-life phase/Retirement phase

Analysis phase

In this phase, the development team analyzes the problem in an existing application or finds new ideas for an application. After identifying the idea, the development team needs to determine the scope of the problem. After identifying the scope, the development team can easily identify the essential components necessary for the product development. The important thing for software development is the system requirement. The system requirement differs based on the software product. The development team should carefully analyze the requirements needed for the product development.

Design phase

This is an important phase in the product life cycle. In this phase, the development team designs the individual components and creates the blue prints. The analysis done in the analysis phase helps to create the design documents. Designs such as database design, functional specification design, and document design take place in this phase. The design needs to be done carefully because the development phase depends upon the design created during the design phase. If the design prepared is well structured, it reduces the time taken in the upcoming stages of the product life cycle.

Development phase

In this phase, the actual development of the product takes place according to the blue print created in the design phase. The team members start writing code for the product. The product is divided into different modules and each member is allotted a separate module to develop the product. The code is written based on the chosen technology. Generation of code takes place after the code is developed. The code is executed after it is generated.

Testing phase

It is essential to test each and every product before it is launched in the market. We must test the developed product to ensure that it meets the specifications stated in the design phase. In this phase, the developed product is tested and reports are prepared. The report describes the errors in the developed products. There are different methods for testing the developed product. Black box testing, unit testing, system testing and many more methods are used for testing the product. After this phase, the life cycle again moves to the development phase to correct the errors identified in this phase. After correcting the errors, the product is again tested. This process continues till the product is found to be error-free. There are some tools available to test the developed product. We can use these tools to test a product and identify the defects. These tools are used to make the testing easy and to get an error-free product.

The test scenarios are written by the testers to check the testing needs of software application. The test scenario drives the test cases which are related to the requirements and designs. Depending upon the type of requirement and design, the test scenarios are addressed as functional and structural. The test scenario should be feasible, clear, complete, and cover all requirements. The test scenario and the test case should be prioritized as per the requirements.

After completing the product testing, versions of completed product are supplied to the clients for testing onsite. The first version is the alpha release and the corrected version is the beta release. Usually the final version is the beta release.

Implementation phase

This is known as First Customer Ship (FCS) in software industry. After the development and testing phase the product moves to the implementation stage. In this phase, the product is taken to the end users.

Maintenance phase

The software maintenance phase is the longest phase in the software life cycle. This phase is distinguished in terms of costs. About 90% of the total life cycle cost of the software is consumed in the maintenance stage. The software maintenance activity is classified into four types. They are perfective, adaptive, corrective and preventive. The maintenance of the software is not performed by the person who creates the product. In this phase, the problems raised by the customers after releasing the product are rectified. The testing team tests the product again and rectifies the errors that are raised by the customers.

End-of-life phase/Retirement phase

The final phase of the life cycle is the retirement phase. This phase is reached after many years of service. In this phase, the product is replaced with a newer version that has enhanced features. Thus, the old product's life cycle comes to an end. This is the end phase for the old product.

1.8   SUMMARY

- Software Engineering is an engineering discipline whose focus is the cost-effective development of high-quality software systems.
- Engineering is an application of well-understood scientific methods to the construction, operation, modification and maintenance of useful devices and systems.
- The principles of software engineering are: give products to customers early, determine the problem before writing the requirements, evaluate design alternatives, use an appropriate process model, put technique before tools, get it right before you make it faster, inspect code, good management is more important than good technology, people are the key to success, follow with care and take responsibility.
- Software is a logical rather than a physical system element.

- Software applications can be compartmentalized into different categories like system software, real time software, business software, engineering and scientific software, embedded software, personal computer software, web-based software, artificial intelligence software, software crisis.
- Objectives of software engineering are maintainability, correctness, reuseability, testability, reliability, portability and adaptability.
- The series of steps involved in developing the product is called the Software Development Life Cycle (SDLC). There are seven phases or stages in SDLC: Analysis phase, Design phase, Development phase, Testing phase, Implementation phase, Maintenance phase and End of life stage.

Software Process and Life Cycle Models

2.1 INTRODUCTION

In the previous unit you have studied the basics of software engineering. A group of software engineers or an engineer in industrial site to resolve a real problem have to integrate a development approach; it includes the process, techniques, layers, tools and standard stages. This approach is frequently referred to as software engineering process or software engineering model.

In production of the Software the centre of attention is on actions directly linked to software development process. Example would be testing, coding, design and maintenance. Every process model identifies a set of activities and they should be executed in the same order advised in the respective model.

In this unit we will study about software process, project and product. We will also study process assessment, software process capability maturity model and various life cycle models like waterfall model, incremental model, and spiral model.

Objectives

After studying this unit, you should be able to:

- Discuss software process, project and product
- Describe capability maturity model
- List and explain various life cycle models

2.2   SOFTWARE PROCESS, PROJECT AND PRODUCT

Software engineering comprises interrelated and recurring entities, which are essential for software development. A software is developed efficiently and effectively with the help of well-defined activities or processes. A process is a sequence of steps involving activities and resources, which produces the desired output.

The following points are noted about software processes:

- Processes use resources subject to given constraints, and produce intermediate and final products.

- Processes are composed of sub-processes that are organized in such a manner that each sub-process has its own process model.

- Each process is carried out with an entry and exit criteria that help in monitoring the beginning and completion of the activity.

- Every process includes guidelines, which explains the objectives of each activity.

- Processes are vital because they impose uniformity on the set of activities.

- A process is regarded as more than just a procedure, tools and techniques, which are collectively used in a structured manner to produce a product.

- Software processes include various technical and managerial issues, which are required to develop a software.

The characteristics of a software process is shown in table 2.1.

Table 2.1 Characteristics of a Software Process

Characteristics	Description
Comprehensibility	The extent to which the process is explicitly defined and the ease with which the process definition is understood.
Visibility	Whether the process activities culminate in clear results or not, so that the progress of the process is visible externally.
Supportability	The extent to which CASE tools can support the process activities.
Acceptability	The extent to which the defined process is acceptable and usable by the engineers responsible for creating the software product.
Reliability	The manner in which the process is designed so that errors in the process are avoided or trapped before they result in errors in the product.
Robustness	Whether or not the process can continue in spite of unexpected problems.
Maintainability	Whether the process can evolve to reflect the changing organizational requirements or identify process improvements.
Rapidity	The speed with which the complete software can be delivered with given specifications.

A project is defined as a specification essential for developing or maintaining a specific product. A software project is developed when software processes or activities are executed for certain specific requirements of the user. Thus, by using a software process, a software project can be easily developed. The activities in a software project comprise various tasks for managing resources and developing products. Figure 2.1 shows that a software project involves people (developers, project managers, end users and so on) also referred to as participants who use software processes to create a product according to user requirements. The participants play a major role in the development of the project and select the appropriate process for the project. In addition, a project is efficient if it is developed within the time constraint. The outcome or the result of a software project is known as a product. Thus, a software project uses software processes to create a product.

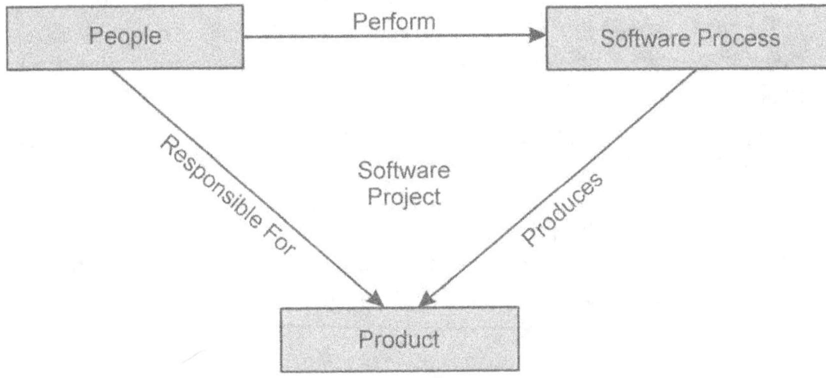

Figure 2.1 Software Project

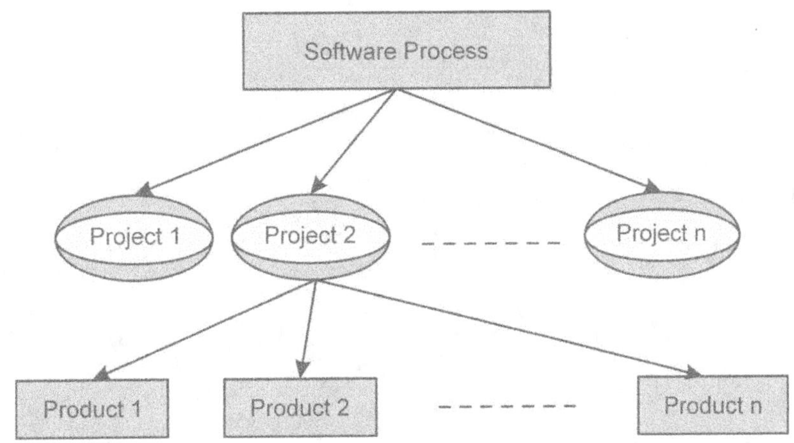

Figure 2.2 Processes, Projects and Products

A software process can consist of many software projects, each of which can produce one or more software products. The interrelationship among these three entities (process, project and product) is shown in figure 2.2. A software project begins with requirements and ends with the accomplishment of the requirements. Thus, a software process should be performed to develop the final software by accomplishing user requirements. Software processes are not specific to the software project.

2.3   PROCESS ASSESSMENT

Within a process improvement context, process assessment provides the means of characterizing the current practice within an organizational unit in terms of the capability of the selected processes. Analysis of the results in the light of the organization's business needs identifies strengths, weakness and risks inherent in the processes. This, in turn leads to the ability to determine whether the processes are effective in achieving their goals and to identify significant causes of poor quality or overruns in time or cost. These provide the drivers for prioritizing improvements to processes.

Process capability determination is concerned with analysing the proposed capability of selected processes against a target process capability profile in order to identify the risks involved in undertaking a project using the selected processes. The proposed capability may be based on the results of relevant previous process assessments or may be based on an assessment carried out for the purpose of establishing the proposed capability. Figure 2.3 shows a process assessment.

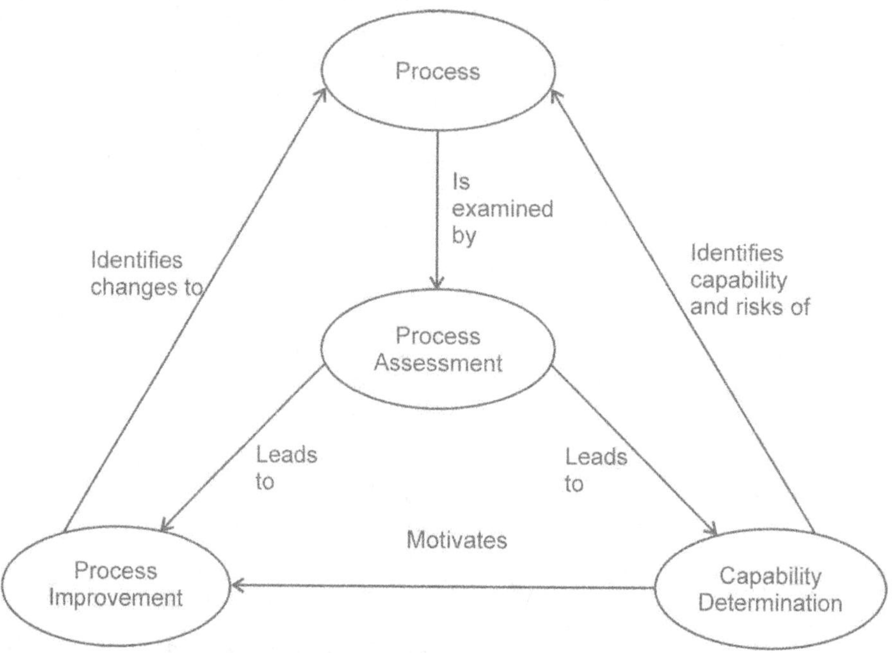

Figure 2.3 Process Assessment

ISO/IEC 15504-2 defines a reference model of processes and process capability that forms the basis for any model to be used for the purposes of process assessment. The reference model comprises a two-dimensional approach to the evaluation of process capability - one dimension defines the processes to be assessed, the other describes the scale for measurement of capability. Any model(s) compatible with the reference model may be used for assessment, and the results of any conformant assessments will be able to be translated into a common base. Each process in the reference model is described by a statement of the purpose of the process, which includes an outline of the intended outcomes of process implementation.

2.4   SOFTWARE PROCESS CAPABILITY MATURITY MODEL

The Capability Maturity Model (CMM) is a standard model used for depicting and measuring the maturity of a software company's development process. It was developed by the software development community along with the Software Engineering Institute (SEI) and Carnegie Mellon University under the direction of United States Department of Defense.

CMM defines five levels (Level 1: Initial, Level 2: Repeatable, Level 3: Defined, Level 4: Managed Level and 5: Optimizing) for process mapping and implementation. These levels represent a model that explains the process maturity of an organization and analyzes the current state of process maturity of an organization. Organizations make use of these levels to assess their maturity levels before moving to the next level. This flexibility to slowly strive towards high process maturity helps these organizations to easily adopt process related changes. They can go from the first level to the fifth level over a period.

CMM is meant for software development organizations. It caters to the field of software engineering, system engineering, project management, software maintenance, risk management, system acquisition, Information Technology (IT), and personnel management.

The widely used and preferred software method of evaluation is CMM. Five quality levels that range from CMM1 to CMM5 are involved in the development of software operating measures. CMM contains various levels and structures. Figure 2.4 shows a structure and components of CMM.

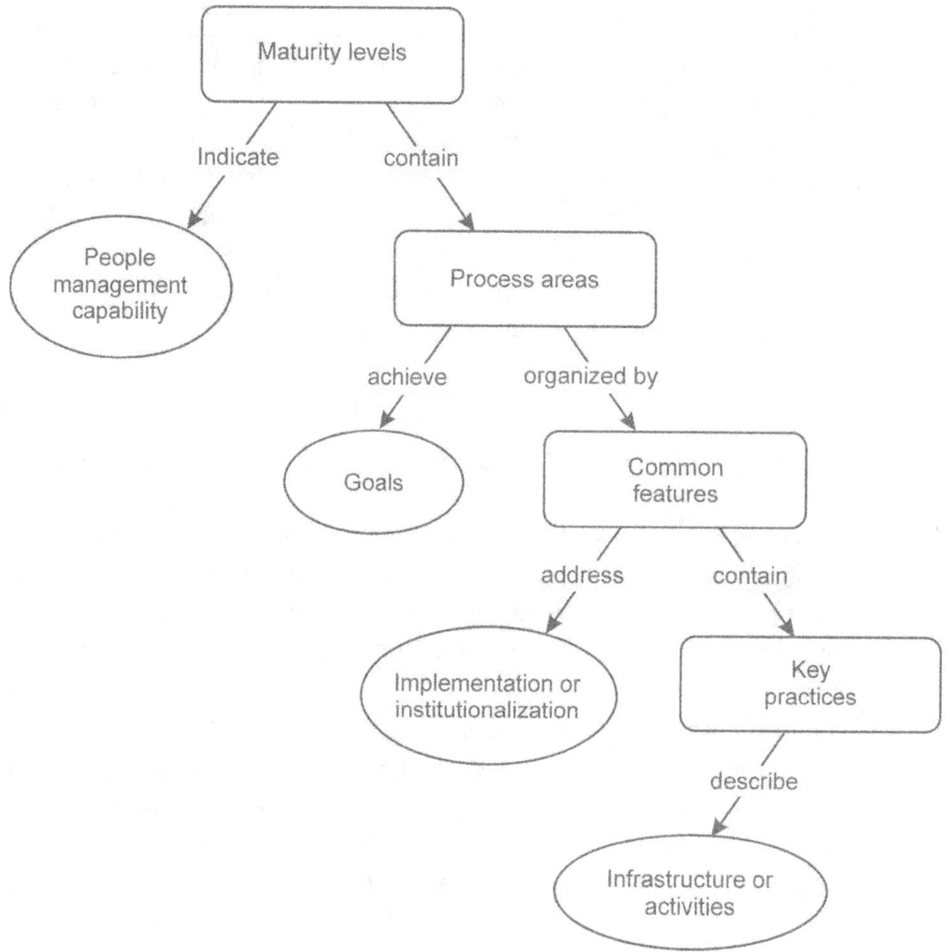

Figure 2.4 Structure and Components of CMM

As depicted in figure 2.4, the main components of CMM are:

- **Maturity levels:** It is the level of process capability an organization possesses. CMM has five maturity levels. The top level is systematically managed by an organization of process optimization, while the initial level is characterized by ad-hoc processes.

- **Process areas:** It is a group of associated activities to attain a set of goals. It also sets up a process capability at the maturity level, example, software project delivery planning.

- **Goals:** It reviews the essential practices of a process area and tells whether a project or an organization has been successful in implementing the process area. The goal also points to the importance and the purpose of each process area.

- **Common features:** These features are the characteristics that determine whether the implementation of the key process area is successful and permanent.

- **Key practices:** It describes the infrastructure and performance of the application of a process. For example, the software delivery schedule plan of a project is designed according to a documented procedure.

2.5   SOFTWARE DEVELOPMENT LIFE CYCLE MODELS

In unit 1, we have discussed phases of software engineering. Organizations make use of various phases of software engineering in their projects. In this section, we will discuss various software development life cycle models. The software development life cycle (SDLC) is a framework defining tasks performed at each step in the software development process. The software development life cycle has many activities involved to make the project successful. The activities are – requirement analysis, design, coding, testing, deployment, maintenance and enhancement. Frequently project teams adopt a life cycle model for their projects. Figure 2.5 shows a software development life cycle model.

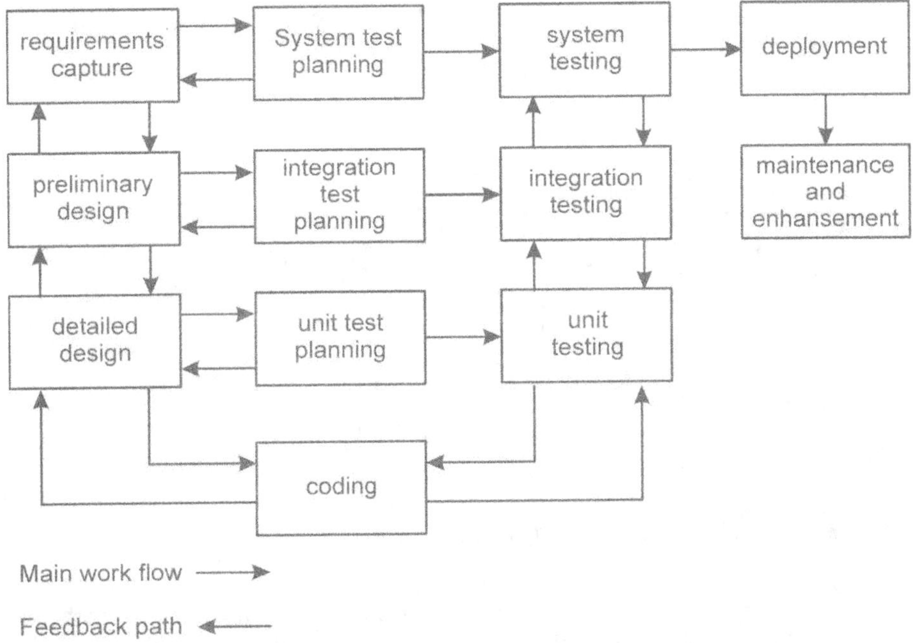

Figure 2.5 Software Development Life Cycle Model

Let us now discuss in detail the life cycle model of a software development project. The software development life cycle model consists of a series of work flows involved in the life cycle. Each step in the work flow performs some activity. The initial stage of the cycle is the requirement analysis stage. In this stage, the requirements necessary for the project is identified. The next stage is the design stage. In this stage, the project design is done. After the design stage, the coding stage begins and this is the development stage. After development, testing is done and it moves to the deployment stage. Final stage is the maintenance and enhancement of the project. There are many types of life cycle models. Each company follows a different life cycle model to develop their project. Some life cycle models used in software development are:

- Waterfall Model
- Spiral Model
- Incremental Model

Let us now discuss in detail these life cycle models.

2.5.1 WATERFALL MODEL

The waterfall model is a common life cycle model. It is also known as linear-sequential life cycle model. This life cycle is simple and easy to understand. Each phase in this model commences only if the previous phase has entirely completed. This life cycle model is used where the requirements are clearly known. If the software development tool is well known, then the waterfall life cycle model is used. Figure 2.6 shows a waterfall life cycle model.

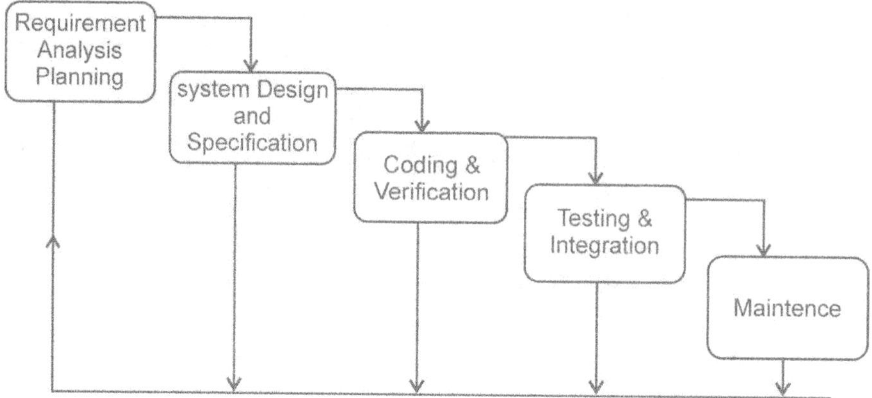

Figure 2.6 Waterfall Life Cycle Model

As shown in figure 2.6, the project begins with the requirement analysis planning. The project planning is done in this phase. After completing the requirement analysis, the design of the project begins. Once the design is completed, coding of the project begins. After completing the coding, the code is integrated and testing is done. The system is installed after the testing is completed. The final phase of the life cycle is the operation and maintenance of the system.

The advantages and disadvantages of waterfall life cycle model are:

Advantages

- This model is very simple and easy to use.

- Easy to manage because each phase has specific deliverables and review process.
- Suitable for small projects where requirements are known clearly.
- The phases are processed and completed one at a time.

Disadvantages

- The scope is adjusted during the life cycle which can adversely impact the project.
- The risk in this model is very high.
- This model is not suitable for long-term projects.
- The software is developed at the later stage of the life cycle.

2.5.2   SPIRAL MODEL

The spiral model is applicable to projects where new technologies are used. The spiral model mainly focuses on risk analysis. The spiral life cycle model has four phases. They are - planning, risk analysis, engineering and evaluation. Software projects repeatedly pass through all these phases in iterations. The project life cycle moves in a spiral in this model. The baseline spiral starts in the planning phase and ends at the evaluation phase.

Figure 2.7 shows a spiral life cycle model.

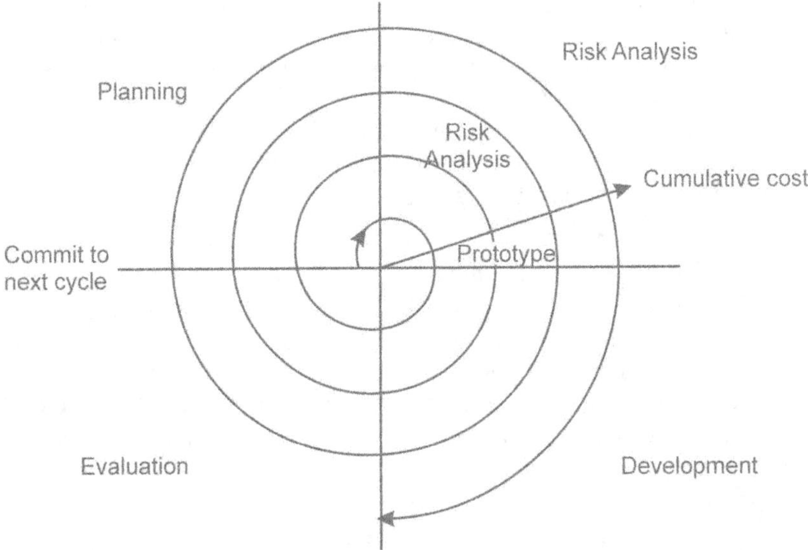

Figure 2.7 Spiral Life Cycle Model

As shown in figure 2.7, the software project passes through all the phases in the life cycle. Each phase has some specific activity to perform. The requirements for the project are gathered in the planning phase. The risks and alternative solutions are identified in the risk analysis phase. At the end of the risk analysis phase, a prototype is produced. In the engineering phase, the software is developed and the testing is done at the end of this phase. In the evaluation phase the customer evaluates the project before it continues to the next spiral.

The advantages and disadvantages of the spiral model life cycle are:

Advantages

- Risk analysis is too high in this life cycle model.
- Used for large and critical projects.
- Software is developed in the early stage of the life cycle.

Disadvantages

- This model is costly to use.
- Success of the project depends on the risk analysis phase.
- Not suitable for small projects.

2.5.3 INCREMENTAL MODEL

The incremental model has same phases that are in waterfall model. But it is iterative in nature. The incremental model has various phases like analysis, design, coding and testing. The incremental model delivers series of releases to the customer. These releases are called increments. More and more functionality is associated with each increment. The first increment is called core product. In this release the basic requirements are implements and then in subsequent increments new requirements are added. The word processing software package can be considered as an example of incremental model. In the first increment only the document processing facilities are available. In the second increment, more sophisticated document producing and processing facilities, file management functionalities are given. In the next increment spelling and grammar checking facilities can be given. Thus, in incremental model progressive functionalities are obtained with each release. Figure 2.8 shows an incremental life cycle model.

Advantages

1. The incremental model can be adopted when there are less number of people involved in the project.
2. With each increment technical risks can be managed.
3. For a very small time span, at least core product can be delivered to the customer.
4. Early feedback is generated, because implementation occurs rapidly for a small sub-set of the software.

Disadvantages

1. At the management and technical level planning is required.
2. It becomes invalid when clients does not accept phased deliverables.

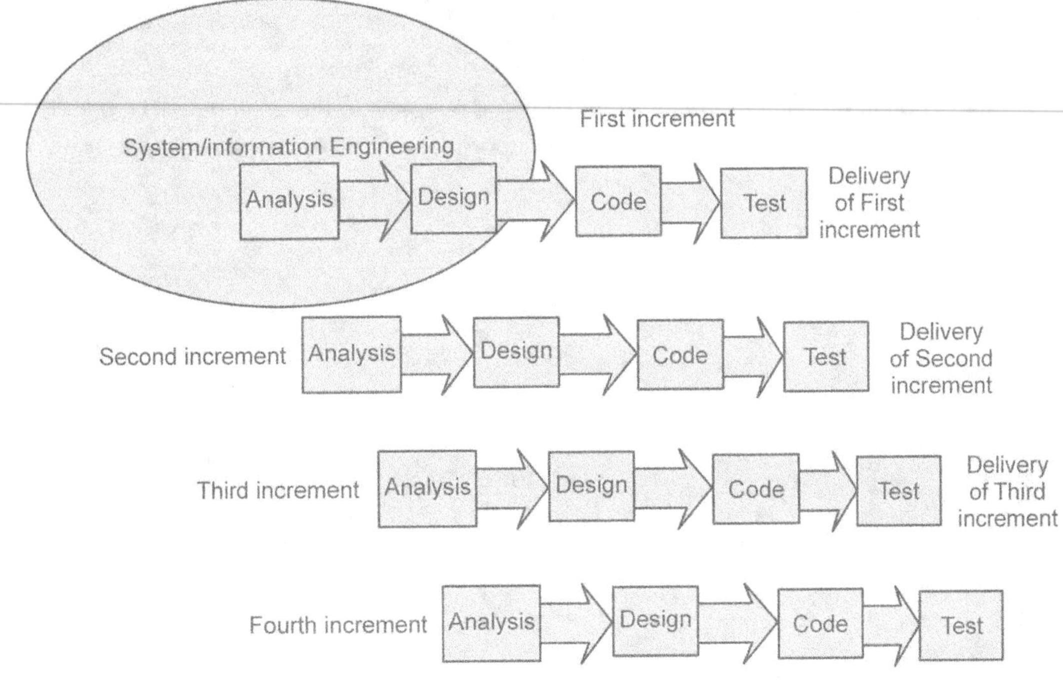

Fig. 2.8 Incremental Life Cycle Model

2.6   SUMMARY

- A process is a sequence of steps involving activities and resources, which produces the desired output.
- A project is defined as a specification essential for developing or maintaining a specific product.
- The outcome or the result of a software project is known as a product.
- Process assessment provides the means of characterizing the current practice within an organizational unit in terms of the capability of the selected processes.
- The Capability Maturity Model (CMM) is a standard model used for depicting and measuring the maturity of a software company's development process.
- The software development project life cycle has many activities involved to make the project successful. The activities are – requirement analysis, design, coding, testing, deployment, maintenance and enhancement. Some life cycle models used in software development are: Waterfall Model, Spiral Model and Incremental Model.

- Waterfall life cycle model is used where the requirements are clearly known.

- The spiral model mainly focuses on risk analysis.

- The incremental model delivers series of releases to the customer. These releases are called increments. More and more functionality is associated with each increment.

3 Software Life-Cycle Model-2

Structure

3.1 INTRODUCTION

In unit 2 we have discussed some of the life cycle models like waterfall model, spiral model and incremental model. Software development projects are often very large projects. A number of people work on such a project for a very long time and therefore the whole process needs to be controlled, progress needs to be monitored, people and resources need to be allocated at the right point in time. Hence, some software life models are used for development of quality software product.

In this unit we will discuss some more life cycle models such as prototyping model, object-oriented model, agile model and extreme programming.

Objectives

After studying this unit, you should be able to:

- Discuss prototyping model
- Explain object-oriented model
- Describe agile model and rapid application development model
- List the advantages and disadvantages of iterative enhancement model
- Discuss V-Model
- List the parameters of extreme programming

3.2 PROTOTYPING MODEL

In prototyping model initially the requirement gathering is done. Developer and customer define overall objectives, identify areas which needs more requirement gathering. Then a quick design is prepared. This quick design represents what will be visible to use-in input and output format. From the quick design a prototype is prepared. Customer or user evaluates the prototype in order to refine the requirements. Iteratively prototype is tuned for satisfying customer requirements. Thus prototype is important to identify the software requirements. When working prototype is built, developer use existing program fragments or program generators to throw away the prototype and rebuild the system to high quality. Certain classes of mathematical algorithms, subset of command driven systems and other applications results can be easily examined without real time interaction and can be developed using prototyping paradigm. Figure 3.1 shows a prototyping model.

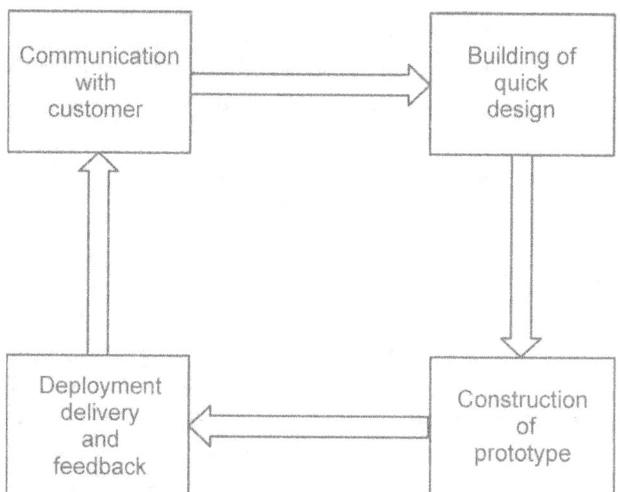

Figure 3.1 Prototyping Model

The advantages and disadvantages of prototyping model are:

Advantages

1. In this methodology a working model of the system is provided, the users get a better understanding of the system being developed.
2. Errors can be detected much earlier.
3. Quick user feedback is available leading to better solutions.

Disadvantages

1. In the first version itself, customer often wants "few fixes" rather than rebuilding of the system. Whereas rebuilding of new system maintains high level of quality.
2. Sometimes developer may make implementation compromises to get prototype working quickly.

3.3   OBJECT–ORIENTED MODEL

The object-oriented approach improves the transitions between the different phases in the software life cycle by using the class concept as the basic unit in all different phases. Classes are initially identified in the problem domain along with their possible interactions in terms of inheritance, aggregation and association relationships. The result of the analysis phase become the inputs to the systems high-level design phase.

The phases in object-oriented development are similar to those in traditional development approaches which includes analysis, system design, detailed design, implementation, testing and maintenance.

Although the phases are very similar to those used in earlier approaches, the activities performed in all the phases of object-oriented development deal with classes, objects and their interactions. Also the phases are not usually performed in a sequential manner.

The activities in each phase are performed iteratively. For example, some parts of the analysis phase may be performed before system design, in contrast, other parts of the analysis phase may be done concurrently with design and even implementation.

Whereas the focus of the analysis phase is mainly problem centered, the system design phase brings in certain practical considerations related to developing an actual computer system. One important example of such a practical consideration deals with user interfaces. Also, unlike the analysis phase, which concentrates primarily on what aspects are to be included in the system, the system design focuses on how these aspects are to be implemented. The main purpose of the design phase is to derive the system structure for the given problem. Moreover, the entire system may be decomposed into subsystems. A subsystem consists of a set of interacting classes that closely cooperate to deliver some portion of the functionality that the system must deliver.

The high-level architecture generated in the system design phase is "fleshed out" during the detailed design phase, the focus is primarily on class design. In this phase, several new classes may appear. These classes are often low-level classes that support the high level classes identified in the problem domain and the interfaces specified in the high-level design. Some new classes may be developed from scratch. However the preferred situation is to reuse existing classes whenever possible. These reusable classes could be found in existing application libraries or class libraries associated with a particular language environment. Another possibility is to use an existing class and specialize it to fulfill the current needs.

The implementation phase uses the results of the detailed design phase to produce the code for the desired system. The detailed design artifact may need to be modified or adapted to the particular object-oriented programming language used.

Compared with traditional development approaches, an object-oriented approach places more emphasis and effort on the analysis and design phase, less emphasis on the testing and implementation phases, and much less effort on maintenance.

3.4 AGILE MODEL

Agile methodology is described as "iterative" and "incremental." In waterfall, development teams have only one chance to get each phase of a project. In an agile methodology, every phase of development that is requirements, design, and so on is continually revisited. Agile Method breaks the product into small incremental builds. These builds are provided in iterations. Each iteration is about one to three months. The team's work cycle is limited to three months and the team re-evaluates project. This "inspect-and-adapt" approach to development greatly reduces development costs and time to market.

In Agile methodology teams can develop software at the same time they are gathering requirements. Agile development helps companies build the right product. Agile allows teams to continuously replan their release to optimize its value throughout development, allowing them to be as competitive as possible in the marketplace.Every iteration involves teams working simultaneously on various areas like planning, requirements analysis, coding, and testing. At the end of the iteration a working product is delivered to the customer. Figure 3.2 shows an agile model.

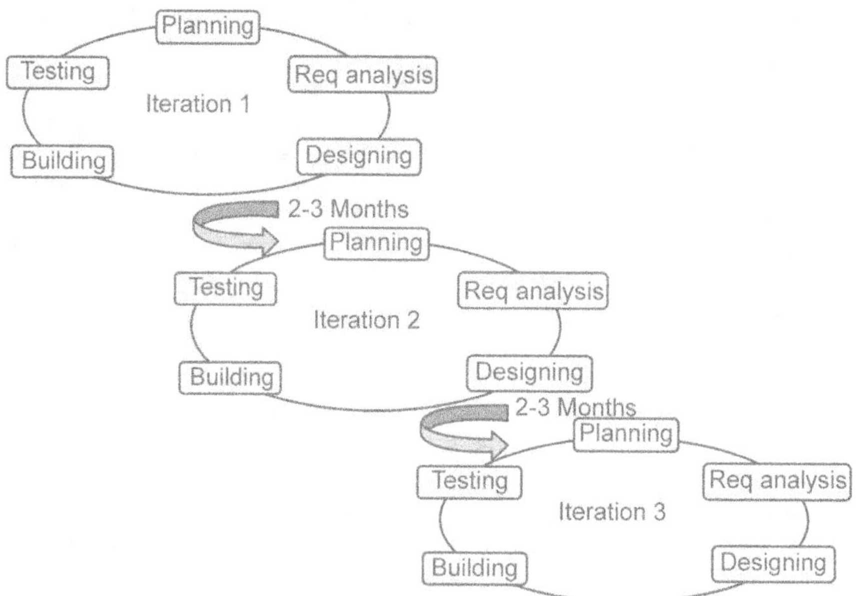

Figure 3.2 Agile Model

The advantages and disadvantages of agile model are:

Advantages

- This model is very simple and easy to use.
- Easy to manage because this model breaks the product in to small modules.
- Suitable for fixed or changing requirements.
- Resource requirements are minimum.
- Enables concurrent development.

Disadvantages

- This model is not suitable for handling complex dependencies.
- Depends heavily on customer interaction, so if customer is not clear, team can be driven in the wrong direction.
- More risk of sustainability, maintainability and extensibility.

3.5   RAPID APPLICATION DEVELOPMENT MODEL

Rapid Application Development (RAD) model is an incremental software development process model that emphasizes an extremely short development cycle. The RAD model is a high speed adaptation of the linear sequential model in which the rapid development is achieved by using component-based construction. If requirements are clear and well understood and the project scope is constrained, the RAD process enables a development team to create a fully functional system within a very short period. Figure 3.3 shows a Rapid Application Development model.

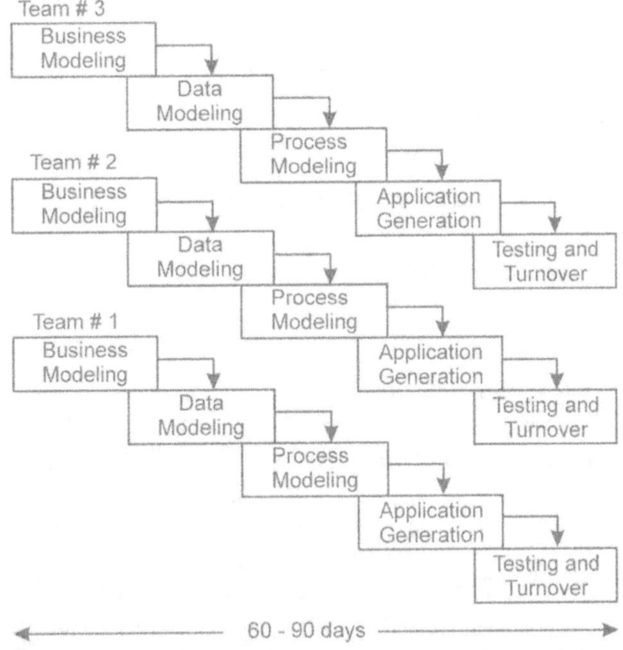

Figure 3.3 Rapid Application Development Model

The Rapid Application Development approach encompasses the following phases:

Business modeling

Here we try to find answers to questions like what information drives the business process. What information is generated? Who generates it? Where does the information go? Who processes it? Etc.

Data modeling

Here the information flow which would have been defined as part of the business modeling phase is refined into a set of data objects that are needed to support the business.

Process modeling

The data objects defined in the data modeling phase are transformed to achieve the information flow necessary to implement a business function. Processing descriptions are created for adding, modifying, deleting, or retrieving a data object.

Application generation

RAD assumes the use of fourth generation techniques. Rather than creating software using conventional third generation programming languages the RAD process works to reuse existing program components (when possible) or create reusable components (when necessary). In all cases, automated tools are used to facilitate construction of the software.

Testing and turnover

Since the RAD process emphasizes reuse, many of the program components have already been tested. This reduces overall testing time. However, new components must be tested and all interfaces must be fully exercised.

The advantages and disadvantages of Rapid Application Development model are:

Advantages

1. RAD generally incorporates short development cycles - users see the RAD product quickly.
2. Flexible and adaptable to changes.
3. RAD realizes an overall reduction in project risk.

Disadvantages

1. Cannot use for small projects.
2. Requires more resources and money to implement RAD.
3. RAD requires developers and customers who are committed to the rapid-fire activities necessary to get a system complete in a much abbreviated time frame. If commitment is lacking from either, RAD projects will fail.
4. Not all types of applications are appropriate for RAD. If a system cannot be properly modularized, building the components necessary for RAD will be problematic. If high performance is an issue and performance is to be achieved through tuning the interfaces to system components, the RAD approach may not work.
5. RAD is not appropriate when technical risks are high (for example, when a new application makes a heavy use of new technology).

3.6 ITERATIVE ENHANCEMENT MODEL

The iterative enhancement model combines elements of the linear sequential model (applied repetitively) with the iterative philosophy of prototyping. In this model, the software is broken down into several modules, which are incrementally developed and delivered. First, the development team develops the core module of the system and then it is later refined into increasing levels of capability of adding new functionalities in successive versions.

Each linear sequence produces a deliverable increment of the software. When an iterative enhancement model is used, the first increment is often a core product. That is, basic requirements are addressed, but many supplementary features (some known, other unknown) remain undelivered. The core product is used by the customer. As a result a plan is developed for the next increment. The plan addresses the modifications of the core product to meet the needs of the customer and the delivery of additional features and functionality. This process is repeated following the delivery of each increment, until complete product is produced. Figure 3.4 shows an iterative enhancement model.

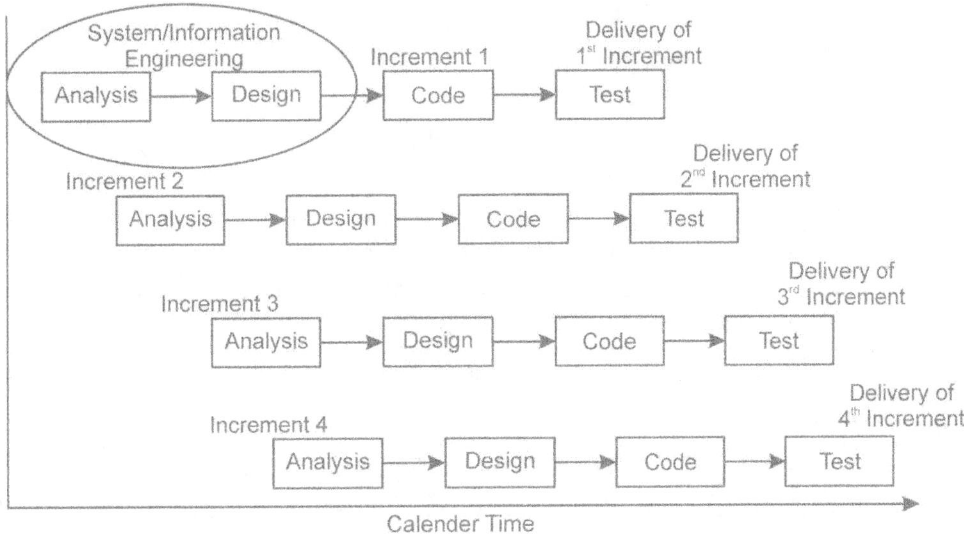

Figure 3.4 Iterative Enhancement Model

The advantages and disadvantages of Iterative enhancement model are:

Advantages

1. The feedbacks from early increments improve the later stages.

2. The possibility of changes in requirement is reduced because of the shorter time span between the design of a component and its delivery.

3. Job satisfaction is increased for developers who see their labors bearing fruit at regular short intervals.

Disadvantages

1. Software breakage, that is, later increments may require modifications to earlier increments.

2. Programmers may be more productive working on one large system than on a series of smaller ones.

3. Some problems are difficult to divide into functional units (modules), which can be incrementally developed and delivered.

3.7 V-MODEL

The extension of Waterfall model is the V-Model. V-Model is also called as verification and validation model. In V-Shape life cycle model, the execution happens in a sequential manner. In this model, the testing phase is planned in parallel with all the phases (requirement analysis, high level design, low level design and coding or implementation). V-model joins coding phase on both the sides, one side is verification phase and other side is validation phase.

Under V-Model, the corresponding testing phase and the development phase is planned in parallel. So there are Verification phases on one side of the V and Validation phases on the other side. Coding phase joins the two sides of the V-Model.

During implementation or coding phase, at the bottom of the V model coding is performed. Once coding is complete, development progresses up the right side of the V model, moving through the test plans developed during the earlier phases. If a problem arises during a testing phase, the life-cycle reverts back to its corresponding development phase. Figure 3.5 shows a V-Model.

The advantages and disadvantages of V-Model are:

Advantages

- This model is very simple and easy to use.
- Suitable for small projects where requirements are known clearly.
- The risk in the model is low because the test plans are prepared at the early stage.

Disadvantages

- In the later stage of development process, it is difficult to change or add requirements.
- The risk in the model is high, if proper test planning is not done.
- This model is not suitable for complex projects.

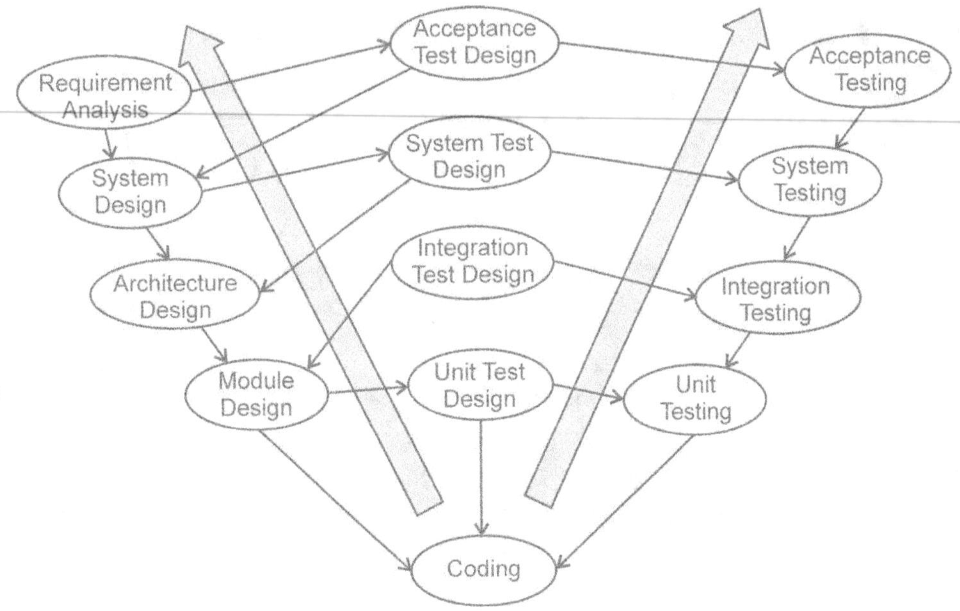

Figure 3.5 V-Model

3.8   SUMMARY

- In prototyping model, a working model of the system is provided, the users get a better understanding of the system being developed.

- The object-oriented approach improves the transitions between the different phases in the software life cycle by using the class concept as the basic unit in all different phases.

- In agile model, every iteration involves teams working simultaneously on various areas like planning, requirements analysis, design, coding, and testing.

- The Rapid Application Development approach encompasses the various phases like business modeling, data modeling, process modeling, application generation, testing and turnover.

- In iterative enhancement model, the software is broken down into several modules, which are incrementally developed and delivered.

In V-Model, the testing phase is planned in parallel with all the phases (requirement analysis, high level design, low level design and coding implementation).

<table>
<tr><td>CHAPTER
4</td><td># Software Requirements</td></tr>
</table>

4.1 INTRODUCTION

In unit 3, we have discussed various life cycle models. Among all the documents produced during a life cycle, software requirement document is most important document. Requirements engineering produces one large document, written in a natural language, and contains a description of what the system will do without describing how it will do it. In many business transactions, a requirement is something that absolutely must happen. The requirements for a system are the description of the services provided by the system and its operational constraints.

In this unit, we are going to study functional requirements, non-functional requirements, user requirements and system requirements. We will also study software requirements documentation.

Objectives

After studying this unit, you should be able to:

- explain functional and non-functional requirements

- discuss user requirements

- discuss system requirements

- explain software requirement documentation

4.2   FUNCTIONAL REQUIREMENTS

A functional requirement defines a function of a system and its components. The functional requirements describe what the system should do. These requirements depend on the type of software being developed, the expected users of the software and the general approach taken by the organisation when writing functional requirements. When expressed as user requirements, the requirements are usually described in a fairly abstract way. However, functional system requirements describe the system function in detail, its inputs, outputs, exceptions and so on.

In order to document the functional requirements of a system, it is necessary to first learn how to identify the high-level functions of the systems by reading the requirement document. The high-level functions would be split into smaller sub-requirements. Once all the high-level functional requirements have been identified these are documented. A function can be documented by identifying the state at which the data is to be input to the system, its input data domain, the output data domain, and the type of processing to be carried on the input data to obtain the output data.

Example 1: Let us first try to document the **withdraw-cash** function of an Automated Teller Machine (ATM) system in the following. The withdraw-cash is a high level requirement. It has several sub-requirements corresponding to the different user interactions.

The functional requirements are:

1. Withdraw-cash

   1.1   Select withdraw amount option.

   1.2   Select account type.

   1.3   Get required amount.

4.3   NON-FUNCTIONAL REQUIREMENTS

Non–functional requirements are the requirements that are not directly concerned with the specific functions delivered by the system. They are related to system properties like reliability, response time and storage requirements. Non-functional requirements may be more critical than functional requirements. If these are not met, the system may be useless. Failing to meet non-functional requirements can mean the whole system is unusable.

For example, aircraft will not be certified as safe for operation, if it does not meet reliability requirements, such as control functions of aircraft not working correctly.

Non-functional requirements may affect the overall architecture of a system rather than the individual components. Figure 4.1 shows different types of non-functional requirements.

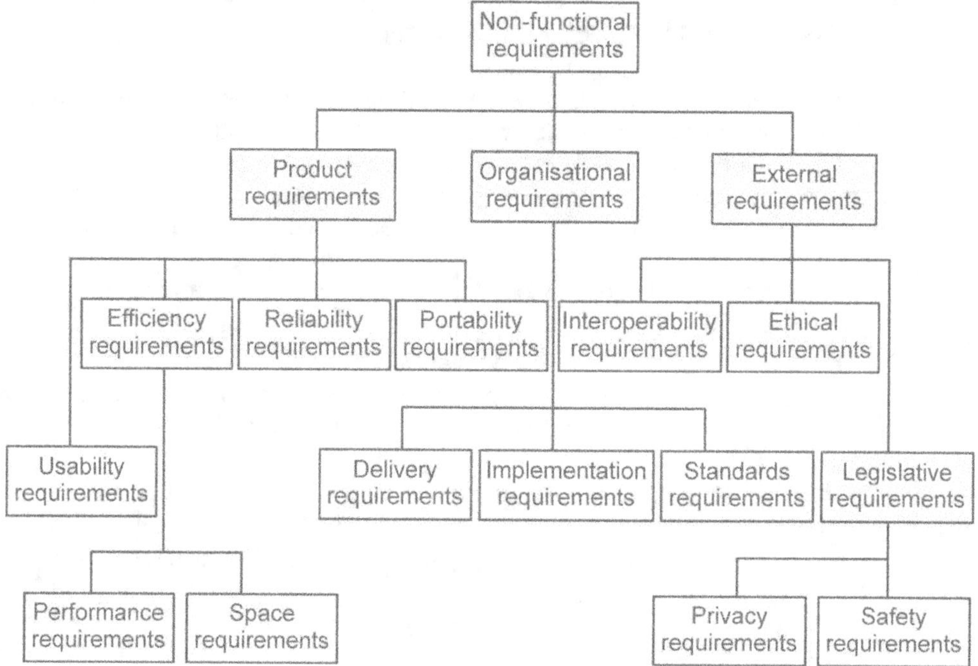

Figure 4.1 Types of Non-Functional Requirements

Three types of non-functional requirements are:

1. **Product Requirements:** These requirements specify product behaviour. One of the Example is performance requirements, the program needs to finish most or all inputs within a certain amount of time. It all depends on how fast the system is executing. Product requirements are classified into usability requirements include well-structured user manuals, informative error messages. Efficiency requirements includes memory utilization, reliability requirements is the ability of a system to perform its required functions under stated conditions for specific period of time. Portability requirements is one in which a system or component can be transferred from one environment to another. The efficiency requirements is categorised into performance requirements and space requirements.

2. **Organisational Requirements:** These requirements include organisational standards that is policies and procedures. Every organisation uses their own standards for developing the software or product. Organisational requirements are classified into delivery requirements, implementation requirements, and standard requirements. Implementation requirements includes programming language or design method and delivery requirements specify when the product and its documentation are to be delivered. Standard requirements includes standards of the organisation.

3. **External Requirements:** These requirements include external factors of the system. External requirements are classified into interoperability requirements, ethical requirements and legislative requirements. Interoperability requirements describe how the system interacts with systems in other organisations. Legislative requirements describes that the system operates within the law. Ethical requirements describes the requirements which are placed on the system will be agreed by users and the general public.

Example 2:

1. **Product Requirement:** The user interface for library system shall be implemented as simple HTML without frames or java applets.

2. **Organizational Requirement:** The system development process and deliverable documents shall conform to the process and deliverables defined as per the organisation standards.

3. **External Requirement:** The system should not disclose any personal information about system users apart from their name.

Table 4.1 shows a metrics for specifying non-functional requirements. These characteristics can be checked whether the system has met its non-functional requirements.

Table 4.1 Metrics for Specifying Non-Functional Requirements

Property	Measure
Speed	<ul><li>Processed transactions/Second.</li><li>User/event response time.</li><li>Screen refresh time.</li></ul>
Size	<ul><li>Number of RAM chips.</li></ul>
Ease of Use	<ul><li>Training time.</li><li>Number of help frames.</li></ul>
Reliability	<ul><li>Mean time to failure.</li><li>Probability of unavailability.</li><li>Rate of failure occurrence.</li><li>Availability.</li></ul>
Robustness	<ul><li>Time to restart after failure.</li><li>Percentage of events causing failure.</li><li>Probability of data corruption on failure.</li></ul>
Portability	<ul><li>Percentage of target-dependent statements.</li><li>Number of target systems.</li></ul>

4.4 USER REQUIREMENTS

The user requirements for a system should describe the functional and non-functional requirements so that they are understandable by system users without detailed technical knowledge. They should only specify the external behaviour of the system and system design characteristics should be avoided, as far as possible. The user requirements should be written in simple language, use simple tables, forms and diagrams.

If the user requirements are not written in simple natural language, then many issues may arise. Some of them are listed below:

1. **Lack of clarity:** It is difficult to read if the requirement document is ambiguous and not clear.

2. **Requirements Confusion:** If the requirements are not clear, all the requirements like functional requirements, non-functional requirements, user requirements and system requirements cannot be differentiated.

3. **Requirements Amalgamation:** Amalgamation means merge. If the requirements are not clear, many various requirements like functional requirements, non-functional requirements, user requirements and system requirements may be merged together as a single requirement.

When writing the user requirements, some guidelines must be followed to minimize misunderstandings:

1. A standard format must be prepared for user requirements and make sure that all requirements definitions obey to that format. Standardising the format makes easier to check the requirements. In the format you may also include information on who proposed the requirements. So that you know whom to consult if the requirement has to be changed.

2. Use language consistently, there should be always difference between mandatory and desirable requirements. Mandatory requirements are the requirements that the system must support and these requirements are compulsory requirements. Desirable requirements are not essential, but it should be included after implementing mandatory requirements.

3. Use proper formatting like font size, color, bold, alignment for text highlighting, to point out the main parts of the user requirements.

Example 3:

User Requirement for Library System: Librarian in the library system should maintain the log file (log file means every request made by the user) to issue, renewal and return the books of the users.

4.5   SYSTEM REQUIREMENTS

System requirements are expanded versions of the user requirements that are used by software engineers as the starting point for the system design. Detailed description of what the system should do including the software system's functions, services, and operational constraints. The system requirements document (sometimes called a functional specification) should define exactly what is to be implemented.

To write the system requirements and user requirements, natural language or simple language is used in order to understand requirements clearly. However, system requirements are more detail than user requirements. System requirements plays an important role while developing the product, and it forms the basis for:

- System architecture and design activities.
- System integration and verification activities.
- Validation and stakeholder's acceptance.
- Communication between the various technical staff that interact throughout the project.

Example 4: System Requirements (this is in detail of user requirements example)

1. User (student, staff) has to register in the library.

2. A unique ID will be given to all users who have registered in the library.

3. Whenever a book is issued to the user, all the book details should be maintained in the log file like, book name, author name, book id and many more. It should also contain date of returning the book.

4. When user wants to renewal or return a book, these details should be maintained by the librarian.

4.6   SOFTWARE REQUIREMENTS DOCUMENT

Software requirements document is also called as Software Requirements Specifications or SRS. User requirements and system requirements both are included in software requirement document. In some situations in a single description it may contain user requirements and system requirements. In other situations user requirements are defined in an introduction and the detailed system requirements may be presented after user requirements.

The requirement document has a various set of users, starting from the senior management of the organisation to the engineers responsible for developing the software. Figure 4.2 shows a user's of a requirement document.

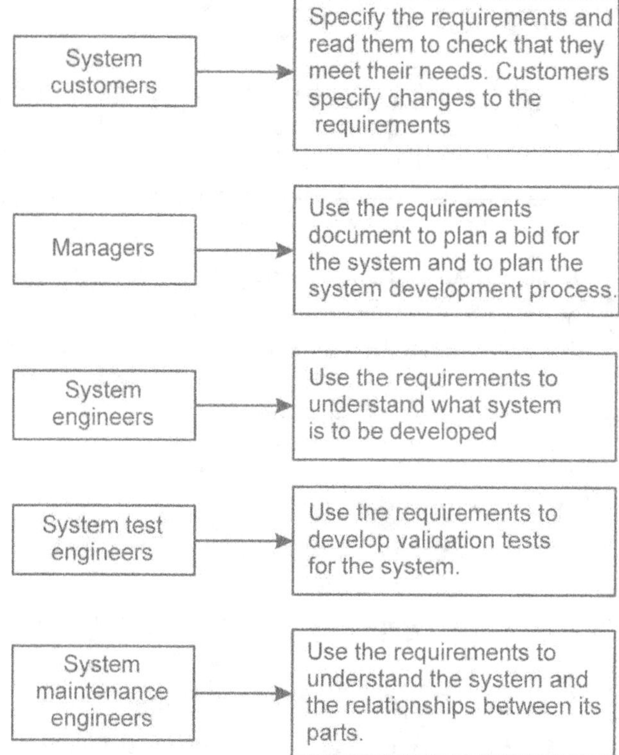

Figure 4.2 Users of a requirements document

Depending on the type of the system the details of the requirements are included that is being developed and the development process used. If an external contractor is developing the system, in that case critical system specifications need to be precise and very detailed. When there is more flexibility in the requirements and where an in-house, iterative development process is used, the requirements document can be much less detailed.

Many organizations have defined standards for requirements. The most widely known standard is IEEE (IEEE - Institute of Electrical and Electronics Engineers). This IEEE standard suggests the following structure for requirements documents:

1. Introduction

    1.1   Purpose of the requirements document.

    1.2   Scope of the product.

    1.3   Definitions, acronyms and abbreviations.

    1.4   References.

    1.5   Overview of the document.

2. **General Description**
   - 2.1   Product perspective.
   - 2.2   Product functions.
   - 2.3   User characteristics.
   - 2.4   General constraints.
   - 2.5   Assumptions and dependencies.
3. **Specific requirements** cover functional, non-functional and interface requirements.
4. **Appendices**
5. **Index**

Although the IEEE standard gives good advice on how to write requirements and how to avoid problems. It is a general framework that can be adapted to define a standard needs of a particular organisation. The information that is included in a requirement document must depend on the type of software being developed and the approach to the development that is used. The designers and programmers use their judgement to decide how to meet the system requirements. For long documents, it is particularly important to include a comprehensive table of contents and document index so that readers can find the information that they need.

4.7   SUMMARY

- Requirements for a software system set out what the system should do and define constraints on its operation and implementation.
- Functional requirements are statements of the services that the system must provide.
- Non-functional requirements, are the requirements that are not directly concerned with the specific functions delivered by the system.
- Non-functional requirements are divided into three categories: product requirements, organisational requirements and external requirements.
- Metrics for specifying non-functional requirements are speed, size, ease of use, reliability, robustness, portability.
- The user requirements for a system should describe the functional and non-functional requirements so that they are understandable by system users without detailed technical knowledge.
- System requirements are detailed explanation of the user requirements.
- User requirements and system requirements both are included in software requirement document.
- The structure of the IEEE standard for the requirement document is: Introduction, general description, specific requirements, appendices and index.

Software Requirement Engineering Process

5.1   INTRODUCTION

In unit 4, we have discussed software requirements. Requirements are established by the client, with help from the software engineer, while the technical decisions often made by the software engineer without much client input – Often times, some of the technical decisions such as which programming languages or tools to use can be given as requirements because the program needs to interoperate with other programs. The goal of software requirement is to completely and consistently specify the technical requirements for the software product in a concise and unambiguous manner.

In this unit, we will discuss feasibility study of software requirements, requirements elicitation, requirements analysis and requirements validation. We will also study software prototyping and requirements management. This unit will enable us to analyse the requirements of both the developer and the user using various principles.

Objectives

After studying this unit, you should be able to:

- explain requirements elicitation and analysis
- describe requirements validation

- discuss software prototyping
- explain requirements management

5.2 FEASIBILITY STUDY

The feasibility study is a study made to decide whether the proposed system is worthwhile. The focus of the feasibility study stage is to determine whether it would financially and technically feasible to develop the software. The feasibility study involves carrying out several activities such as collection of basic information relating to the software like different data items that would be input to the system, the processing required to be carried out on these data, the output data required to be produced by the system, as well as various constraints on the development. These collected data are analyzed to perform the following:

Development of an Overall Understanding of the Problem: It is necessary to first develop an overall understanding of what the customer requires to be developed. For this, only the important requirements of the customer need to be understood and the details of various requirements such as the screen layouts required in the Graphical User Interface (GUI), specific formulas or algorithms required for producing the required results.

Formulation of the Various Possible Strategies for Solving the Problem: In this activity, various possible high-level solution schemes to the problem are determined.

Evaluation of the Different Solution Strategies: The different identified solution schemes are analysed to evaluate their benefits and shortcomings. Such evaluation often requires making approximate estimates of the resources required, cost of development, and development time required. The different solutions are compared based on the estimations that have been worked out. Once the best solution is identified, all activities in the later phases are carried out as per this solution. At this stage, it may also be determined that none of the solution is feasible due to high cost, resource constraints or some technical reasons. This scenario would, of course, require the project to be abandoned.

Feasibility study should be done with the help of project managers who is going to handle that particular project, software engineers who are about to develop that system, technical experts and customers who will be using the system. Typically, feasibility study should be completed within two to three weeks. Finally, the feasibility study report has to be prepared.

5.3 REQUIREMENTS ELICITATION AND ANALYSIS

After performing feasibility study the requirements elicitation and analysis can be done. Requirements elicitation means discovery of all possible requirements. After identifying all possible requirements the analysis on these requirements can be done. Software engineers communicate the end-users or customers in order to find out certain information such as: application domain, expected services from the system, the expected performance level of the system. From this information even constraints of the system can be decided.

5.3.1 STAKEHOLDERS

This is a commonly used term in software engineering. The stakeholder means the persons who will be affected by the system. For example: end-user, system maintenance engineers or software engineers can be stakeholders. Following is the list of problems encountered in understanding the requirements of the system.

Unrealistic expectations: Stakeholders sometimes unable to specify what they want exactly. Sometimes they specify unrealistic demands.

Differences in the requirements: Different stakeholders specify different requirements. The requirement engineer has to resolve the conflicts in the requirements with proper communication with the stakeholders.

Economic and business environment: The economic and business environment is dynamic due to which there may be change in the requirements or change in the stakeholders. Both these things may affect the requirement analysis process.

Political changes: Sometimes political factors affect heavily on the need for the system. Hence, there may be change in the requirements or stakeholders which ultimately affect the requirement elicitation and analysis

5.3.2 REQUIREMENT ELICITATION AND ANALYSIS PROCESS

The requirement elicitation and analysis process of the spiral model is shown in Fig.5.1.

The process activities are:

- **Requirement Discovery:** By having effective communication with the customers the requirements can be identified. Requirement discovery means finding all relevant information about the system. The sources of information for requirement gathering are: document, system stakeholders and specification some other system which is of similar kind. Various methods of requirement discovery are discussions or interviews, observations and so on.

- **Requirements Classification and Discovery:** All the unstructured requirements can be categorized systematically depending upon their nature and they are arranged in groups.

- **Requirement Prioritization:** There are some conflicting requirements. Hence, the requirements are prioritized first. If there are some unrealistic requirements then negotiations are made and only realistic prioritized requirements are collected. If any conflict occurs then it's resolved by requirement engineers.

- **Requirement Documentation:** Once all requirements are finalized, accordingly prepare the document this is called as requirement document.

Requirements elicitation and analysis is a critical process in software development. It is conducted with the following objectives:

- Identify the customers need
- Evaluate the system concept for feasibility
- Perform economic and technical analysis
- Allocate functions to hardware, software, people, database and other system elements
- Establish cost and schedule constraints

Create a system definition that forms for all subsequent engineering work. A variety of techniques are used to determine what the users and customers really want.

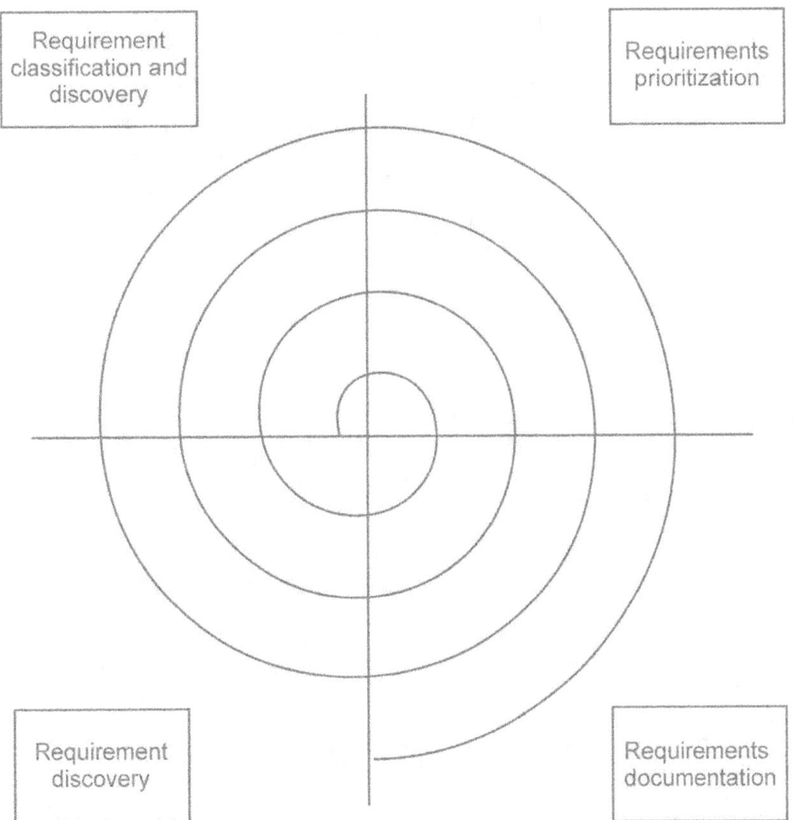

Figure 5.1 Requirement Elicitation and Analysis Process

5.4 REQUIREMENTS VALIDATION

Requirement validation is a process in which it is checked that whether the gathered requirements represent the same system that customer really wants. In requirements validation the requirement errors are fixed. Requirements checking can be done in the following manner:

- **Validity:** Does the system provide the functions which best support the customer's needs?
- **Consistency:** Are there any requirements conflict?
- **Completeness:** Are all functions required by the customer included?
- **Realism:** Can the requirements be implemented according to budget and technology?
- **Verifiability:** Can the requirements be checked?

Requirements validation techniques

The work product produced as a consequence of requirements engineering are assessed for quality during a validation step. The validation process ensures that all software requirements have been stated unambiguously, there are no inconsistences, and that the work products follow organisation standards established by the process. This ensures that the right work product is built. A technical review is the primary mechanism for requirements validation. This is usually done in a team. The team includes members from software developers, customers, users and other stakeholders. Figure 5.2 shows a requirement validation techniques.

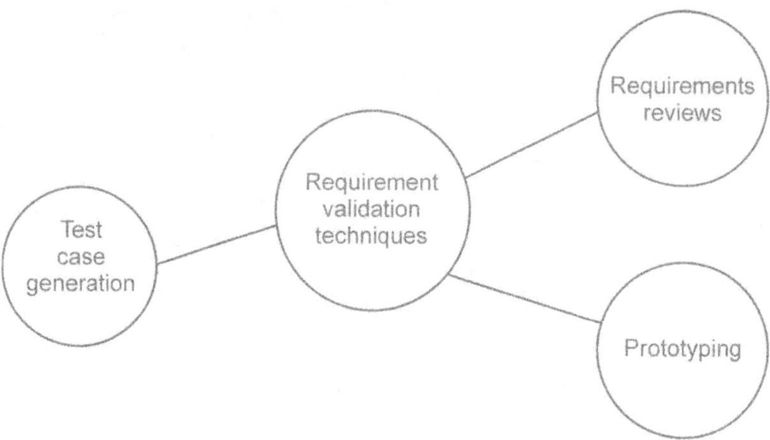

Figure 5.2 Requirement Validation Techniques

- **Requirements Reviews:** Requirement review is a systematic manual analysis of the requirements. Reviews may be formal (with completed documents) or informal. Good communications should take place between developers, customers and users. Such a healthy communication helps to resolve problems at an early stage.
- **Prototyping:** The requirements can be checked using executable model of system.
- **Test–case Generation:** In this technique, the various tests are developed for requirements. The requirement check can be carried out with verifiability this includes whether the requirements realistically testable, comprehensibility this

includes whether the requirement properly understood, traceability this includes whether the origin of the requirement clearly stated and adaptability this describes can the requirement be changed without a large impact on other requirements.

5.5   SOFTWARE PROTOTYPING

Software prototyping is defined as a rapid development of software to evaluate the requirements. Prototype is developed to facilitate the developers to understand the requirements for the system. Prototype is necessary at the start of the analysis because creating model is the only way through which requirements can be efficiently derived. The model then grows into production software. Thus, the prototype is considered, to reduce risk which in-turn reduces requirement risks.

The use of system prototypes is to help customers and developers to understand the system requirements. Figure 5.3 shows a Software prototyping activities. Under software prototyping, various activities are carried out those are:

(a)   **Requirements Elicitation:** User can perform various experiments with the prototype to check the system support.

(b)   **Requirements Validation:** Prototype can show errors and omissions in requirement.

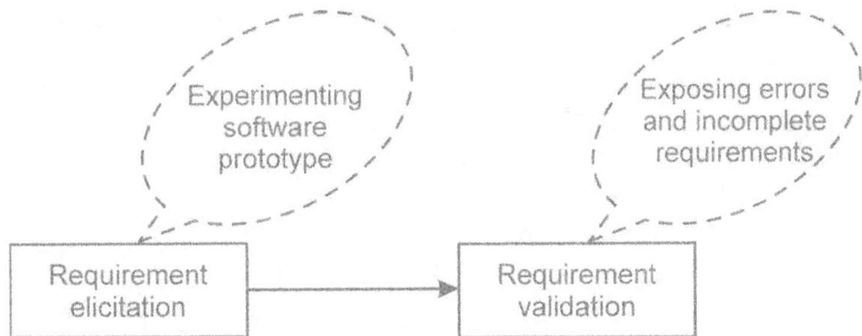

Figure 5.3 Software Prototyping Activities

The benefits of software prototyping are given below:

- If any requirement is missing or confusing then that can be identified.
- Prototype can serve as a basis for deriving system specification.
- Design quality can be improved.
- Development efforts may get reduced.
- System usability can be improved.

In many situations, it is not possible to completely specify a problem at an early stage. Prototyping offers an alternative approach that results in a demonstrable model of the software from which requirements can be refined. The prototype paradigm can be either closed-ended or open-ended. The closed-ended approach is often called throwaway prototyping. Using this approach a prototype serves a rough demonstration of requirements. It is then discarded and the software is engineered using a different paradigm. An open-ended approach, called evolutionary prototyping, uses the prototype as the first part of an analysis activity that will be continued into design and construction.

The important difference between the objectives of close-ended and open-ended prototyping is:

The objective of close-ended prototyping is to validate or derive the system requirements. The objective of open-ended prototyping is to deliver a working system to end-users.

Closed-ended Prototyping: The principle function of the prototype is to clarify requirements and provide additional information for managers to assess process risks. After evaluation, the prototype is thrown away. It is not used as a basis for further system development. The close-ended process model assumes that the prototype is developed from an outline system specification, delivered for experiment and modified until the client is satisfied with its functionality.

At this stage, a conventional software process model is entered, a specification is derived from the prototype and the system is re-implemented in a final production version. Components from the prototype may be reused in the production-quality system.

Figure 5.4 shows a Closed-ended prototyping.

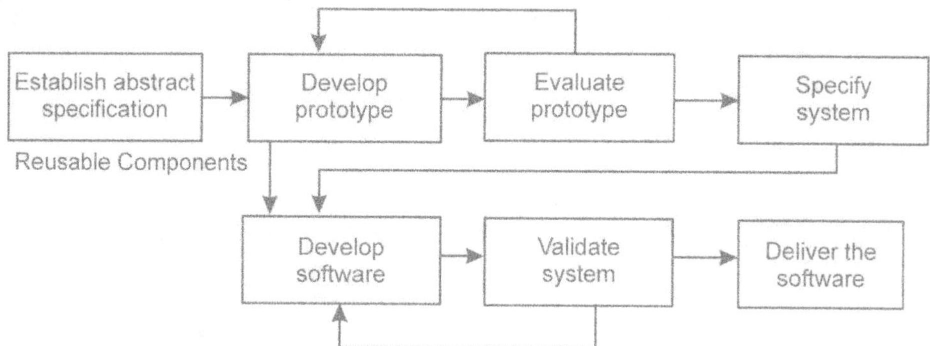

Figure 5.4 Closed-ended Prototyping

Customers should avoid close-ended prototype due to the following reason:

- System characteristics like performance, security, reliability and so on have been ignored during closed-ended prototype development. It will be impossible to incorporate these non-functional requirements into the prototype. The prototype have gone through multiple, uncontrolled changes to meet the user requirements, which are not documented for long-term maintenance.

Open-ended Prototyping: It is based on the idea of developing an initial version of the system, exposing this to the user, refining this through many stages, until an adequate system has been developed. Open-ended prototyping is adopted to develop system where it is difficult to establish a detailed system specification. It allows systems to be developed and delivered rapidly and system development costs are reduced.

The main problems associated with open-ended prototyping are given below:

- Prototypes usually evolve so quickly, that it is not cost-effective to produce large system documentation, hence it is difficult to assess the progress.
- The basic structure of the prototype tends to get corrupt because of the continual changes. Hence, maintenance becomes more difficult and costly.
- Highly skilled and motivated individuals adopt this process model and not generally suitable for software engineering teams.

5.6 REQUIREMENTS MANAGEMENT

Requirements management is the process of managing the changed requirements during requirement engineering process and system development.

Below are the some of the reasons where requirements get change:

- Requirements are always incomplete and inconsistent. New requirements occur during the process as business needs change and a better understanding of the system is developed.
- System customers may specify the requirements from business perspective that can conflict with end user requirements.
- During the development of the system, its business and the technical environment may get changed.

5.6.1 REQUIREMENTS MANAGEMENT PLANNING

Many things should be planned during requirement process. Traceability is concerned with relationship between requirements and the system design. Using traceability the requirement finding becomes easy. Various types of traceability are:

Source Traceability: These are basically the links from requirement to stakeholders who propose these requirements.

Requirements Traceability: These are the links between dependent requirements.

Design traceability: These are the links from requirements to design.

Example: Traceability information is typically represented by a traceability matrix. If one requirement is dependent upon the other requirement then in that row-column cell 'D' is mentioned (shown in table 5.1) and if there is a weak relationship between the requirements then corresponding entry can be denoted by 'R' which is shown in table 5.1

Table 5.1 Traceability Matrix

Requirement iD	A	B	C	D	E	F
A		D			R	
C				R		
D			D			R
E						

5.6.2   REQUIREMENT CHANGE MANAGEMENT

The requirement change management is a technique that can be applied to the processes in which requirements may get changed. The need for requirement change management is that even though the changes are made consistently in the requirements it is possible to incorporate those changes in a controlled manner. Figure 5.5 shows stages of requirement change management process. The requirement change management process can be applied in three stages.

(a)   Problem analysis and change specification

(b)   Change analysis and costing

(c)   Change implementation

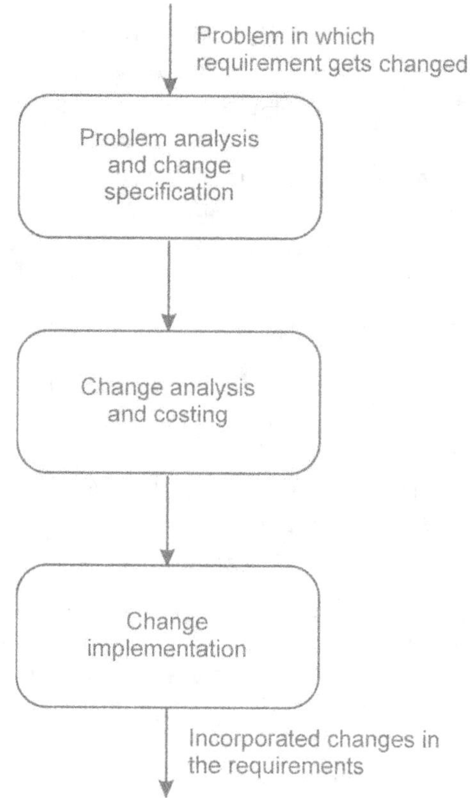

Figure 5.5 Requirement Change Management Process

Problem analysis and change specification: When requirement change request is made for some particular problem then the problem with the older requirement is mentioned or sometimes simply change specification is given. Then first of all, problem analysis or change specification is analysed in order to validate the required change. If necessary the feedback of this analysis is given to the person who is demanding such change.

Change analysis and costing: Following actions are carried out in this stage:

- The effect of change is assessed using traceability information.
- The cost of such change is estimated.
- After getting the cost of changes the decision is made on whether to go for implementation of these changes or not.

Change Implementation: Once it is decided to implement the proposed changes in the requirement, the requirement document has to be modified. The requirement document has to either re-written or re-organised. This can be achieved by making the modularity in the requirement specifications, so that it becomes easy to change individual section without affecting other part of requirement document.

5.7 SUMMARY

- The main focus of the feasibility study stage is to determine whether it would financially and technically feasible to develop the software.
- In feasibility study the collected data are analysed to perform development of an overall understanding of the problem, formulation of the various possible strategies for solving the problem, evaluation of the different solution strategies.
- Requirements elicitation means discovery of all possible requirements. After identifying all possible requirements the analysis on these requirements can be done.
- Problems encountered in understanding the requirements of the system are Unrealistic expectations, Differences in the requirements, Economic and business environment and political changes.
- Requirement Elicitation and Analysis Process activities are requirement discovery, requirements classification and discovery, requirement prioritization and requirement documentation.
- The validation process ensures that all software requirements have been stated unambiguously, there are no inconsistences, and that the work products follow organisation standards established by the process.
- Requirement validation technique includes requirements reviews, prototyping, test–case generation
- Software prototyping is defined as a rapid development of software to evaluate the requirements. Prototype is developed to facilitate the developers to understand the requirements for the system.
- Software prototyping activities are requirement elicitation and requirement validation.

- The prototype paradigm can be either closed-ended (throwaway prototyping) or open-ended (evolutionary prototyping).
- Requirements management is the process of managing the changed requirements during requirement engineering process and system development.
- The requirement change management is a technique that can be applied to the processes in which requirements may get changed. The need for requirement change management is that even though the changes are made consistently in the requirements it is possible to incorporate those changes in a controlled manner.
- The requirement change management process includes problem analysis and change specification, change analysis and costing, change implementation.

6 Software Reliability

6.1 INTRODUCTION

In unit 5, we have seen software requirement engineering process. For any software organization consistency or reliability is the significant vigorous attribute. End-users end up in lofty expenses if the software delivered is unreliable. Developers of the defective or unreliable systems possibly will obtain bad name for their quality and lose further business prospectus in future.

The Software consistency or Reliability is generally defined as possibility of operation with no failures for a particular time in a particular setting for a particular purpose. It is a kind of measure how well software system provides the services needed by the user. For example software installed in an aircraft will be 99.99% reliable during an average flight of five hours. This means that a software failure of some kind will probably occur in one flight out of 10000.

In this unit, we will study software reliability, software reliability metrics. We will also cover programming for reliability and software reuse.

Objectives

After studying this unit, you should be able to:
- define software reliability and differentiate between the terms fault, error and failure
- explain software reliability metrics
- describe programing for reliability
- explain the benefits of software reuse

6.2 SOFTWARE RELIABILITY

Reliability is usually defined as the probability of failure-free operation for a specified time in a specified environment for a specific purpose. Software reliability is a function of the number of failures experienced by a particular user of that software. A software failure occurs when the software is executing. It is a situation in which the software does not deliver the service expected by the user. Software failures are not the same as software faults although these terms are often used interchangeably.

If you measure software reliability in one environment, you cannot assume that the reliability might be similar in another environment where the system is used in a different way. For example, let's say that you measure the reliability of a word processor in an office environment where most users are uninterested in the operation of software. They follow the instructions for its use and do not try to experiment with the system. If you measure the software reliability in an university environment, then the reliability might be quite different. Here students may explore the boundaries of the system and use the system in unexpected ways. These may result in system failures that did not occur in the more constrained office environment.

Human perceptions and patterns of use are also significant. For example say a car has a fault in its wiper system that results in intermittent failures of the wipers to operate correctly in heavy rain. The reliability of that system as perceived by a driver depends on where they live and use the car. A driver in wet climate will probably be more effected by this failure than a driver in dry climate. The wet climate driver perception will be that the system is unreliable, whereas the driver in dry climate may never notice the problem.

In software reliability, it is helpful to distinguish between the terms fault, error and failure.

Failure: An event that occurs at some point in time when the software does not deliver a service as expected by its user.

Error: A mistake in software can lead to system behaviour that is unexpected by system users.

Fault: A characteristic of a software system that can lead to a system error. For example, failure to initialize a variable could lead to that variable having the wrong value when it is used.

6.3 SOFTWARE RELIABILITY METRICS

Metrics which have been used for software reliability specification are shown in table 6.1. The choice of which metric should be used depends on the type of system to which it applies and the requirements of the application domain. For some systems, it may be appropriate to use different reliability metrics for different sub-systems.

Table 6.1 Reliability Metrics

Metric	Explanation
Probability of Failure on Demand (POFOD)	The probability that the system will fail when a service request is made. A POFOD of 0.01 means that one out of thousand service requests may result in failure
Rate Of Failure Occurrence (ROCOF)	This metric sets out the probable number of system failures that are likely to be observed relative to a certain time period (e.g., an hour) or to the number of system executions.
Mean Time To Failure (MTTF)	The average time between observed system failures. An MTTF of 500 means that one failure can be expected every 500 time units.
Availability (AVAIL)	The probability that the system is available for use at a given time. Availability of 0.998 means that the system is likely to be available for 998 of every 1,000 time units.

In some cases, system users are most concerned about how often the system will fail, perhaps because there is a significant cost in restarting the system. In such cases, a metric the Mean Time To Failure (MTTF) or rate of failure occurrence metric base should be used.

In other cases, it is essential that a system should always meet a request for service because there is some cost in failing to deliver the service. The number of failures in some time period is less important. In those cases, a metric based on the Probability of Failure on Demand (POFOD) should be used. Finally, users or system operators may be mostly concerned when a request for service made the system should be readily available for service. They will incur some loss if the system is unavailable. Availability (AVAIL) takes into account the repair or restart time.

There are three kinds of measurement, which can be made when assessing the reliability of a system:

1. System failures are decided based on the inputs which is used to measure POFOD.
2. The time (or number of transaction) between system failures is used to measure ROCOF and MTTF.
3. The elapsed repair or restart time when a system failure occurs. Given that the system must be continuously available; this is used to measure AVAIL.

Time is a factor in all of this reliability metrics. It is essential that the appropriate time units should be chosen if measurements are to be meaningful. Time units, which may be used, are calendar time, the number of transactions or processor time.

In systems that spend much of their time waiting to respond to a service request, such as telephone switching systems, the time unit that should be used is processor time. If you use calendar time, then this includes the time when the system was doing nothing.

Calendar time is an appropriate time unit to use for systems that are in continuous operation. For example, monitoring systems such as alarm systems and other types of process control systems fall into this category.

There are various types of software failures that affect the software reliability of the system. Examples of different types of software failures are:

Failure Class	Description
Transient	This type of failure happens with specific inputs
Permanent	This type of failure happens with all inputs
Recoverable	System can recover without operator intervention
Unrecoverable	Operator intervention needed to recover from failure
Non-corrupting	Failure does not corrupt system state or data
Corrupting	Failure corrupts system state or data

6.4 PROGRAMMING FOR RELIABILITY

In this, there is a general requirement for more reliable systems in all application domains. Customers expect their software to operate without failures and to be available when it is required. Improved programming techniques, better programming languages and better quality management have led to very significant improvements in reliability for most software. However, for some systems, such as those, which control unattended machinery, these 'normal' techniques may not be enough to achieve the level of reliability required. In these cases, special programming techniques may be necessary to achieve the required reliability. Some of these techniques are seen in this chapter.

Reliability in a software system can be achieved using three strategies:

- **Fault avoidance:** This is the most important strategy, which is applicable to all types of system. The design and implementation process should be organized with the objective of producing fault-free systems.

- **Fault tolerance:** In this, even though the system fails, facilities are provided in the software to continue the operations.

- **Fault detection:** In this, the faults are identified before the software is put into operation.

6.4.1 FAULT AVOIDANCE

A good software process should be oriented towards fault avoidance rather than fault detection and removal. It should have the objective of developing fault-free software. Fault-free software means software, which conforms to its specification. Of course, there may be errors in the specification or it may not reflect the real needs of the user so fault-free software does not necessarily mean that the software will always behave as the user wants.

Fault avoidance and the development of fault-free software rely on:

1. The availability of an exact system specification, which is a clear description of what, must be implemented.
2. The adoption of an organizational quality philosophy in which quality is the driver of the software process. Programmers should expect to write bug-free program.
3. The adoption of an approach to software design and implementation which is based on information hiding and encapsulation and which encourages the production of readable programs.
4. The use of a strongly typed programs language so that possible errors are detected by the language compiler.
5. Restriction on the use of programming construct, such as pointers, which are inherently error-prone.

Achieving fault-free software is virtually impossible if low-level programming languages with limited type checking are used for program development. Figure 6.1 shows an increasing cost of residual fault of removal

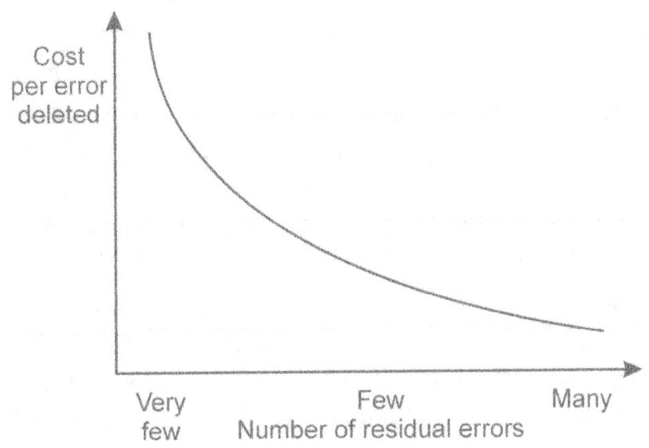

Figure 6.1 The Increasing Cost of Residual Fault of Removal

We must be realistic and accept that human errors will always occur. Faults may remain in the software after development. Therefore, the development process must include a validation phase, which checks the developed software for the presence of faults. This validation phase is usually very expensive. As faults are removed from a program, the cost of finding and removing remaining faults tends to rise exponentially. As the software becomes more reliable, more and more testing is required to find fewer and fewer faults.

Structured programming and error avoidance

Structured programming is a programming using only while loops and if statements as control constructs and designing using a top-down approach. This programming does not use any go to statements. The adoption of structured programming was an important milestone in the development of software engineering because it was the first step away from an undisciplined approach to software development.

Go to statement was an inherently error-prone programming construct. The disciplined use of control structures force programmers to think carefully about their program. Hence they are less likely to make mistakes during development. Structured programming means programs can be read sequentially and are therefore easier to understand and inspect. However, avoiding unsafe control statements is only the first step in programming for reliability.

If the use of these constructs is minimized, then the faults are less likely to be introduced into programs, these constructs include:

1. **Floating-point numbers:** Floating-point numbers are inherently imprecise. They present a particular problem when they are compared because representation imprecision may lead to invalid comparisons. Fixed-point numbers, where a number is represented to a given number of decimal places, are safer as exact comparisons are possible.

2. **Pointer:** Pointer refers a location in the memory. They cause errors because they allow 'aliasing'. This means the same memory location can be accessed using different names. Aliasing makes programs harder to understand so that errors are more difficult to find. However, it is often impractical to avoid the use of pointers.

3. **Dynamic memory allocation:** Program memory is allocated at run-time rather than compile-time. The danger with this is that the memory may not be de-allocated so that the system eventually runs out of available memory. This can be a very intelligent type of errors to detect as the system may run successfully for a long time before the problem occurs.

4. **Parallelism:** Parallelism is dangerous because of the difficulties of predicting the effects of timing interactions between parallel processes. Timing problems generally cannot be identified by program check and the irregular combination of circumstances, which might effect a timing problem. Parallelism is necessary but its use should be carefully controlled to minimize inter-process dependencies. Programming language facilities, such as Ada tasks, help avoid some of the problems of parallelism as the compiler can detect some kinds of programming errors.

5. **Recursion:** The process of function calling itself repeatedly is known as recursion. Its use can result in very concise programs but it can be difficult to follow the logic of recursive programs. Errors in using recursion may result in the allocation of the system's memory as temporary stack variables are created.

6. **Interrupts:** Interrupts are a means of forcing control to transfer to a section of code irrespective of the code currently executing. The problem with the interrupt is, it might effect a complex operation to be terminated.

6.4.2 FAULT TOLERANCE

In fault-tolerance system the operations are continued even after system failures are occurred, even though there is a failure in some of its components the system enables to continue operating properly. Some of the features of fault tolerance are seen below:

1. **Failure detection:** This will detect the failure of the system. Failure may be due to hardware or software.

2. **Damage assessment:** This will identify the damaged parts of the system, which have been affected by the failure.

3. **Fault recovery:** Fault recovery is a process that involves restoring an error state to an error-free state.

4. **Fault repair:** This involves modifying the system so that the fault does not recur. In many cases, software failures are transient, due to a peculiar combination of system inputs. No repair is necessary and normal processing can resume immediately after fault recovery.

If there are no faults in the system, there would not seem to be any chance of system failure. However, 'fault-free' does not mean 'failure-free'. It can only mean that the program corresponds to its specification. The specification may contain errors or omissions or incorrect assumptions about the system's environment. We can never demonstrate that the system is completely fault-free. In systems that have the highest reliability and availability requirements, you need to use the redundant and diverse approaches of fault avoidance and fault tolerance.

6.5 SOFTWARE REUSE

Software reuse is the process of creating software systems from existing software rather than building them from scratch. The design process in most engineering disciplines is based on reuse of existing system or components. For example in mechanical or electrical engineers do not specify a design in which every component has to be manufactured specially. They base their design on components that have been tried and tested in other systems. These are not just small components, but includes major sub-systems such as engines, condensers or turbines.

Software products are expensive, therefore the software project managers are always worried about the high cost of software development, and are desperately looking for way-outs to cut development cost. A possible way to reduce development cost is to reuse parts from previously developed software. In addition to reduced development cost and time, reuse also leads to higher quality of the developed products since the reusable components are ensured to have high quality.

Reuse-based software engineering is a comparable software engineering strategy where the development process is geared to reusing existing software. Although the benefits of reuse have been recognized for many years, it is only in the past 10 years that there has been a gradual transition from original software development to reuse-based development. The move to reuse-based development has been in response to demands for lower software production and maintenance costs, fast delivery of systems and increased software quality. More and more companies see their software as a valuable asset and promoting reuse to increase their return on software investments.

Apart from libraries such as window system libraries, there is no common base of reusable software components, which is known by all software engineers. However, this situation is slowly changing. We need to reuse our software assets rather than redevelop the same software again and again. Demands for lower software production and maintenance costs along with increased quality can only be met by widespread and systematic software reuse. Reuse of program is just not mean to reuse existing code or modules. Designs and requirements are likely reuse. Reusing of intangible products of the software development process has latent gains, such as requirements, would be bigger than those from reusing modules code. Reuse –based software engineering is an approach to development that tries to maximize the reuse of existing software. The software units that are reused may be of radically different sizes. For example, the reuse of software can consider at a number of different levels:

1. **Application System Reuse:** The whole of an application system may be reused. The key problem here is ensuring that the software is portable; it should execute on several different platforms.
2. **Sub-system Reuse:** Major sub-systems of an application may be reused. For example, a pattern-matching system developed as part of a text processing system may be reused in a database management system.
3. **Module or Object Reuse:** Components of a system representing a collection of functions may be reused. For example, an Ada package or a C++ object implementing a binary tree may be reused in different applications.
4. **Function Reuse:** Software components, which implement a single function, such as a mathematical function, may be reused.

One of the advantage of software reuse is cost reduction. Some of the benefits of reusing software is given below:

Reduced Process Risk: The cost of existing software is already known, while the costs of development are always a matter of judgement. This is an important factor for project management because it reduces the margin of error in project cost estimation. This is particularly true when relatively large software components such as sub-systems are reused.

Effective Use of Specialists: Instead doing the same work over and over, these application specialists can develop reusable software that encapsulates their knowledge.

Standards Compliance: Some standards, such as user interface standards, can be implemented as a set of standard reusable components. For example, in a user interface if menus are implemented using reusable components, the same menu format is applied to all applications like (word, power point, excel and many more) so that standard or common user interface is maintained and users become more familiar and makes less mistakes while using the menus.

Accelerated Development: Bringing a system to market as early as possible is often more important than overall development costs. Reusing software can speed up system production because both development and validation time should be reduced.

However, there are also costs and problems associated with reuse. In particular, Systematic reuse does not just happen, it must be planned and introduced through an organisation. Companies such as Hewlett-Packard have also been more popular in their reuse programs. Some of the problems with software reuse are seen below:

Increased Maintenance Costs: If the source code of a reused software system or component is not available then maintenance costs may be increased because the reused elements of the system may become increasingly incompatible with system changes.

Lack of Tool Support: CASE toolsets may not support development with reuse. It may be difficult or impossible to integrate these tools with a component library system. The software process assumed by these tools may not take reuse into account.

Rewrite Software: Some software engineers prefer to rewrite components because they believe they can improve on them. This is partly to do with trust and partly to do with the fact that writing original software is seen as more challenging than reusing others peoples software.

Creating and Maintaining a Component Library: Populating a reusable component library and ensuring the software developers can use this library can be expensive. The current techniques for classifying, cataloguing and retrieving software components are immature.

Finding, Understanding and Adapting Reusable Components: Software components have to be discovered in a library, and sometimes adapted to work in a new environment. Engineers must be reasonably confident of finding a component in the library before they will include a component search as part of their normal development process.

6.6   SUMMARY

- Reliability is usually defined as the probability of failure-free operation for a specified time in a specified environment for a specific purpose.
- In software reliability, there are various reliability metrics such as Probability of Failure on Demand (POFOD), Rate Of Failure Occurrence (ROCOF), Mean Time To Failure (MTTF), Availability (AVAIL).
- There are various types of software failures that affect the software reliability of the system. Examples of different types of software failures are: Transient, permanent, recoverable, unrecoverable, non-corrupting and corrupting.
- In programming for reliability, customers expect their software to operate without failures and to be available when it is required.
- Reliability in a software system can be achieved using three strategies such as fault avoidance, fault tolerance and fault detection.
- Structured programming is a programming using only while loops and if statements as control constructs and designing using a top-down approach.   This programming does not use any go to statements.

- If the use of these constructs is minimized, then the faults are less likely to be introduced into programs, these constructs include floating-point numbers, pointer, dynamic memory allocation, parallelism, recursion, interrupts.
- Some of the features of fault tolerance are failure detection, damage assessment, fault recovery and fault repair.
- Software reuse is the process of creating software systems from existing software rather than building them from scratch.

Software Design

Structure

7.1 INTRODUCTION

In unit 6, we have seen software reliability, software design is an essential phase of the software engineering process for creating and evaluating software models that guide the construction effort for developing high-quality software systems on time and within budget. Design is an integral part of every engineering discipline. Airplanes, bridges, buildings, electronic devices, cars and many other products of similar complexity are all designed. In civil engineering, designs are used to specify detailed plans for developing physical and naturally built environments, such as bridges, roads, canals, dams, and buildings. In electrical engineering, designs are used to capture, evaluate, and specify the detailed qualitative and quantitative description of solutions for telecommunication systems, electrical systems and electronic devices. In mechanical engineering, designs are used for analyzing, evaluating and specifying technical features required to construct machines and tools such as industrial equipment, heating and cooling systems, aircrafts, robots and medical devices. In all other engineering disciplines, design provides a systematic approach for creating products that meet their intended functions and user's expectations.

In this unit we will study, basics of software design, data design, architectural design, component level design and user interface design. We will also see fundamental design basics such as module and modularization. Finally we will cover design techniques.

Objectives

After studying this unit, you should be able to:

- discuss software design
- describe data design, architectural design
- explain component level design and user interface design
- discuss design techniques

7.2 BASICS OF SOFTWARE DESIGN

Software design is the process of transforming functional and non-functional requirements into models that describe the technical solution before development begins. To achieve this, the concept of software design, its activities and tasks must be well understood so that a problem-solving framework for designing quality into software products can be established. In today's modern software systems, there are numerous design principles, processes, strategies and other factors affecting how designers execute the software design phase.

A software design is a process of problem solving and planning for a software solution. The design model resides at the core of the software engineering process consisting of several entities and relationship between these entities. The design is baseline for any detailed implementation. It helps in interoperability between the designers of sub systems.

It gives prior information of the system maintenance that the designers intend for.

Every phase of SDLC has a detailed document as an outcome. Software design document is also one such outcome which an architect designs after obtaining a detailed requirement specification from the customers. There are primarily three main types of notations used in the design document:

(a) **Graphical Notations:** This notation is used to represent co-relation among the entities involved in a design using certain modelling languages such as Unified Modeling Language (UML). It provides an abstract picture of the software at early stages of Software Development Life Cycle (SDLC).

(b) **Program Description Languages:** Program Design Language (or PDL, for short) is a method for designing and documenting methods and procedures in software. It is related to pseudo code, but unlike pseudo code, it is written in plain language without any terms that could suggest the use of any programming language or library.

(c) **Informal Text:** The design is an explanation is expected to be more readable and hence the design is explained using natural language text called informal text.

Any design problem is solved using the following three approaches:

1. **Detailed Study and Understanding of the Problem:** The problem must be analyzed from different perspectives or views in order to check if all the requirements are met according to the design requirements.

2. **Identify the Core Features of at Least One Possible Solution:** It is useful to detect more number of solutions and to evaluate each of them. The choice of solution depends on designers view based on his/her experience, the availability of reusable components and the level of simplicity of the desired solutions.

   Designers prefer to choose familiar solutions though they are not optimal as they have better understanding of pros and cons of using a familiar solution.

3. **Describe all the Abstracted Information Used in the Solution:** Before releasing any formal document, the designer must write an informal design description. This may be analyzed by developing the solution in detail. Errors and omissions in the high-level design will be detected during this analysis. Such errors are corrected before the design is documented.

7.2.1 DESIGN PROCESS

A general model of a software design is a directed graph. The target of the design process is the creation of a graph without any inconsistencies. Nodes in this graph represent entities in the design entities such as process function or types. The link represents relation between these design entities such as calls, uses and so on. Software designers do not arrive at a finished design graph immediately but develop the design iteratively through a number of different versions. The design process involves adding formality and detail as the design is developed with constant backtracking to correct earlier, less formal, designs. The starting point is an informal design, which is refined by adding information to make it consistent and complete as shown in figure 7.1.

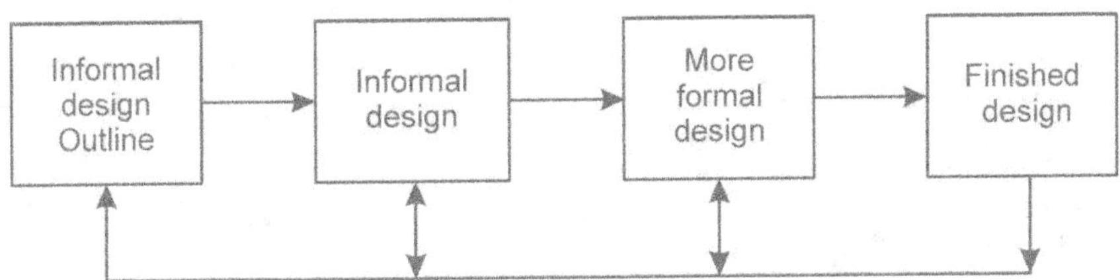

Figure. 7.1 The Progression from an Informal to a Detailed Design

A general model of the design process shown in figure 7.2 suggests that the design process stages are sequential in nature, but the activities of the design process will be proceeding in parallel. The activities which are shown below are part of designing the large software systems.

1. **Architectural Designs** the sub-systems making up the system and their relationships are identified and documented.

2. **Abstract Specification** for each sub-system, one to produce the abstract specification and the constraints.
3. **Interface Design** for each sub-system, its interface with other sub-systems is designed and documented. This interface specification must be unambiguous as it allows the sub-system to be used without knowledge of the sub-system operation.
4. **Component Design** Services are allocated to different components and the interfaces of these components are designed.
5. **Data Structure Design** the data structures used in the system implementation is designed in detail and specified.
6. **Algorithm Design** the algorithms used to provide services are designed in detail and specified.

This process is repeated for each sub-system until the components identified can be mapped directly into programming language components such as packages, procedures or functions.

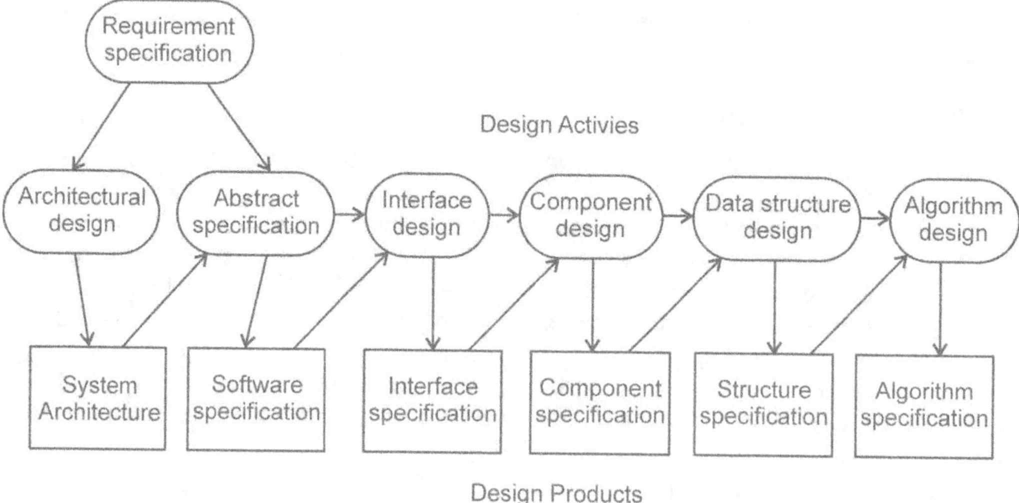

Figure 7.2 A General Model of the Design Process

7.3   DATA DESIGN

The data design is basically the model of data that is represented at the high level of abstraction. The data design is then progressively refined to create implementation specific representations. Various elements of data design are:

Data Object – the data objects are identified and relationship among various data objects can be represented using entity relationship diagrams or data dictionaries.

Databases – using software design model, the data models are translated into data structures and databases at the application level.

Data Warehouses – at the business level useful information is identified from various databases and the data warehouses are created. For extracting or navigating the useful business information is stored in the data warehouse.

Guidelines for Data Design are Listed below:

Apply Systematic Analysis on Data: Represent data objects, relationships among them and data flow along with the contents.

Identify Data Structures and Related Operations: For the design of efficient data structures all the operations that will be performed on it should be considered.

Establish Data Dictionary: The data dictionary explicitly represents various data objects, relationships among them and the constraints on the elements of data structures.

Defer the Low-Level Design Decisions until Late in the Design Process: Major structural attributes are designed first to establish an architecture of data. And then low-level design attributes are established.

Use Information Hiding in the Design of Data Structures: The use of information hiding helps in improving quality of software design. It also helps in separating the logical and physical views.

Apply a Library of Useful Data Structures and Operations: The data structures can be designed for reusability. A use of library of data structure templates (called as abstract data types) reduces the specification and design efforts for data.

Use a Software Design and Programming Language to Support Data Specification and Abstraction: The implementation of data structures can be done by effective software design and by choosing suitable programming language.

7.4 ARCHITECTURAL DESIGN

Requirements of the software should be transformed into an architecture that describes the softwares top-level structure and identifies its components. This is accomplished through architectural design (also called as system design), which as a preliminary 'blueprint' from which a software can be developed.

Large systems can be decomposed into sub-system that provides some related set of services. The initial design process of identifying this sub-system and establishing a framework for sub-system control and communication is called Architectural design.

Architectural design comes before detailed system specification, it should not include any design information. Architectural design is necessary to structure and organize the specification. This model is the starting point for the specification of the various parts of the system.

An architectural design performs the following functions:

- It provides a level of abstraction at which the software designers can specify the system behaviour (such as function and performance).

- It serves as the conscience for a system as it evolves. By characterizing the crucial system design assumptions, a good architectural design guides the process of

system enhancement indicating what aspects of the system can be easily changed without compromising system integrity.
- It evaluates all top-level designs.
- It develops and documents top-level design for the external and internal interfaces.
- It improves preliminary versions of user documentation.
- It describes and documents preliminary test requirements and the schedule for software integration.

Sources of Architectural Design
- Information regarding the application domain for the software to be developed.
- Using data-flow diagrams.
- Availability of architectural patterns and architectural styles.

Architectural design occupies a pivotal position in software engineering. During architectural design the crucial requirements such as performance, reliability, costs, etc., are addressed. This job is clumsy as the software engineering model is shifting from huge, stand-alone, built from-scratch systems to componentized, evolvable, standards-based and product line-oriented systems. Also, an important task for designers is to understand exactly how to continue from requirements to architectural design. To avoid these problems, designers accept strategies like reusability, componentization, platform-based, standards-based and many more.

With the architectural design the responsibility of developers, participants in the architectural design phase should also include user representatives, systems engineers, hardware engineers, and operational personnel. In reviewing the architectural design, the project management should ensure that all parties are consulted in order to minimize the risk of incompleteness and error.

Architectural Design Representation
Architectural design can be represented using various models, such as:
- **Structural Model:** This shows an architecture as a systematic collection of program components.
- **Framework Model:** This tries to recognize repeatable architectural design pattern met in similar types of applications which leads to rise in the level of abstraction.
- **Dynamic Model:** This states the behavioral features of the software architecture and shows how the structure or system configuration changes as the function changes due to change in the external environment.
- **Process Model:** This specifies on the design of the business or technical process, which must be implemented in the system.
- **Functional Model:** This denotes the function hierarchy of the system. There is no generally accepted process model for architectural design. The process depends on application knowledge and on the skill and intuition of the system architect. For this process, the following activities are usually necessary:

1. **System Structuring:** The system is structured into a number of principal sub-systems where a sub-system is an independent software unit. Communications between sub-systems are identified.

2. **Control Modeling:** A general model of the control relationships between the parts of the system is established.

3. **Modular Decomposition:** Each identified sub-system is decomposed into modules. The architect must decide on the types of module and their interconnections.

During any of these process stages, it may be necessary to develop the design in more detail to find out if architectural design decision allows the system to meet its requirements. The output of the architectural design process is an architectural design documents. This consists of a number of graphical representations of the system models along with associated descriptive text. It should describe how the system is structured into sub-systems and how each sub-system is structured into modules.

7.5   COMPONENT-LEVEL DESIGN

As quickly as the first iteration of architectural design is complete, component-level design takes place. Component-level design is created by transforming the structural elements defined by the software architecture into procedural descriptions of software components. These components are derived from the analysis model where data-flow-oriented element (present in the analysis model) serves as the base for the derivation. A component, also known as module, resides within the software architecture and serves one of the following three roles:

- **A Control Component**, which co-ordinates the invocation of all other components present in the problem domain.
- **A Problem Domain Component**, which implements a complete or partial function as required by the user.
- **An Infrastructure Component** supports functions, which in turn support the processing required in the problem domain.

Component-level design is used to define the data structures, algorithms, interface description and communication mechanisms allocated to each module. The module or component can be defined as a modular building block for the software. Though, the importance of component varies according to how software engineers use it, the modular design of the software should exhibit the following sets of properties:

- **Provide Simple Interfaces:** Simple interfaces reduce the number of interactions that must be considered when verifying that a system performs its intended function. Simple interfaces also make it easier to reuse components in different circumstances. Reuse is a major cost saver. Not only does it reduce the time spent in coding, designing and testing but also allows development costs to be amortized over many projects.
- **Ensure Information Hiding:** The benefits of modularity automatically do not follow the act of subdividing a program. Each module should encapsulate information that is not available to the rest of a program. This reduces the cost of subsequent design changes. For example, a module may encapsulate related functions which can benefit from a common implementation or which are used in many parts of a system.

Modularity has become an accepted method in each engineering discipline. With the overview of modular design, difficulty of software design has significantly reduced, change in the program is facilitated that has encouraged parallel development of systems. To attain effective modularity, design thoughts such as functional independence are reflected to be very important.

7.6 USER INTERFACE DESIGN

User interface determine the way in which users interact with the software. The user interface design creates an effective communication medium between a human and a computer machine. It provides easy and intuitive access to information as well as efficient interaction and control of software functionality. For this, it is necessary for the designers to understand what the user requires from the interface.

Since the user is central while developing the software, user interface must also be central while designing the software. It is important to first know the user for whom the user interface is being designed before designing the user interface. Direct contact between end-users and developers often improves the user interface design. The result of this communication helps the designers to know the users goals, and needs.

While designing the user interface software engineer communicates the user and according to his thinking about the interface, software engineer draws the sketches. Get it approved from the user and then work on defining objects and corresponding actions.

7.6.1 USER INTERFACE RULES

Designing a good and efficient user interface is a common objective among software designers. But what makes a user interface look good. Software engineering strive to achieve a good user interface by following three rules namely ease of learning, efficiency of use and aesthetic appeal.

- **Ease of learning:** ease of learning describes how quickly and effortlessly users learn to use the software. Ease of learning is especially important for new users. However, even an experienced users face a learning experience problem while attempting to expand their usage of the product or when using a new version of the software. Here, the principle of state visualization is applied, which states that each change in the behaviour of the software should be accompanied by a corresponding change in the appearance of the interface. Generally, to ease the task of learning, designers make use of the following tools:

  - **Affordance:** provides clues that suggest what a machine or tool can do and how to use it. For example, the style of a door handle on the doors of many departmental stores, offices and shops suggest whether to pull a door or push a door to open it. If the wrong style door handle is used, people struggle with the door. In this case, the door handle is more than just a tool for physically helping you to open the door, it is also an affordance showing you how the door opens. Similarly, software designers while developing user interface should offer hints as to what each part does and how it functions.

  - **Consistency:** Designers strive to maintain consistency within the interface. Every aspect of the interface, including minor details, such as font usage and colours is kept consistence when the behaviour is consistent. Here the principle of coherence (i.e., behaviour of the program should be internally and externally consistent) is applied. Internal consistency means that the programs behaviour must make 'sense' with respect to other parts of the program. For example, if one attribute of an object (for example colour) is modified using a pop-up menu, then it is expected that other attributes of the object will also be edited in a similar manner. External consistency means that the program is consistent with the environment in which it runs. This includes consistency with both the operating system and other suite of applications that run within that operating system.

- **Efficiency of Use:** once a user knows how to perform tasks, then efficiency can be evaluated reasonably only if users are no longer engaged in learning how to do the task and are rather engaged in performing the task. A few guidelines help in designing an efficient interface.

  (a) The task should require minimal physical actions. The desire of experienced users for hot keys and to shortcuts to pull-down menu actions is a well-known example of reducing the number of actions required to perform a task

  (b) The task should require minimal effort as well.

- **Aesthetically Pleasing:** Today, look and feel is one of the biggest USPs (Unique Selling Points) while designing a software. An attractive user interface improves the sales because a buyer likes to have things that looks attractive. An attractive user interface makes the user feel better (as it provides ease of use), while using the product. Many software organizations focus specifically on designing software, which has an attractive look and feel so that they can attract customers/users towards their products.

7.6.2   USER INTERFACE DESIGN PROCESS

User interface design is an iterative process in which each design process occurs more than once. Each time the design step gets elaborated in more detail. Following are the commonly used interface design steps.

- During the analysis step define interface objects and corresponding actions or operations.
- Define the major events in the interface. These events depict the user actions. Finally model these events.
- Analyse how the interface look like from user's point of view.
- Identify how the user understands the interface with the information provided along with it.

The user interface design activity starts with the identification of user, task and environmental requirements. After this, user states are created and analyzed to define a set of interfaces objects and actions. These objects then form the basis for the creation of screen layout, menus, icons and much more.

While designing the user interface, the following points must be remembered:

- Follow the rules stated in section 7.6.1. Any interface that fails to achieve any of these rules to a reasonable degree needs to be redesigned.

- Determine how interface will be implemented.

- Consider the environment (like operating system, development tools, display properties and so on).

7.7 FUNDAMENTAL DESIGN CONCEPTS

In today's modern software systems, software design plays a key role in the development of software products; however, it is only one phase of the complete software engineering life cycle. Software design was introduced as a systematic and intelligent process for generating, evaluating and specifying designs for devices, systems or processes. Software designs provide blueprints that capture how software systems meet their required functions and how they are shaped to meet their planned quality. Formally, software engineering design is defined as the process of identifying, evaluating, validating and specifying the architectural, detailed, and construction models required to build software that meets its intended functional and non-functional requirements.

The term software design is used interchangeably in practice as a means to describe both the process and product of software design. From a process perspective, software design is used to identify the phase, activities, tasks and interrelationship between them required to model software's structure and behavior before construction begins. From a product development perspective, software design is used to identify the design artifacts that result from the identified phase, activities, and tasks, therefore, these products by themselves or collectively, are referred to as a software design. Design products vary according to several factors, including design perspective, language, purpose and their capabilities for evaluation and analysis. For example, designs can be in architectural form, using architectural notations targeted for specific stakeholders. These types of design can be presented using block diagrams, Unified Modeling Language (UML) diagram. In other cases, design can be in detailed form, where the system is used to model structural and behavioral aspects. These can include software models that contain class diagrams, object diagrams, sequence diagrams or activity diagrams. Other design products include models that represent interfaces, data or user interface designs.

During the software design phase, the system is decomposed to allow optimum development of the software, requirements are mapped to conceptual models of the operational software, roles are assigned to software teams on the same or remote sites, well-known interfaces for software components are created, quality attributes are addressed and incorporated into the design of the system; the user interface is created, the softwares capability is analyzed, functions and variable names are identified, design documentation goals are established and the foundation for the rest of the software engineering life cycle is also established.

7.7.1   MODULE

Software architecture and design patterns represents modularity, that is software is divided into named and addressable components, sometimes called modules that are integrated to satisfy problem requirements.

It has been stated that "modularity is the single attribute of software that allows a program to be intellectually manageable". Monolithic software (i.e., a large program composed of a single module) cannot be easily grasped by a software engineer. The number of control paths, span of reference, number of variables and overall complexity would make understanding close to impossible. To illustrate this point, consider the following argument based on observations of human problem solving.

Consider two problems, p1 and p2. If the perceived complexity of p1 is greater than the perceived complexity of p2, it follows that the effort required to solve p1 is greater than the effort required to solve p2. As a general case, this result is intuitively obvious. It does take more time to solve a difficult problem.

It also follows that the perceived complexity of two problems when they are combined is often greater than the sum of the perceived complexity when each is taken separately. This leads to a "divide and conquer" strategy – it's easier to solve a complex problem when you break it into manageable pieces. This has important implications with regard to modularity and software.

It is possible to conclude that, if we subdivide software indefinitely, the effort required to develop it will become negligibly small. The effort (cost) to develop an individual software module does decrease as the total number of modules increases. Given the same set of requirements, more modules means smaller individual size. However, as the number of modules grows, the effort (cost) associated with integrating the modules also grows.

We can modularize a design (and the resulting program) so that development can be more easily planned, software increments can be defined and delivered, changes can be more easily accommodated, testing and debugging can be conducted more efficiently and long-term maintenance can be conducted without serious side effects.

7.7.2   MODULARIZATION

Modularization is one of the most important design principles in software design. Modularity allows software systems to be manageable at all levels of the development life cycle. That is, the work products of the requirements, design, construction and testing efforts can all be modularized to efficiently carry out the operations. In the design phase, modularization is the principle that drives the continuous decomposition of the software system until fine grained components are created. Modularization plays a key role during all design activities, including software architecture and detailed construction design, when applied effectively, it provides a roadmap for software development starting from coarse-grained components that are further modularized into fine-grained components directly related to code. If applied properly, modularization can lead to designs that are easier to understand, resulting in systems that are easier to develop and maintain. Efficient modularization can be achieved by following and applying the principles of abstraction and encapsulation. With proper modularization, software systems can be decomposed into modules that allow the systems complexity to be manageable and allow the system to be efficiently built, maintained and reused.

7.8 DESIGN TECHNIQUES

A more methodical approach to software design is purposed by structured methods, which are sets of notations and guidelines for software design. Budgen (1993) describes some of the most commonly used methods such as structured design, structured systems analysis, Jackson System Development and various approaches to object-oriented design.

The use of structured methods involves producing large amounts of diagrammatic design documentation. CASE tools have been developed to support particular methods. In many projects, the structured methods are applied successfully. As they use standard notations and produce the standard design documents, they can reduce the cost.

Irrespective of who applies the mathematical method, they always produce the same results. The term structured methods suggests that from the specification, the designers should generate the designs which are similar to each other. Notations set of activities, rules, guidelines and report formats are included by the structured method. Following models are supported by the structured method:

1. **A Data-Flow Model:** In this model, by using the transformations in the data the system will be modeled.

2. **An Entity-Relation Model:** The logical data and structures used are described by this model.

3. **A Structural Model:** Documents the components of the system and interactions between them.

4. If the method is **Object-Oriented** it will include an inheritance model of the system, a model of how objects are composed of other objects and, usually, an object-use model which shows how objects are used by other objects.

The other system models like state transition diagram, entity life histories enhance the above models. Most methods suggest a centralized repository for system information or a data dictionary should be used. No one method is better or worse than other methods: the success or other methods often depends on their suitability for an application domain.

7.9 SUMMARY

- Software design is the process of transforming functional and non-functional requirements into models that describe the technical solution before development begins.
- There are primarily three main types of notations used in the design document: graphical notations, program description languages, and informal text

- The data design is basically the model of data that is represented at the high level of abstraction. Various elements of data design are: data object, databases and data warehouses.
- Architectural design comes before detailed system specification, it should not include any design information. Architectural design is necessary to structure and organize the specification.
- Architectural design can be represented using various models, like: structural model, framework model, dynamic model, process model and functional model.
- Component-level design is created by transforming the structural elements defined by the software architecture into procedural descriptions of software components.
- A component, also known as module, resides within the software architecture and serves one of the following three roles: A control component, A problem domain component and an infrastructure component.
- Component-level design is used to define the data structures, algorithms, interface description and communication mechanisms allocated to each module.
- User interface determine the way in which users interact with the software. The user interface design creates an effective communication medium between a human and a computer machine.
- In the design phase, modularization is the principle that drives the continuous decomposition of the software system until fine grained components are created.
- Various models that are supported by the structured method are A data-flow model, an entity-relation model, structural model, If the method is object-oriented it will include an inheritance model of the system

Object Oriented Design

8.1 INTRODUCTION

In unit 7, we have seen software design. The design should be specific to the problem and also general enough to address future problems and requirements. The goal of object-oriented programming is to make development easier, quicker, and more natural by raising the level of abstraction to the point where applications can be implemented in the same terms in which they are described in the application domain. It must be possible to find pertinent objects, factor them into classes at the right granularity, and establish key relationships among them.

In this unit, we will study objects and classes, relationship. We will also study an object oriented design process, object identification and design model such as sequence model and state diagram.

Objectives

After studying this unit, you should be able to:

*   describe objects and object classes
*   explain object oriented design process
*   discuss various design models

8.2   OBJECT AND OBJECT CLASSES

Objects: An object is a real world entity, comprising of data and methods to manipulate the data. We can have many objects nested inside one object. We are aware of the meaning of an object, but we have to describe the exact use of an object in software development.

Every real time entity can be called as an object, such as person, a place or a thing. It can be noun or noun phrase, either physical or conceptual. Some examples of objects of the college are shown in table 8.1:

Table 8.1

Object name	Description of the object
Kushal	An employee of the college. A physical entity
Computer	A department of the college. A conceptual entity
Sruthi	Head of the computer department and also an employee of the college.
Vindya	An employee of the computer department and also an employee of the college.

The objects kushal, sruthi and vindya have similarity. They can be categorized into a group (class) such as 'Employee'.

An object contains data and functions as its integral parts. In the object terminology, the data integral to an object are called attributes of the object and functions are called methods. This is shown in figure 8.1. In the example stated above, the objects can have different attributes such as emp_id, emp_name, designation, address, basic pay etc. These attributes distinguish one object from another. The methods that operate on the data (attribute) of the object are also the integral parts of the object. An object has an unique identity and refers to a single entity from a group of entities.

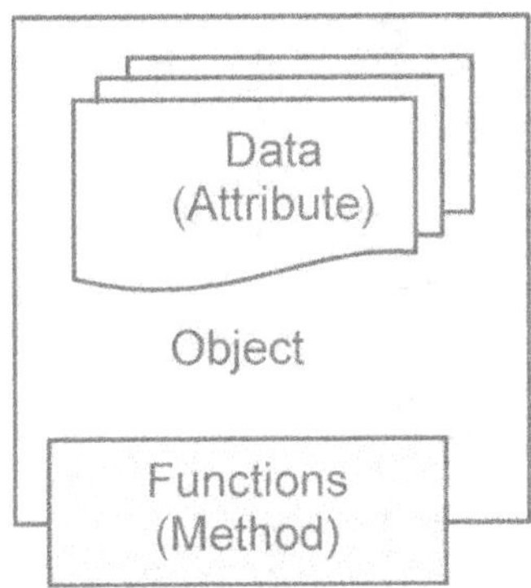

Figure 8.1 Structure of an Object

Object Classes

Now that we have seen the way to define an object using attributes, let us study the way to group these objects. Objects are grouped into a class. The class definition is given below.

Definition: An object class is defined as a group of objects with the same structure and behavior.

We usually identify the properties and behavior of a real world entity very easily. For example, we can easily identify a computer or a typewriter, based on the properties and behavior of a computer and a typewriter. Also, we can group all the properties of the particular object, say a computer, and call it as a class.

All objects belong to some particular class and every object is identified as an instance (occurrence) of that class. A class helps us to easily classify the objects and inherit properties from other classes. Classes define the properties of an object. For example, an object XYZ or let us say an instance XYZ of the class 'computer' has the property 'price'. This property can have different values such as Rs.36000, Rs.25000 etc.

We can call the class as a template for an object. Every object of a class has the same format and responds to the same instructions. For example, a class named 'Student' will have different objects of students (A, B, C) under it () which is shown in figure 8.2.

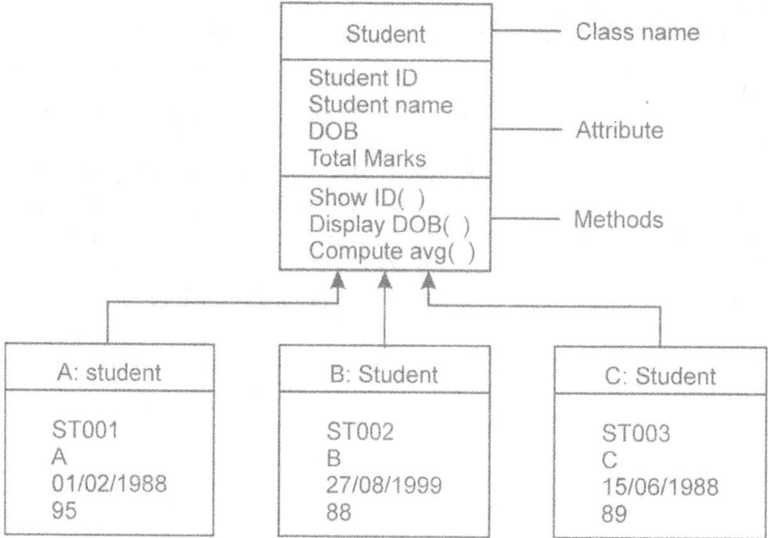

Figure 8.2 Example of a Class

Here, the student represents group of students. All these students are instances of the class and are individually identified as objects. The Student class can have unlimited number of such instances. The data associated with every object is managed by the object itself, but the instructions are managed by the class. If two students A and B of the class Student, are given an instruction to display their Date of birth using the 'Display DOB()' method, both the students respond equally to the instruction, but with their own unique DOBs. In object oriented programming, we use predefined classes for which we create different instances and solve the problem.

8.3   RELATIONSHIPS

A relationship provides a channel through which an instances of classes communicate with each other. They represent connection among instances of classes. Relationships are classified as follows:

- A Kind-Of relationship.
- Is-A relationship.
- Has-A relationship / Part-Of-relationship.

   Consider for a moment the similarities and differences among the following objects/classes: Automobile, Ford, truck, Car and Engine. We can make the following observations:

- A truck is a kind of an automobile.
- A car is a (different) kind of an automobile.
- An engine is a part of an automobile.
- An automobile has an engine.
- The ford is a car.

A-Kind-Of Relationship

Taking the example of a human being and an elephant, both are 'kind-of' relationship. As human beings and elephants are 'kind-of' mammals (living thing), they share the attributes and behaviors of mammals. Human being and elephants are subset of the mammals class. The following figure 8.3 depicts the relationship between the Mammals and Human Being classes:

Figure 8.3 Example for A-Kind-of Relationship

Is-A Relationship

Let's take an instance of the human being class – peter, who 'is –a' human being and, therefore, a mammal. The following figure 8.4 depicts the 'is –a' relationship.

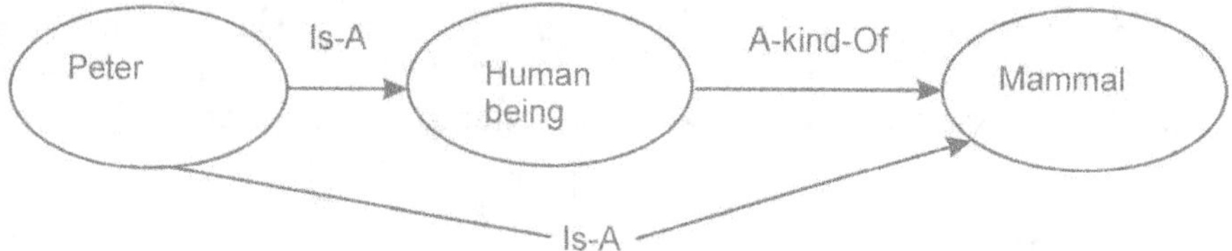

Figure 8.4 Example for Is-A Relationship

Has-A Relationship/Part-Of Relationship

A human being has a heart. This represents **has-a** relationship. Heart is a part of the human being. This represents **part-of** relationship. The figure 8.5 depicts the relationship between a human being and a heart.

Figure 8.5 Example for Has-A/Part-Of Relationship

8.4   OBJECT ORIENTED DESIGN PROCESS

In object oriented design process, we have to revisit the classes identified during the analysis phase so as to implement it in the design. We have to add more classes and attributes if required. Let us see the step by step process of object oriented design.

8.4.1 ACTIVITIES IN OBJECT ORIENTED DESIGN PROCESS

The activities in object oriented design process using unified approach are shown in figure 8.6.

In the OOAD design approach as shown in figure 8.6, we have three phases. The first phase deals with the designing of classes and applying the design axioms to it. Here we have to create the UML diagrams, define class associations and hierarchy.

In the second phase, we have to create the mirror classes for access layer corresponding to every class created in the first phase. We have to eliminate the redundant classes and use method classes to refine the class structure.

Third phase deals with designing view layer classes. Here we have to use the view level interface and create macro classes according to the axioms and corollaries. Here, we test the usability and user satisfaction also.

Finally, repeat the process until an effective design it formed. We can iterate each phase individually, different number of times to refine it.

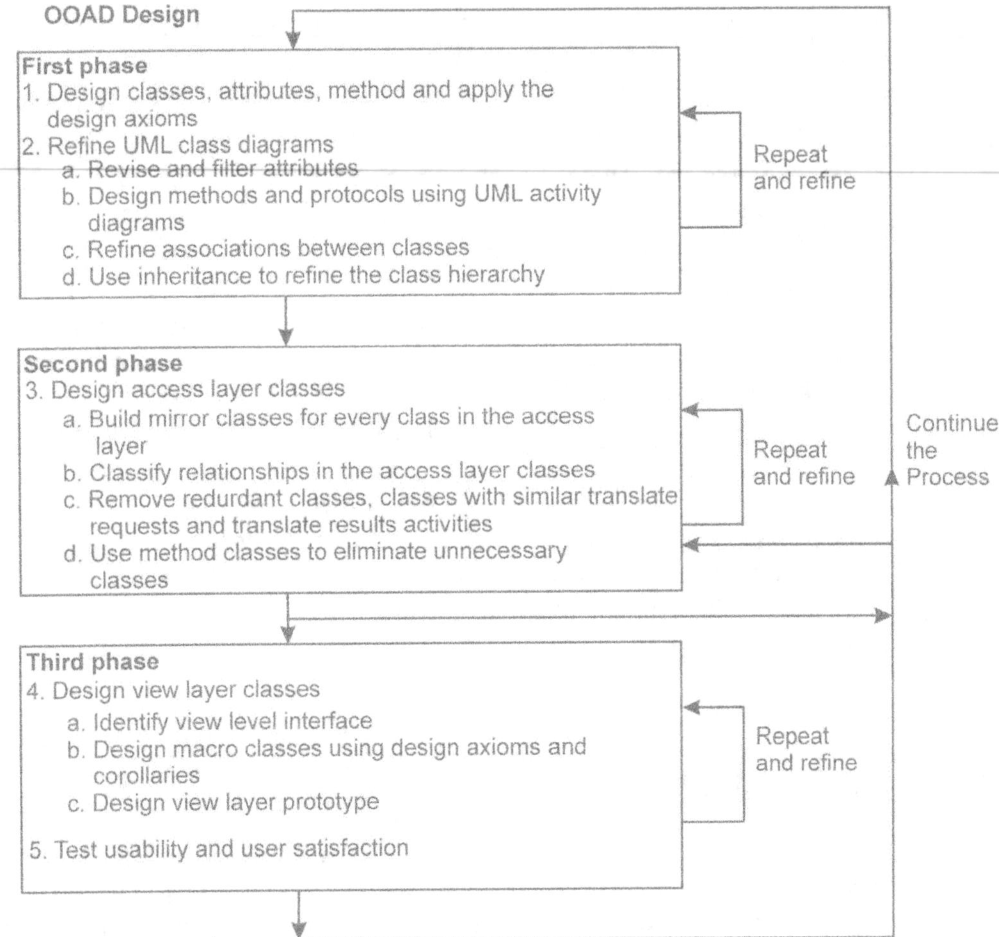

Figure 8.6 The Object Oriented Design using Unified Approach

Using the UML class diagrams, we can create an inheritance structure. We can find out the classes to be created and the classes to be reused. We can create specific subclasses and super classes if required. In object oriented systems, iteration is considered as a good practice. We have to follow a step by step approach while designing and the design should match the user requirements.

8.5   OBJECT IDENTIFICATION

The main problem in object-oriented design is identifying the objects that make up the system, their attributes and associated operations (methods). There is no simple formula, which allows objects to be identified. Designers must use their skill and experience in this task.

There are several plans that are made to identify objects, some of them are discussed below:

- **Use grammatical analysis** of a natural language description of a system. Objects and attributes are nouns, operations or services are verbs.

- **Use tangible entities** (things) in the application domain such as aircraft, roles such as manager, events such as request, interactions such as meetings, locations such as offices, organizational units such as companies, and so on.

- **Use a behavioral approach** in which the designer first understands the overall behavior of the system. The various behaviors are assigned to different parts of the system and an understanding derived of who initiates and participates in these behaviors. Participants who play significant roles are recognized as objects.

- **Use a scenario-based analysis** where various scenarios of system use are recognized and analyzed in turn. As individual scenario is analyzed, the team responsible for the analysis must recognize the required objects, attributes and operations. A method of analysis called Class-Responsibility-Collaboration (CRC) cards whereby analysts and designers take on the role of objects is effective in supporting this scenario-based approach.

These approaches are not limited. Good designers may use all of them when trying to identify objects.

8.6 DESIGN MODELS

Design models show the objects or object classes in a system and, the relationships between the entities. Design models essentially are the bridge between the system requirements and the system implementation. However, they also have to include enough details for programmers to make implementation decisions.

An important step in the design process, is to choose which design model is essential and the level of details of these models. This depends on the type of system that is being developed. There are two types of design models to describe an object-oriented design:

1. Static models describe the static nature of the system using object classes and their relationships.

2. Dynamic models describe the dynamic structure of the system and show the interactions between the system objects (not the object classes).

Unified Modeling Language (UML) provides twelve different static and dynamic models that may be produced to document a design. Some of them are seen below:

1. Subsystem models that show logical groupings of objects into coherent sub-systems. These are denoted using a form of class diagram where each sub-system is shown as a package. Subsystem models are static models.

2. Sequence models that show the sequence of object interactions. These are denoted using a UML sequence diagram. Sequence models are dynamic models.

3. State machine models that show how individual objects change their state in response to events. These are represented in the UML using state chart diagrams. State machine models are dynamic models.

Figure 8.7 shows the objects in the sub-systems in the weather station. For example, the commscontroller object is linked with the weatherstation object, and the weatherstation object is linked with the data collection package. This means that this object is linked with one or more objects in this package.

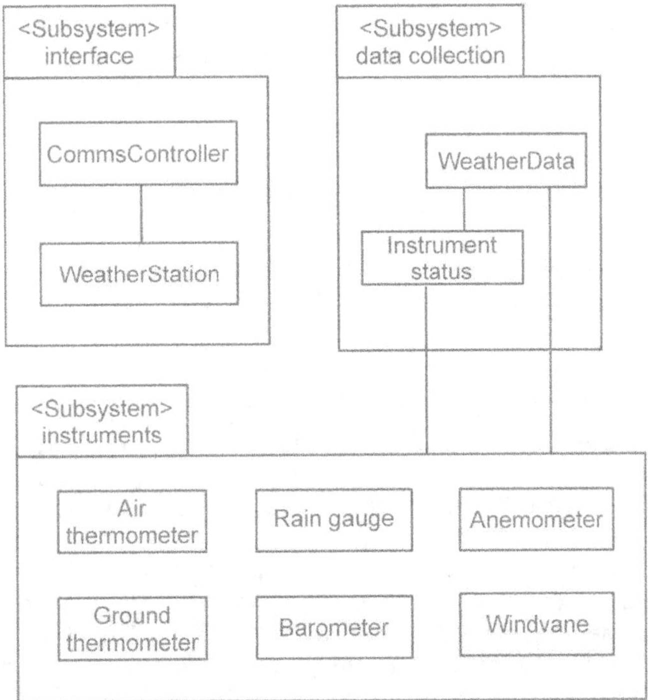

Figure 8.7 Weather Station Packages

8.6.1 SEQUENCE MODEL

Sequence models are dynamic models that document for each mode of interaction in which sequence of the object interactions takes place. Figure 8.8 is an example of a sequence model that shows the operations involved in collecting the data from a weather station, in a sequence model:

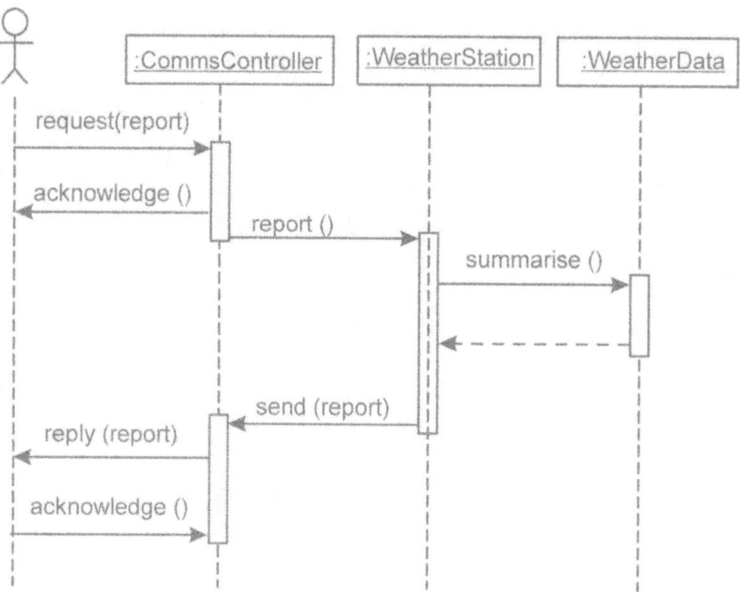

Figure 8.8 Sequence of Operations – Data Collection

1. The objects involved in the interaction are arranged horizontally with a vertical line linked to each object.
2. Time is denoted vertically so that time progresses down the dashed vertical lines. Therefore, the sequence of operations can be read easily from the model.
3. Labelled arrows linking the vertical lines represent interactions between objects. These are not data flows but denote messages or events that are fundamental to the interaction.
4. The thin rectangle on the object lifeline denotes the time when the object is controlling the object in the system. An object takes over control at the top of this rectangle and relinquishes control to another object at the bottom of the rectangle. If the hierarchy of calls, control is not relinquished until the last return then the initial method call has been completed.

Figure 8.8 shows the sequence of interactions when the external mapping system requests the data from the weather station. Read the sequence diagram from top to bottom:

1. An object that is an instance of commscontroller (:commscontroller) receives a request from its environment to send a weather report. It acknowledge receipt of this request. The half-arrowhead on the acknowledge message indicates that the message sender does not expect a reply.

2. This object sends a message to an object that is an instance of weatherstation to create a weather report. The instance of commscontroller then suspends itself (its control box ends). The style of arrowhead used indicates that the commscontroller object instance and the weatherstation object instance are objects that may execute concurrently.

3. That object that is an instance of weatherstation sends a message to a weatherdata object to summarise the weather data. in this case, the squared-off style of arrowhead indicates that the instance of weatherstation waits for a reply.
4. This summary is computed and the control returns to the weatherstation object. The dotted arrow indicates a return of control.
5. This object sends a message to commscontroller requesting it to transfer the data to the remote system. The weatherstation object then suspends itself.
6. The commscontroller object sends the summarized data to the remote system, receives an acknowledgement, and then suspends itself waiting for the next request.

From the sequence diagram, we can see that the commscontroller objects and the weatherstation objects are actually concurrent processes, where execution can be suspended and resumed. Essentially, the commscontroller object instance listens for messages from the external system, decodes these messages and initiates weather station operations.

8.6.2 STATE MACHINE MODEL

Sequence diagrams are used to model the combined behaviour of a group of objects, but you may also want to summarize the behaviour of a single object in response to the messages it can process. To do this, you can use a state machine model that show how the object instance changes state depending on the messages that it receives.

Figure 8.9 is a state chart for the weatherstation object that shows how it responds to request for various services. Read the figure 8.9 as follows:

1. If the object state is shutdown then it can only respond to a startup() message. It then moves into a state where it is waiting for further messages. The unlabeled arrow with the black blob denotes that the shutdown state is the initial state.
2. In the waiting state, the system expects further messages. If a shutdown() message is received, the object returns to the shutdown state.
3. If a reportweather() message is received, the system moves to the summarizing state. When the summary is complete, the system moves to s transmitting state where the information is transmitted through the commscontroller. It then returns to the waiting state.
4. If a calibrate() message is received, the system moves to the Calibrating state, then the Testing state, and then the Transmitting state, before returning to the Waiting state. If a test() message is received, the system moves directly to the Testing state.
5. If a signal from the clock is received, the system moves to the Collecting state, where it is collecting data from the instruments. Each instrument is instructed in turn to collect its data.

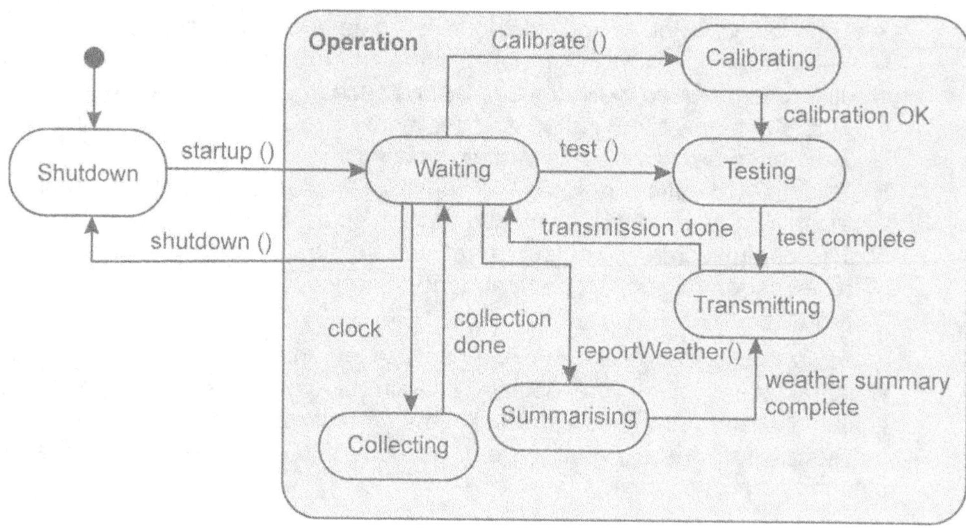

Figure 8.9 State Diagram for Weather Station

8.7 SUMMARY

- An object is a real world entity, comprising of data and methods to manipulate the data. Every real time entity can be called as an object, such as person, a place or a thing.
- An object contains data and functions as its integral parts. In the object terminology, the data integral to an object are called attributes of the object and functions are called methods.
- An object class is defined as a group of objects with the same structure and behaviour.
- A relationship provides a channel through which an instances of classes communicate with each other. They represent connection among instances of classes. Relationships are classified as follows: A Kind-Of relationship, Is-A relationship, Has-A relationship / Part-Of-relationship.
- In object oriented design process, we have to revisit the classes identified during the analysis phase so as to implement it in the design.
- There are several plans that are made to identify objects, some of them are: Use grammatical analysis, Use tangible entities, Use a behavioral approach, Use a scenario-based analysis and many more.
- Design models show the objects or object classes in a system and, the relationships between the entities. There are two types of design models to describe an object-oriented design: static models and dynamic models.
- Static models describe the static nature of the system using object classes and their relationships.

- Dynamic models describe the dynamic structure of the system and show the interactions between the system objects (not the object classes).
- Unified Modeling Language (UML) provides twelve different static and dynamic models to document a design.
- Sequence models that show the sequence of object interactions. These are denoted using a UML sequence diagram. Sequence models are dynamic models.
- State machine models that show how individual objects change their state in response to events. These are represented in the UML using state chart diagrams. State machine models are dynamic models.

Software Implementation

9.1   INTRODUCTION

In Chapter 8 we have studied object oriented design, after finalizing, reviewing and approving the software design, one or more programming team begin coding the software. Coding is done with the help of suitable programming languages. A number of languages are available for coding. But certain types of languages will be ideal for certain specific applications. Selection of coding language and use of coding standards are decided after considering different factors. These factors include the operating system used, nature of application, number of simultaneous users and many more.

The implementation phase of software development is concerned with translating design specifications into source code. The primary goal of implementation is to write source code and internal documentation so that the code to its specification can be easily verified. This goal can be achieved by making the source code as clear. Simplicity and clarity are the hall mark of good programs.

In this unit we study structured coding techniques, coding styles, coding methodology. We will also study code verification techniques, coding tools, code documentation, coding standards and guidelines

Objectives

After studying this unit, you should be able to:

- explain structured coding techniques
- describe coding styles and coding methodology
- explain code verification techniques
- list coding tools
- discuss code documentation
- explain coding standards and guidelines

9.2   STRUCTURED CODING TECHNIQUES

The goal of structured coding is to linearize control flow through a computer program so that the execution sequence follows the sequence in which the code is written, i.e., readability of code, which eases understanding, debugging, testing, documentation, and modification of programs. It also facilitates formal verification of programs. Source code clarity is enhanced by structured coding techniques, by good coding style, by appropriate supporting documents, by good internal comments and by the features provided in modern programming languages.

9.2.1   SINGLE-ENTRY, SINGLE-EXIT CONSTRUCTS

In 1966, Bohm and Jacopini demonstrated the sequencing, selection among alternative actions, and iterations are a sufficient set of constructs for describing the control flow for an algorithm. An algorithm can be written using sequencing, selection and iteration.

A modified version of the Bohm-Jacopini theorem can be stated as follows:

Any single-entry, single-exit program segment that has all statements on some path from the entry to the exit can be using only sequencing, selection and iteration.

A sufficient set of single-entry, single-exit constructs for specifying control flow in algorithm is:

- Sequencing: S1; S2; S3
- Selection: IF B THEN S1 ELSE S2
- Iteration: WHILE B DO S

The single-entry, single-exit property permits nesting of constructs within one another in any desired fashion. Each statement might be an assignment statement, a procedure call, an IF...THEN...ELSE, or a WHILE...DO. Statements of the latter forms may in turn contain nested statements. The most important aspect of the single-entry, single-exit property is that linearity of control flow is retained, even with nesting of constructs. The set of structured constructs selected for use in any particular application, is primarily matter of notational convenience.

9.3   CODING STYLES

As a part of software development plan, a coding style specifies the style for writing code. A coding style should be realistic, easy to learn and practical. The main advantage of using a coding style is that code written by various developers will look as if it is written by one person. The style should be adhered by all developers without exception. Moreover, it should adhered during both the development and the maintenance of the software.

Coding style is a primary influence on software maintenance. During the entire period that the product source exists, it has been developing and maintained by many people, and is sometimes passed from one company to another. Moreover, a specific coding style is characteristic of each person, and code maintained by different people often looks almost unreadable. To avoid this issue, coding style guides were developed. For example coding style guide for C prescribes having two files (MyModule.c and MyModule.h), where .c is the implementation file and .h is the interface file. A unified coding style is an important factor in code trustworthiness, since it lowers the probability of a bug and makes the code more understandable and self-explanatory.

9.4   CODING METHODOLOGY

Coding methodology refers to a set of well-documented procedures and guidelines used in the analysis, design and implementation of programs. Coding methodology includes a diagrammatic notation for documenting the results of the procedure. It also includes an objective set of criteria for determining whether the results of the procedure are of the desired quality or not. To use coding methodology, a number of steps are followed, such as:

A. The software development team begins its work by reviewing and understanding the design and requirements specification documents. These documents are essential for understanding user requirements and creating a framework for the software code.

B. In case the software development team is unable to understand user requirements correctly and further clarification is required, the queries are sent back to the user. The software development team also returns the requirements that are understood by them.

C. After the requirements are clearly understood by the software development team, the design and specification are implemented in source code, supporting files and the header files. While writing the software code, the coding style guidelines should be followed. In some cases, there may be a proposal of change in hardware or software specifications. However, the requests for change are implemented only after the approval of the user.

D. When the software code is completely written, it is compiled along with other required files.

E. Code inspection and reviews are conducted after the compilation. These methods are used to correct and verify errors in the software code.

F. Software testing is carried out to detect errors and correct in each module of the software code, its integration with hardware, the type of errors and so on.

G. After the software code is tested, the software is delivered to the user along with the relevant code files, header files and documentation files.

In case further change and clarification are required in the design or software requirements specification (SRS) documents, the software development team raises a query, which is sent to the user with the document containing what the software development team understood from the documents sent by the user. Changes are made only when the user has a positive response to the queries raised by the software development team.

9.5　CODE VERIFICATION TECHNIQUES

Code verification is the process used for checking the software code for error introduced in the coding phase. The objective of code verification process is to check the software code in all aspects. This process includes checking the consistency of user requirements with the design phase. The code verification process does not concentrate on proving the correctness of programs. Instead, it verifies whether the software code has been translated according to the requirements of the user or not.

The code verification techniques are classified into two categories, namely, dynamic and static techniques. The dynamic technique is performed by executing some test data. The outputs of the program are tested to find errors in the software code. This technique follows the conventional approach for testing the software code. In the static technique, the program is executed conceptually and without any data. In other words, the static technique does not use any traditional approach as used in the dynamic technique. Some of the static techniques commonly used are code reading, static analysis, symbolic execution, code inspection and reviews. Figure 9.1 shows a static techniques.

Code Reading

Code reading is a technique that concentrates on how to read and understand a computer program. It is essential for a software developer to know code reading. The process of reading a software program in order to understand it is known as code reading or program reading. In this process, attempts are made to understand the documents, software specifications, or software designs. The purpose of reading programs is to determine the correctness and consistency of the code. In addition, code reading is performed to enhance the software code without entirely changing the program or with minimal disruption in the current functionality of' the program. Code reading also aims at inspecting the code and removing (fixing) errors from it.

Static Analysis

Static analysis comprises a set of methods used to analyze the source code or object code of the software to understand how the software functions and to set up criteria to check its correctness. Static analysis studies the source code without executing it and gives information about the structure of model used, data and control flows, syntactical accuracy, and much more.

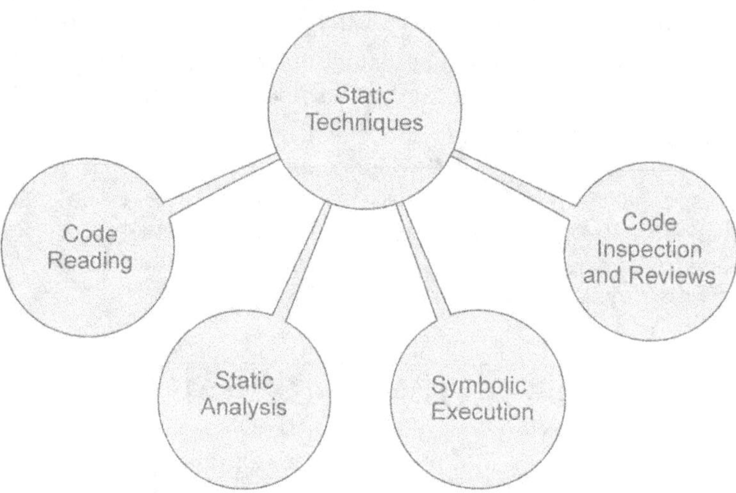

Figure 9.1 Static Techniques

Symbolic Execution

Symbolic execution concentrates on assessing the accuracy of the model by using symbolic values instead of actual data values for input. Symbolic execution, also known as symbolic evaluation, is performed by providing symbolic inputs, which produce expressions for the output.

Code Inspection and Reviews

The inspection process is carried out to check whether the implementation of the software code is done according to the user requirements. This technique is a formal and systematic examination of the source code to detect errors. During this process, the software is presented to the project managers and the users for a comment of approval. Before providing any comment, the inspection team checks the source code for errors.

9.6 CODING TOOLS

The coding tools make the work simple, efficient and fast. The advantage of using coding tools is that developers need not know the details of the rules and the syntax of the programming languages. Apart from the availability of different programming tools, several other tools are also available for such varied operations like image editing, text editing, web authoring etc. Image editing and text editing tools are indispensable for content generation of web pages. Packages such as dream weaver and front page are widely accepted for creating and managing websites. These have user-friendly interfaces. Java applets and activeX controls can be embedded in web pages.

Hot Metal PRO is another tool having additional features for getting data from external sources to a web page. Also different visual elements can be added to web pages. Front Page helps in the creation of different types of frames, draw tables and add rich and dynamic graphics to the site. Powerful functionality can be added by using this tool. Database functions help to make direct access to database and access information. HTML editor helps in editing HTML code. Several java development tools are also available for database applications. Oracle form builder helps in the creation of several forms. Form builder helps in avoiding manual coding for the creation of different forms. Forms can be easily converted to HTML files for creation of web pages. Using oracle reports, it is possible to create reports easily. Different wizards provided along with these tools make the selection of reports and the coding easier. Wizards are also available in other common database management systems like MS Access, SQL Server, IBM DB2, etc. Since several types of coding languages and coding tools are available, the choice regarding the selection of the right tool or the language for coding depends on factors such as the kind of application, frequency of web content access, technology used, etc.

While writing a software code, several coding tools are used along with the programming language to simplify the tasks of writing a software code. The coding tools vary from one programming language to another as they developed according to a particular programming language. However, sometimes a single coding tool can be used in more than one programming language. Generally, coding tools comprise text editors, supporting tools for a specific programming language, and the framework required to run the software code. Some of the commonly used coding tools are listed in table 9.1.

Table 9.1 Coding Tools

Coding Tools	Language	Description
JBuilder	Java, XML	Used to speed up web applications and database applications. It provides interfaces to application servers such as Web Logic, WebSphere and EAServer as an editor and visual flow designer. In addition, it provides the J2SE and J2EE support in Java, enhanced performance tools, and code audits.
Dreamweaver	HTML, ASP.NET	Used for the server-side scripting of languages such as ASP.NET and HTML. In addition, it is used for performing functions such as creation of websites, database connections, querying a database, formatting the output of software code, and displaying multiple records.
Eclipse	Java	Used for Integrated Development Environment (IDE) for Java. It is a cross-platform tool integrated with other coding tools of Java and relatively easy to set up.

Table 9.1 *Contd...*

Coding Tools	Language	Description
Ant	Java	Used for writing code in Java. In addition, it is a cross-platform tool and is flexible to use as any action being performed repeatedly can be standardized using Ant.
Junit	Java	Used for testing a framework by creating tests for the software code that are to be repeated as often as required.

In addition to the programming language and coding tools, there are some software programs that are essential to run the software code. For example, a debugger is used to detect the source of program errors by performing a step-by-step execution of the software code. A debugger breaks program execution at various levels in the application program. It supports features, such as breakpoints, displaying or changing memory and so on. Similarly, compilers are used to translate programs written in a high-level language into their machine language equivalents.

9.7   CODE DOCUMENTATION

Code documentation is a manual-cum-guide that helps in understanding and correctly utilizing the software code. The coding standards and naming conventions written in a commonly spoken language in code documentation provide enhanced clarity for the designer. Moreover, they act as a guide for the software maintenance team (this team focuses on maintaining software by improving and enhancing the software after it has been delivered to the end user) while the software maintenance process is carried out. In this way, code documentation facilitates code reusability.

While writing a software code, the developer needs proper documentation for reference purposes. Programming is an ongoing process and requires modifications from time to time. When a number of software developers are writing the code for the same software, complexity increases. With the help of documentation, software developers can reduce the complexity by referencing the code documentation. Some of the documenting techniques are comments, visual appearances of codes, and programming tools. **Comments** are used to make the reader understand the logic of a particular code segment. The **visual appearance of a code** is the way in which the program should be formatted to increase readability. The **programming tools** in code documentation are algorithms, flowcharts, and pseudo-codes.

Code documentation contains source code, which is useful for the software developers in writing the software code. The code documents can be created with the help of various coding tools that are used to auto-generate the code documents. In other words, these documents extract comments from the source code and create a reference manual in the form of text or HTML file. The auto-generated code helps the software developers to extract the source code from the comments. This documentation also contains application programming interfaces, data structures, and algorithms. There are two kinds of code documentation, namely, internal documentation and external documentation.

Internal Documentation

Documentation which focuses on the information that is used to determine the software code is known as internal documentation. It describes the data structures, algorithms, and control flow in the programs. There are various guidelines for making the documentation easily understandable to the reader. Some of the general conventions to be used at the time of internal documentation are header comment blocks, program comments, and formatting. Header comment blocks are useful in identifying the purpose of the code along with details such as how the c0ge functions and how each segment of code is used in the program.

Since software code is updated and revised several times, it is important to keep a record of the code information so that internal documentation reflects the changes made to the software code. Internal documentation should explain how each code section relates to user requirements in the software. Generally, internal documentation comprises the following information.

1. Name, type, and purpose of each variable and data structure used in the code
2. Brief description of algorithms, logic, and error-handling techniques
3. Information about the required input and expected output of the program
4. Assistance on how to test the software
5. Information on the upgradations and enhancements in the program.

External Documentation

Documentation which focuses on general description of the software code and is not concerned with its detail is known as external documentation. It includes information such as function of code, name of the software developer who has written the code, algorithms used in the software code, dependency of code on programs and libraries, and format of the output produced by the software code. Generally, external documentation includes structure charts for providing an outline of the program and describing the design of the program.

External documentation is useful for software developers as it consists of information such as description of the problem along with the program written to solve it. In addition, it describes the approach used to solve the problem, operational requirements of the program, and user interface components. For the purpose of readability and proper understanding, the detailed description is accompanied by figures and illustrations that show how one component is related to another. External documentation explains why a particular solution is chosen and implemented in the software. It also includes formulas, conditions, and references from where the algorithms or documentation are derived. External documentation makes the user aware of the errors that occur while running the software code. For example, if an array of five numbers is used, it should be mentioned in the external documentation that the limit of the array is five.

9.8 CODING STANDARDS AND GUIDELINES

Good developers always follow the coding standards and guidelines while writing the code. Code written using the standards and guidelines are easy to review, understand and debug. It is also easy to maintain and enhance the code if it follows the standards and guidelines.

Advantages of coding standards:

Figure 9.2 shows the advantages of coding standards.

- **Reusability**: It is easy to use parts of code as it is written in standard code.
- **Maintainability**: It is easy to identify bugs, easy to add new features.
- **Readability**: Coding standard increases easy reading.
- **Understandability**: It is easy to understand – this is not the same as readability, example: relative code may be readable, but not understandable.
- **Robustness**: Code that can handle unexpected inputs and conditions.
- **Reliability**: Code i.e., unlikely to produce wrong results.

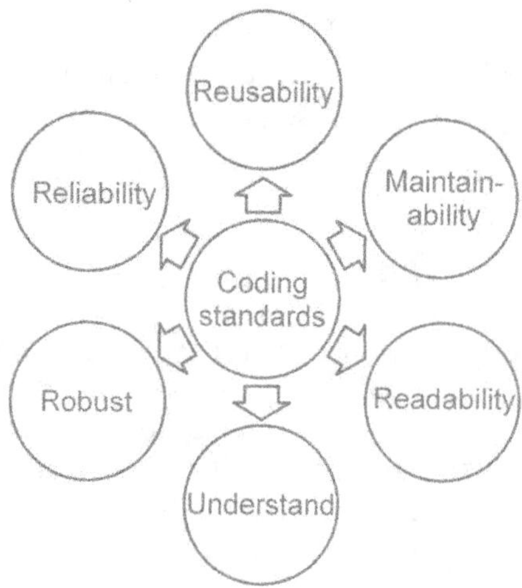

Figure 9.2 Coding Standards

The sample coding standards and guidelines are as follows:

- Write comments before writing the code.
- Use meaningful names for variables and functions. (try to avoid single character variable names and function names).
- Avoid extremely long names.
- Format the code properly using the standards specific to the programming language.
- Use tools to improve coding standards if possible.
- Prefix "is" for Boolean variable – for example: is Open+True

- Comment should explain "why" instead of "How" , why a particular algorithm was chosen.
- Comments should be blended into the code.
- Avoid deeply nested code.
- Never use " Go To" Statement.
- Don't duplicate the code.
- Avoid using multiple inheritance.

9.9   SUMMARY

1. Source code clarity is enhanced by structured coding techniques, by good coding style, by appropriate supporting documents, by good internal comments and by the features provided in modern programming languages.
2. A coding style should be realistic, easy to learn and practical. The main advantage of using a coding style is that code written by various developers will look as if it is written by one person.
3. Coding methodology refers to a set of well-documented procedures and guidelines used in the analysis, design and implementation of programs.
4. The objective of code verification process is to check the software code in all aspects.
5. The code verification techniques are classified into two categories, namely, dynamic and static techniques.
6. Code reading is a technique that concentrates on how to read and understand a computer program.
7. The coding tools make the work simple, efficient and fast. The advantage of using coding tools is that developers need not know the details of the rules and the syntax of the programming languages.
8. Code documentation is a manual-cum-guide that helps in understanding and correctly utilizing the software code.

Structure

10.1 INTRODUCTION

In Chapter 9, we have studied about software implementation, now we will see software maintenance, in most of the field's maintenance means it's about repairing things that break or wear out. But in software field, the nature of software is such that it never breaks or wears out. Software is an intangible thing, having no particular physical form, and so there is not anything to break or wear out. Software can have errors in it. The software can be modified to do new things. The thing is, software errors are not due to material weakness, but rather to errors made when the software was being built or errors made as the software is being changed. So software maintenance is about fixing those errors as they are discovered and making those changes as they become necessary.

In this unit we will study, Software re-engineering, Change management. We will also study configuration management, maintenance tools and techniques.

Objectives

After studying this unit, you should be able to:

- explain software reengineering process model
- discuss objectives of change management
- list the tasks of configuration management
- discuss impact analysis

10.2   SOFTWARE RE-ENGINEERING

Re-engineering is a rebuilding activity, and we can better understand the re-engineering of information systems if we consider an analogous activity; the rebuilding of a house. Consider the following situation; if you purchased a house in another state. You've never actually seen the property, but you acquired it at an reasonable low price, with the warning that it might have to be completely rebuilt. How would you proceed?

- Before you can start rebuilding, it would seem reasonable to inspect the house. To determine whether it is in need of rebuilding, you would create a list of criteria so that your inspection would be systematic.
- Before you tear down and rebuilt the entire house, be sure that the structure is weak. If the house is structurally sound, it may be possible to "remodel" without rebuilding.
- Before you start rebuilding be sure you understand how the original was built. Take a peek behind the walls. Understand the wiring, the plumbing, and the structural internals. Even if you trash them all, the insight you'll gain will serve you well when you start construction.
- If you begin to rebuild, use only the most modern, long-lasting materials. This may cost a bit more now, but it will help you to avoid expensive and time-consuming maintenance later.
- If you decide to rebuild, be disciplined about it. Use practices that will result in high quality–today and in the future.

These principles focus on the rebuilding of a house, they apply equally well to the re-engineering of computer-based systems and applications.

To implement these principles, we apply software re-engineering process model that defines six activities, shown in Figure10.1. In some cases, these activities occur in a linear sequence, but this is not always the case. For e.g., it may be that reverse engineering may have to occur before document restricting can commence.

The re-engineering paradigm shown in Figure 10.1 is a cyclical model. This means that each of the activities presented as a part of the paradigm may be revised. For any particular cycle, the process can terminate after any one of these activities.

Inventory analysis: Every software organization should have an inventory of all applications. The inventory can be nothing more than a spreadsheet model containing information that provides a detailed description (e.g., size, age, business critical) of every active applications by storing the information according to business critically, longevity, current maintainability, and other locally important criteria, candidate for reengineering work.

It is important to note that the inventory should be revisited on a regular cycle. The status of applications (e.g. Business critically) can change as a function of time, and as a result, priorities for re-engineering will shift.

Document restructuring: Weak documentation is the trademark of many legacy systems. But what we do about it? What are our options?

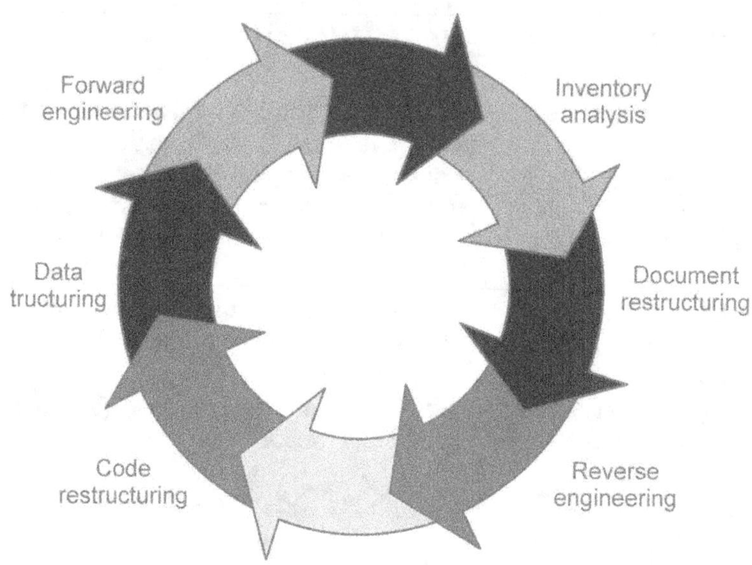

Figure 10.1 A Software Re-engineering Process Model

1. Creating documentation is too time consuming. If the system works, we'll live with what we have. In some cases, this is correct approach. It is not possible to re-create documentation for hundreds of computer programs. If a program is relatively static, is coming to the end of its useful life, and is unlikely to undergo significant change.
2. Documentation must be updated, but we have limited resources. We'll use a "document when touched" approach. It may not be necessary to fully re-document an application. Rather, those portions of the system that are currently undergoing change are fully documented. Over time, a collection of useful and relevant documentation will evolve.
3. The system is business critical and must be fully re-documented. Even in this case, an intelligent approach is to prepare documentation to an essential minimum.

A software of organization must choose the one that is most appropriate for each case.

Reverse Engineering: Reverse engineering is the process of analyzing software with the objective of recovering its design and specification. The software source code is usually available as input to the reverse engineering process. Reverse engineering is different from re-engineering. Reverse engineering purpose is to derive the design or specification of a system from its source code, while the objective of re-engineering is to produce a new, more maintainable system.

Code Restructuring: The common type of re-engineering is code restructuring. Some legacy systems have a relatively solid program architecture, but individual modules were coded in a way that makes them difficult to understand, test, and maintain. In such cases, the code within the suspect modules can be restructured.

To accomplish this activity, the source code is analyzed using structuring tool, Violations of structured programming constructs are noted and code is then restructured. The resultant restructured code is reviewed and tested to ensure that no anomalies have been introduced, internal code documentation is updated.

Data structuring: A program with weak data architecture will be difficult to adapt and enhance. In fact, for many applications, data architecture has more to do with the long-term viability of a program that the source code itself.

Unlike code restructuring, which occurs at a relatively low level of abstraction, data structuring is a full-scale re-engineering activity. In most cases, data restructuring begins with a reverse engineering activity. Data object and attributes are identified, and existing data structures are reviewed for quality.

When data structure is weak (e.g., Flat files are currently implemented, when a relational approach would greatly simplify process), the data reengineered. Because data architecture has a strong influence on program architecture and algorithms that populate it, changes to the data will invariably result in either architectural or code-level changes.

Forward Engineering: In an ideal word, applications should be rebuilt using an automated 're-engineering engine'. The old program would be fed into the engine, analyzed, restructured, and then regenerated in a form that exhibited the best aspects of software quality. In the short term, it is unlikely that such an 'engine' will appear, but CASE vendors have introduced told that provide a limited subset of these capabilities that addresses specific application domain. More important these re-engineering tools are becoming increasingly more sophisticated.

Forward engineering, also called renovation or reclamation, not only recovers design information from existing software, but uses this information to alter or reconstitute the existing system in an effort to improve its overall quality. In most cases, reengineered software reimplements the function of the existing system and also adds new functions and/or improves overall performance.

10.3   CHANGE MANAGEMENT

Change management evaluates and plans the change process. It makes sure that a change is made in the most efficient way possible. It ensures that the proper procedures are followed. This in turn ensures the quality and continuity of IT services of the organization.

10.3.1   ELEMENTS OF CHANGE MANAGEMENT

Change management is the correct application of tools, skills, processes and principles required for making a suitable change. The three main elements of change management are:

- Set of tools, skills, processes and principles.
- Acceptance of change by the people.
- Achievement of the desired results of the project.

Let us now see these elements.

Set of tools, skills, processes and principles

Change management uses a number of tools to bring about a successful change. A communication plan and training plan are two of the most widely used tools. The change management process describes the sequence of activities that should be followed for a particular project. Generally, there are three phases. They are:

- Preparing the change
- Managing the change
- Reinforcing the change

Change management uses the skill of almost everyone in the organization. However, the contribution of executives, managers, leaders and supervisors is more important. Change management uses certain principles for proper implementation.

Acceptance of change by the people

When a change is made in an organization, the job of every individual changes. Changes that make an impact on the jobs of people need structure and planning to address the change of the people involved. An important aspect of managing changes that impact employees is to understand how each individual successfully makes the change. The success of a change depends on the adaptability of the individuals involved.

Achievement of the desired results of the project

Having a change management process increases the probability of a project to achieve its objectives on a large scale. It also increases the probability of maintaining the schedule and budget. This clause is important while discussing change management with executives, managers, leaders, and supervisors.

10.3.2 OBJECTIVES OF CHANGE MANAGEMENT

The objectives of change management include the following:

- Ensure that the reason for change is clear.
- Identify the important people who will be involved in the change activities.
- Define the sponsorship, communication and involvement to all the stakeholders.
- Plan the activities and involvement of change sponsors.
- Plan how and when a certain activity should be carried out.
- Deliver appropriate messages.
- Assess the impact of the people and the organization.
- Plan activities that take care of the impact of the change.
- Ensure that people who are involved and are affected by the change understand the change properly and have proper guidance during this time.

- Assess the training needs due to the change and plan how this will be implemented.
- Have success indicators and ensure these are measured regularly.

10.3.3 ISSUES OF CHANGE MANAGEMENT

Some of the common issues faced by the change management are:

- **Technology** – A technology change like software change, a new hardware, change in operating system or even a procedural adjustment causes discomfort and problems for many. The IT departments generally implement changes with limited considerations for training and how people may react to the change.
- **Mergers or acquisitions** – If the company purchases or starts a new business, it may create doubts in the mind of the existing employees about their career. They will fear all kinds of changes that may happen. Generally, mergers or acquisitions bring in changes such as a change of role, leadership, or even termination.
- **New leadership** – The change of CEO or leadership departments compels the staff to make adjustments that may not be easy. If the person has been holding the position for a long time the adjustment becomes even more difficult.
- **Staff changes** – Addition or removal of members changes the dynamics of the team and the organization.
- **Office relocation** – It is not important if one is moving nearby or far away. The important aspect is ensuring that employees know the new location and assurance that the required facilities are available. This helps them to work with a relaxed mind.

10.4 CONFIGURATION MANAGEMENT

The process of defining, recording, and reporting the status of Configuration Items (CI) within a system is known as configuration management. Configuration management also verifies the correctness of a configuration item. Configuration management is a must have process in any security plan. It offers a logical model of the IT infrastructure in the form of documentation. It also keeps track of versions of configuration items and authorizes or forbids use of hardware and software.

10.4.1 TASKS OF CONFIGURATION MANAGEMENT

Configuration management involves teams that perform certain tasks. These tasks are iterative, incremental, and are bound by time-constraints. Figure10.2 shows the flow of the configuration management process.

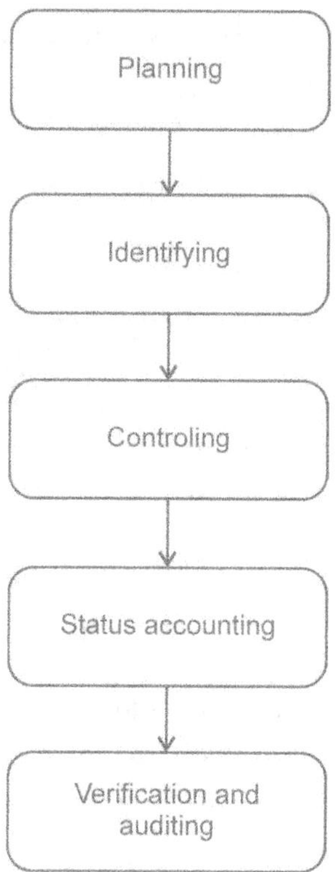

Figure 10.2 Configuration Management Process

The tasks of configuration management involve:

1. Planning
2. Identifying
3. Controlling
4. Status accounting
5. Verification and auditing

Planning

Planning involves the following steps:

- Definition scope, objectives, policies, rules and regulations of configuration management plan.
- Confirmation of the associated policies, rules, responsibilities, and regulations that govern a particular task in an organization.
- Schedule of time for every process. Make a schedule of the start time as well as the end time.
- Assignment of roles and responsibilities to every member of the group, so that there is a clear understanding of the tasks to be done.
- Instructions to the team members to follow a suitable and uniform naming convention.

Identifying

Identifying Configuration Items (CIs) is the next step after planning. This step involves:

- Recognition of each CI's configuration structure.
- Identification of connectivity between the CIs and their documentation.
- Placing related documents together.
- Allocation and identification of different versions of various CIs.
- Recording of each version of the CI into the database.

Controlling

Controlling involves addition of only genuine CIs in the database. The control task must focus on:

- Ensuring entry of all the components in the Configuration Management Database (CMDB).
- Supervising the status of all the components of CI.
- Updating the dependencies of CI.
- Reporting the license status.

Status accounting

Status accounting involves:

- Recording of past and present data of a particular CI in order to avail details of each CI to the users.
- Inclusion of version number, validity period, status, and repairing details in the record.

Verification and Auditing

The configuration management team has to verify the data addition into database and conduct periodic audits. The purpose of audits is to ensure similarity in the Configuration Management Database (CMDB) data and actual configuration of the organization's IT infrastructure.

If the CMDB includes CIs like documentation, Service Level Agreements (SLAs), and personnel, the manual audits should involve the backup action of these CIs. Audits have to be carried out frequently. They need to be done:

- After a new CMDB is implemented
- Before and after major changes in infrastructure
- When CMDB is suspected of containing incorrect or incomplete information.

Audits have to concentrate more on the following aspects:

- Using correct naming convention in CI records
- Updating CI status
- Communicating with change management
- Checking for fulfilment of defined levels of scope and detail
- Finding the match between CMDB structure and the real IT structure.

10.5 SOFTWARE MAINTENANCE TOOLS AND TECHNIQUES

Over the years many tools and techniques have been developed that directly or indirectly concern software maintenance. Some of the tools and techniques are seen below:

Software Configuration Management: Already we have studied configuration management in section 10.4. In this section we discuss in more detail. Configuration management is practiced by establishing a configuration control board because many maintenance-related changes are requested by users or customers to correct failures or make enhancements. The board oversees the change process, and its membership includes parties like customers, users and developers. Each highlighted problem is handled in the following manner.

1. A user, developer or customer who discovers a problem uses a formal change control form to record all associated symptoms. Similarly, in the case of enhancement, all relevant information is recorded.
2. The configuration control board is formally informed of the proposed change.
3. The board meets and discusses the proposed change.
4. After making a decision about the change requested, the board prioritizes the change and assigns appropriate individuals to make the change.
5. The designated individuals identifies the problem source and the high-lights the changes required. Working with the test copy, the assigned individual tests and implements the changes.
6. The designated individual's works with the software program librarian to control and track the change or modification installation in the operational system and update associated documentation.
7. A change report describing the changes made is filed by the designated individual.

Impact Analysis

Software maintenance depends on the customer or user requirements. A requirement translating into a seemingly minor change is frequently more extensive; consequently, more costly to implement than anticipated. Under such circumstances a study of the impact of the change could provide useful information, especially where the change is complex and sophisticated.

Impact analysis can be defined as the determination of risks associated with the proposed change, including the estimation of effects on factors such as effort, resources and schedule.

Maintenance Reduction

Reduction is the amount of maintenance which helps to increase maintenance productivity. A maintenance staff armed with the latest knowledge, skills and techniques can improve significant productivity and quality improvements.

Some methods for reducing software maintenance are as follows:

- Use of portable languages, operating systems and tools.

- Use preventive maintenance approaches, such as using limits for tables that are reasonably greater than possibly be required.
- Highlight possible enhancements and design the software so that it can easily incorporate those enhancements.
- Consider human factors in areas such as screen layouts during software design. This is one source of frequent changes or modifications.
- Introduce structured maintenance that employs approaches for documenting currently existing systems and includes guidelines for reading programs etc.

10.6 SUMMARY

- Re-engineering is a rebuilding activity.
- software reengineering process model has various activities like inventory analysis, document restructuring, reverse engineering, Code restructuring, Data structuring, Forward Engineering.
- Change management evaluates and plans the change process.
- The three main elements of change management are: Set of tools, skills, processes and principles, Acceptance of change by the people, Achievement of the desired results of the project.
- The change management process describes the sequence of activities that should be followed for a particular project. Generally, there are three phases. They are: Preparing the change, Managing the change, Reinforcing the change.
- Some of the common issues faced by change management are: Technology, Mergers or acquisitions, New leadership, Staff changes, Office relocation.
- The process of defining, recording, and reporting the status of Configuration Items (CI) within a system is known as configuration management.
- The tasks of configuration management involve: Planning, Identifying, Controlling, Status accounting, Verification and auditing.
- Over the years many tools and techniques have been developed that directly or indirectly concern software maintenance.

11 Software Testing Strategies

Structure

11.1 INTRODUCTION

In chapter 10, we have studied software maintenance, now we will see software testing strategies, the main aim of testing is to identify all the defects existing in the software product. Testing is a process of identifying the program behavior for the set of sample test input. If it behaves as expected, then it is fine otherwise we need to note the condition under which failure occurs and later debug and correct the error. For this purpose, we need to define different test case design methods and testing techniques. The low-level testing is used to test the modules for correct implementation whereas the high-level testing is for testing the system against the requirements of the customer.

In this unit, we will study, a strategic approach to software testing, test strategies for convention software, Black-box and white box testing, validation and system testing, and debugging.

Objectives

After studying this unit, you should be able to:

- discuss the generic characteristics of software testing
- describe testing strategies for convention software
- differentiate whit box and black box testing
- explain validation testing
- define system testing, stress testing and performance testing
- describe debugging

11.2 A STRATEGIC APPROACH TO SOFTWARE TESTING

Testing activity can be planned and conducted systematically; hence, to very specific test case design methods are defined called as templates.

A number of software testing has been proposed in the literature. All provide the software developer with a template for testing and all have the following generic characteristics.

- Testing begins at module level or class or object level in object-oriented systems and works Outward toward the integration of the entire computer based system.
- Different techniques are appropriate at different points in time.
- Testing is conducted by the developer of the software and, an independent test group for large projects.
- Testing and debugging are different activities, but debugging must be accommodated in any testing state.

How should a strategy be?

- A strategy for software testing must accommodate low-level tests that are necessary to verify that a small source code segment has been correctly implemented as well as high-level tests that validate major customer requirements.
- A strategy must provide guidance for the practitioner and a set of milestones for the manager. Because the steps of the test strategy occur at a time when deadline pressure begins to rise, progress must be measurable and problems must surface.

11.3 TESTING STRATEGIES FOR CONVENTION SOFTWARE

The software engineering process may be viewed as a spiral, illustrated in figure 11.1, initially system engineering defines the roll of software and leads to software requirements and analysis, where the information domain, function, behavior, performance, constraints, and validation criteria for software are established. Moving inward along the spiral, we come to design and finally to coding.

To develop computer software, we spiral in along streamlines that decrease the level of Abstraction on each turn.

The strategy for software testing may also be viewed in the context of the spiral.

Unit testing begins at the start of the spiral and concentrates on each unit of the software as implemented in source code. Testing progresses by moving outward along the spiral to **integration testing**, where the focus is on design and the construction of the software architecture. Talking another turn outward on the spiral, we encounter.

Validation testing where requirements established as part of software requirements analysis are validated against the software that has been constructed. Finally, we arrive at system testing where the software and other system elements are tested as a whole.

To test computer software, we spiral out along streamlines that broaden the scope of testing with each turn.

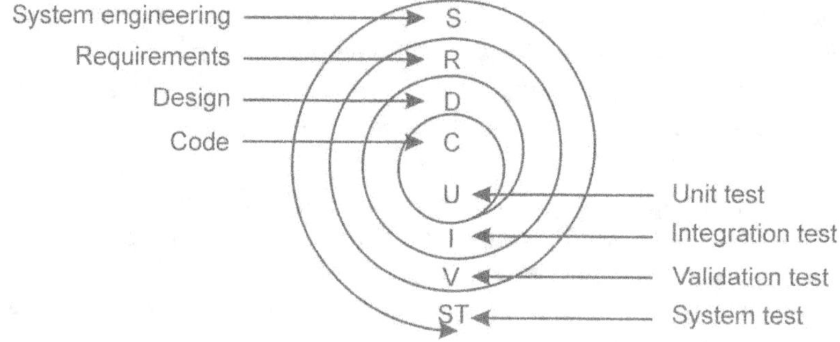

Figure 11.1 Testing Strategy

Considering the process from a procedural point of view testing within the context of software engineering is a series of four steps that are implemented sequentially.

The steps are shown in Figure 11.2 initially tests focus on each module individually, assuring that it functions as a unit hence the name **unit testing**. Unit testing makes heavy use of white-box testing techniques, exercising specific paths in a module's control structure to ensure complete coverage and maximum error detection. Next, modules must be assembled or integrated to form the complete software package. **Integration testing** addresses the issues associated with the dual problems of verification and program construction. Black-box test case design techniques are most prevalent during integration, although a limited amount of white -box testing may be used to ensure coverage of major control paths. After the software has been integrated (constructed), sets of high-order test are conducted. Validation criteria (established during requirements analysis) must be tested. **Validation testing** provides final assurance that software needs all functional, behavioral and performance requirements. Black-box testing techniques are used exclusively during validation.

The last high-order testing step falls outside the boundary of software engineering and into the broader context of computer system engineering. Software once validated must be combined with other system elements (e.g., hardware, people, and databases). **System testing** verifies the tall elements mesh properly and that overall system function/performance is achieved.

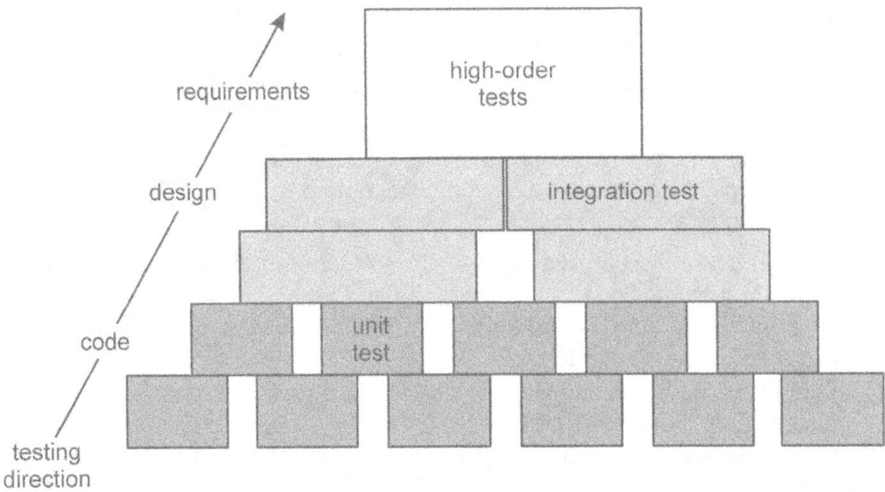

Figure 11.2 Software Testing Steps

11.4 BLACK-BOX TESTING

Black Box Testing is also called as functional testing. In this testing, the tester just focuses on inputs and outputs of the software system without having any internal knowledge of the program. Black box testing is often used for validation.

In this method the software's functional requirements are focused. That is, black-box testing enables the software engineer to derive sets of input conditions that will fully exercise all functional requirements for a program. Black box testing is opposite to white box testing, which can be used to uncover the errors which are not detected during white box testing.

In the following categories, attempt to find the errors are made by the black box testing methods:

1. errors because of missing or incorrect functions, (2) errors at interface, (3) data structure errors or data base access which is external, (4) errors in behavior or performance, and (5) errors in initialization and termination of the software.

Equivalence partitioning is a black-box testing technique that segregates the input data to different testing possibilities/cases. An ideal test case alone can detect various classes of errors, thus reducing the number of test cases.

Test case design for equivalence partition is in relevance with the evaluation of the input equivalence. An equivalence class would be present if the set of objects in the preceding section can be conjugated/associated in relation that are symmetric, transitive and reflexive. An equivalence class represents the validity state for input conditions.

Typically, an input condition is specific numeric value, a range of values, a set of related values, or a Boolean condition. According to the following guidelines one can define the equivalence classes:

1. One valid and two invalid equivalence classes are defined, if a range is specified by the input condition.
2. One valid and two invalid equivalence classes are defined, if specific value is required by the input condition
3. One valid and one invalid equivalence classes are defined, if member set is specified by the input condition
4. One valid and one invalid equivalence classes are defined, if Boolean is the input condition.

As an example, consider an automated banking application where data is maintained as part of it. By using the personal computer, the user can access the bank by entering the password which is of six digits and then follow the commands that trigger the different banking functions. During the log-on sequence, the software supplied for the banking applications data in the form

Area code – blank or three-digit number

Prefix – three-digit number not beginning with 0 or 1

Suffix – four-digit number

Password – six digit alphanumeric string

Commands – check, deposit, bill pay, and the like

The input conditions associated with each data element for the banking applications can be specified as

Area code: Input condition, Boolean-the area code may or may not be present.

Input condition, range-values defined between 200 and 999, with specific exceptions.

Prefix: Input condition, range-specified value >200

Input condition, value-four-digit length

Password: Input condition, Boolean-a password may or may not be present.

Input condition, value-six-character string.

Command: Input condition, set-containing commands noted previously.

The test cases for each data item can be developed by applying the above guidelines and then executed. The test cases are selected in such way that at once the largest number of equivalence class attributes should be exercised.

11.5 WHITE BOX TESTING

White box testing is a testing technique that takes internal logic and structure of the code into account. White box testing is also called as structural testing or glass box testing or open box testing or unit testing. In order to perform white box testing on an application, the tester needs to possess knowledge of the internal working of the code. The tester needs to have a look inside the source code and find out which part of the code is behaving inappropriately. White box testing is often used for verification.

White box testing is a test case design method that uses the control structure of the procedural design to derive test cases.

The white box testing technique does the following,

1. Ensures that all the different path the code execution can take place is tested at least once,
2. Executes all the possible combination of logical decision making in the code,
3. Execute all loops at their boundaries and within their operational bounds, and
4. Ensures the validity of internal data structure by exercising them

Now let's discuss various white box testing techniques:

Basis path testing

Basis path testing is a white-box testing technique first proposed by Tom McCabe. This method helps the test case designer to compute the measure of logical complexity of the design and use this measure as the basis for fixing the set of execution paths. The test cases developed through basis path testing method are guaranteed to execute each statement of the program at least once from the coverage point of view,

Flow Graph Notation

Flow graphs can be used to represent control flow in a program and can help in the derivation of the basis set. Each flow graph node represents one or more procedural statements. The edges between nodes represent flow of control. An edge must terminate at a node, even if the node does not represent any useful procedural statements. A region in a flow graph is an area bounded by edges and nodes. Each node that contains a condition is called a predicate node. Cyclomatic complexity is a metric that provides a quantitative measure of the logical complexity of a program. It defines the number of independent paths in the basis set and thus provides an upper bound for the number of tests that must be performed.

Notation for representing control flow is shown in figure 11.3.

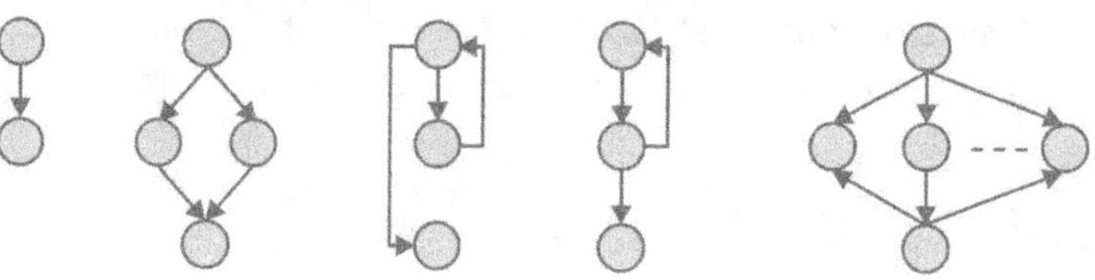

Figure 11.3 Flow Graph Notations

On a flow graph:

- Arrows called *edges* represent flow of control
- Circles called *nodes* represent one or more actions.
- Areas bounded by edges and nodes are called *regions*.
- A predicate node is a node containing a condition

Any procedural design can be translated into a flow graph. Note that compound Boolean expressions at tests generate at least two predicate node and additional arcs.

Cyclomatic complexity

Cyclomatic complexity is software metric that provides a quantitative measure of the logical complexity of a program. If the cyclomatic complexity is referred in terms of basis path testing, the complexity derived provides the number of independent tests to be carried out to visit all statements at least once. An *independent path* is any path through the program that introduces at least one new set of processing statements or a new condition. Cyclomatic complexity provides a measure of independent paths possible in the software which is a direct measure of complexity of the application. When stated in terms of a flow graph, an independent path must move along at least one edge that has not been traversed before the path is defined. For example, a set of independent paths for the flow graph illustrated in figure 11.4 is given below:

Path 1: 1-11.

Path 2: 1-2-3-4-5-10-1-11

Path 3: 1-2-3-6-8-9-10-1-11

Path 4: 1-2-3-6-7-9-10-1-11

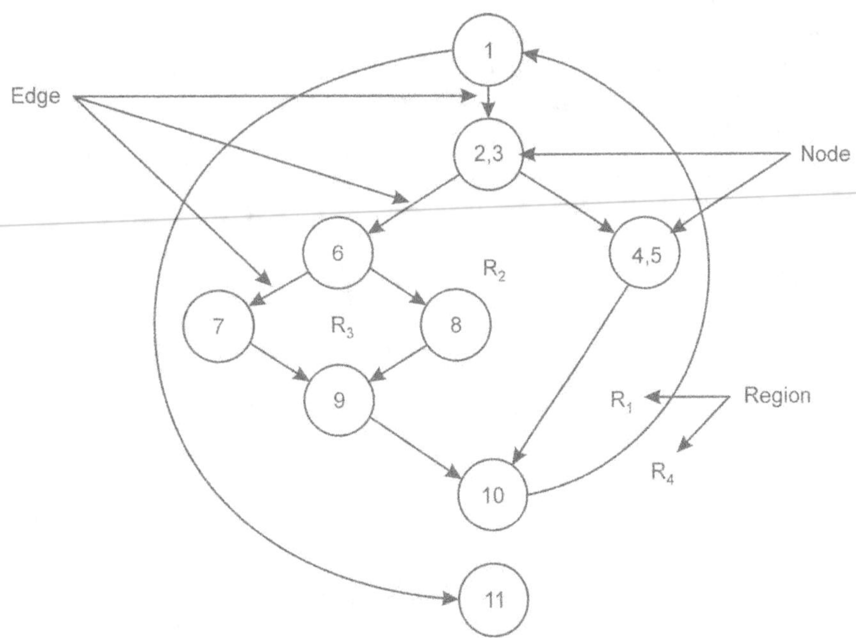

Figure 11.4 An Example Flow Graph

Note that each new path introduces a new edge. The path 1-2-3-4-5-10-1-2-3-6-8-9-10-1-11 is not considered to be an independent path because it is simply a combination of already specified paths and does not traverse any new edges. Cyclomatic Complexity is computed in one of three ways:

1. The number of regions of the flow graph corresponds to the cyclomatic complexity.
2. Cyclomatic complexity, $V(G)$, for a flow graph, G, is defined as $V(G) = E - N + 2$. Where E is the number of flow graph edges, N is the number of flow graph nodes.
3. Cyclomatic complexity, $V(G)$, for a flow graph, G, is also defined as $V(G) = P + 1$. Where P is the number of predicate nodes contained in the flow graph G.

Referring again to the flow graph in figure 11.4, the cyclomatic complexity can be computed using each of the algorithms just noted:

1. The flow graph has four regions.

2. $V(G) = 11$ edges $- 9$ nodes $+ 2 = 4$.

3. $V(G) = 3$ predicate nodes $+ 1 = 4$.

Therefore, the cyclomatic complexity of the flow graph in figure 11.4 is 4.

Control structure testing

Control structure testing as name suggests focusses on testing the control statements or loops in the software. The different types of control structure testing are listed as follows:

Loop testing:

Loops are fundamental to many algorithms and need thorough testing. There are four different classes of loops: simple, concatenated, nested, and unstructured (See Figure 11.5).

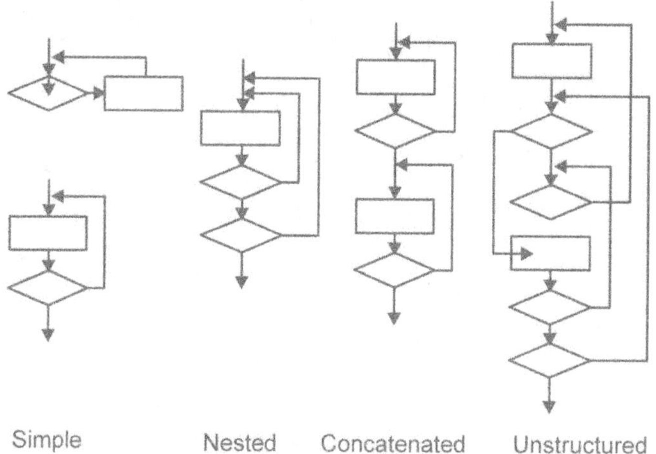

Figure 11.5 Loop Structures

- ***Simple loops,*** Suppose n is the number of passes allowed through the loop, the testing would involve
  - Skip loop entirely
  - test with only one pass
  - test with the passes
  - try with m passes where $m<n$.
  - (n-1), n, and (n+1) passes through the loop.

- ***Nested loops*** : *For nested loops test as follows*
  - Start with inner loop. Set all other outer loops with terminal conditions attaching minimum value.
  - Conduct simple loop testing on inner loop.
  - extend towards outer loops
  - Complete the testing continuing in same fashion covering all the loops.
- ***Concatenated loops***
  - If the loops are not inter-dependent execute the test as simple loops.
  - If the loops are dependent, then carry out the testing as nested loops.
- ***Unstructured loops***
  - Do not test this code, instead redesign the solution

Advantages of White Box testing

(i) Since the tester has the pre-requisite knowledge on the software, the testing becomes more effective as tester can define meaningful set of test data and test conditions.

(ii) White box testing helps in code optimization.

(iii) It helps in removal of un-necessary code from the application as these can cause some unknown defects in the long run of the application.

Disadvantages of White Box testing

(i) For performing white box testing the tester should have the knowledge of the code and internal structure of the application. This prerequisite increases the cost of testing.

(ii) Though white box testing intends to test the internal structure of the application, it is impossible to look at every line of code and various code combinations that execution can take place.

11.6 VALIDATION TESTING

Validation can be defined in many ways, but a simple definition is that validation succeeds when software functions in a manner that can be reasonably expected by customer.

Reasonable expectations are defined in the software requirement specification - a document that describes all user-visible attributes of the software. The specification contains a section titled "Validation Criteria". Information contained in that section forms the basis for a validation testing approach.

11.6.1 VALIDATION TEST CRITERIA

A test plans outlines the classes of tests to be conducted and a test procedure defines specific test cases that will be used in an attempt to uncover errors in conformity with requirements. Both the plan and procedure are designed to ensure that:

- All functional requirements are satisfied
- All performance requirements are achieved
- Documentation is correct and human-engineered and
- Other requirements like portability, error recovery, and maintainability are met.

11.6.2 CONFIGURATION REVIEW

An important element of the validation process is a configuration review. The intent of the review is to ensure that all elements of the software configuration have been properly developed, are catalogued, and have the necessary detail to support the maintenance phase of the software life cycle.

11.6.3 ALPHA AND BETA TESTING

If software is developed as a product to be used by many customers, it is impractical to perform formal acceptance tests with each one. Most software product builder's use a process called alpha beta testing to uncover errors that only the end user seems able to find.

Alpha testing is a type of acceptance testing; performed to identify all possible issues/bugs before releasing the product to everyday users or public. The focus of this testing is to simulate real users by using black box and white box techniques. The aim is to carry out the tasks that a typical user might perform. Alpha testing is carried out in a lab environment and usually the testers are internal employees of the organization.

The **beta** test is conducted at one or more customer sites by the end user(s) of the software. Unlike alpha testing the developer is generally not present; therefore the beta test is "live".

Application of the software in an environment that cannot be controlled by the developer.

The customer records all problems (real/imagined) that are encountered during beta testing and reports these to the developer at regular intervals. Because of problems reported during beta test, the software developer makes modification and then prepares for release of the software product to the entire customer base.

11.7 SYSTEM TESTING

System testing is the testing to make sure that by keeping the software in different environments (for example, Operating Systems) it still works. System testing is done with full system implementation and environment. System testing is actually a series of different tests whose primary purpose is to fully exercise the computer-based system. Although each test has a different purpose, all work to verify that all system elements have been properly integrated and perform allocated functions.

A classic system testing problem is "finger pointing". This occurs when an error is uncovered, and each system element developer blames the other for the problem. The software engineer should anticipate potential interfacing problems and

1. Design error-handling paths that test all information coming from other elements of the system;
2. Conduct a series of tests that simulate bad data or other potential errors at the software interface;
3. Record the results of tests to use as "evidence" if finger pointing does occur; and
4. Participate in planning and design of system tests to ensure that software is adequately tested.

In the section, we see the types of system tests that are worthwhile for software - based system.

11.7.1 RECOVERY TESTING

Many computer-based systems must recover from faults and resume processing within a pre-specified time. In some cases, a system must be fault tolerant; that is, processing faults must not cause overall system function to cease. In other cases, a system failure must be corrected within a specified period of time or severe economic damage will occur.

Recovery testing is a system test that forces the software to fail in a variety of ways and verifies that recovery is properly performed. If recovery is automatic (performed by the system itself), re-initialization, check pointing, mechanism, data recovery, and restart are each evaluated for correctness. If recovery requires human intervention, the mean time to repair is evaluated to determine whether it is within acceptable limits.

11.7.2 SECURITY TESTING

Security testing attempts to verify that protection mechanisms built into a system will in fact protect it from improper penetration.

During security testing, the tester plays the role(s) of the individual who desires to penetrate the system. Anything goes! The tester may attempt to acquire passwords through external clerical means, may attack the system with custom software designed to break down any defenses that have been constructed; may overwhelm the system, thereby denying service to others; may purposely cause system errors, hoping to penetrate during recovery; may browse through insecure data, hoping to find the key to system entry; and so on.

Given enough time and resources, good security testing will ultimately penetrate a system. The role of the system designer is to make penetration cost greater than the value of the information that will be obtained.

11.7.3 STRESS TESTING

Stress test is designed to confront programs with abnormal situations. In essence, the tester who performs stress testing asks: "How high can we crank this up before it fails"?

Stress testing executes a system in a manner that demands resources in abnormal quantity, frequency, or volume. The tester attempts to break the program.

11.7.4 PERFORMANCE TESTING

Performance testing is designed to test run-time performance testing occurs throughout all steps in the testing process. Even at the unit level, the performance of an individual module may be assessed as white- box tests are conducted. However, it is not until all system elements are fully integrated that the true performance of a system can be ascertained. Performance tests are often coupled with stress testing.

11.8 DEBUGGING

Software testing is a process that can be systematically planned and specified. Test case design can be conducted, a strategy can be defined, and results can be evaluated against prescribed expectations.

Debugging occurs as a consequence of successful testing. That is, when a test case uncovers an error, debugging is the process that results in the removal of the error. Debugging is not testing, but it always occurs as consequence of testing.

11.8.1 THE DEBUGGING PROCESS

The debugging process begins with the execution of a test case. As shown in figure 11.6, the debugging process begins with the execution of a test case. Results are assessed and a lack of correspondence between expected and actual is encountered. In many cases, the non-corresponding data is a symptom of an underlying cause as yet hidden. The debugging process attempts to match symptom with cause, thereby leading to error correction.

The debugging process attempts to match symptom with cause, there by leading to error correction.

The debugging process will always have two outcomes:

1. The cause will be found, corrected, and removed
2. The cause will not be found.

In the latter case, the person performing debugging may suspect a cause, design a test case to help validate his/her suspicion, and work toward error correction in iterative fashion.

Some characteristics of bugs provide some clues:

1. The symptom and the cause may be geographically remote. That is, the symptom may appear in one part of a program, while the cause may actually be located at a site that is far removed. Highly coupled program structures exacerbate this situation.
2. The symptom may disappear (temporarily) when another error is corrected.
3. The symptom may actually be caused by no errors (e.g., round-off inaccuracies).
4. The symptom may be caused by human error that is not easily traced.
5. The symptom may be a result of timing problems, rather than processing problems.
6. It may be difficult to accurately reproduce input conditions (e.g., a real-time application in which input ordering is indeterminate).
7. The symptom may be due to causes that are distributed across a number of tasks running on different processors.

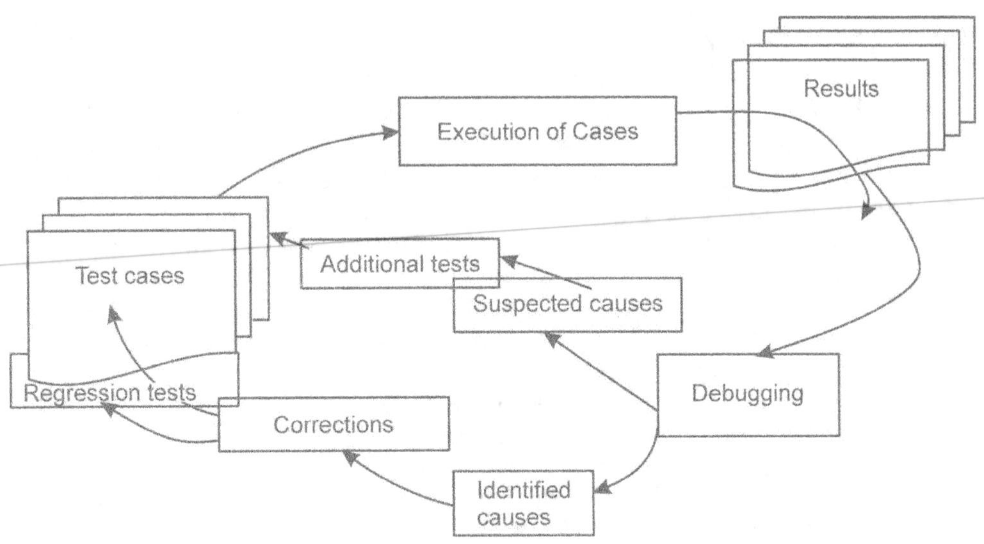

Figure 11.6 Debugging Process

11.8.2 DEBUGGING APPROACH

In general, three categories for debugging approaches may be proposed.

♦ Brute force
♦ Back tracking
♦ Cause elimination

The brute force category of debugging is probably the most common and efficient method for isolating the cause of a software error. Brute force debugging methods are applied when all methods of debugging fail. Using a philosophy, memory dumps are taken, run time traces are invoked and the program is loaded with WRITE statement. When this is done, one finds a clue by the information produced which leads to cause of an error.

Back tracking is a common debugging approach that can be used successfully in small programs. Beginning at the site where a symptom has been uncovered, the source code is traced backward (manually) until the site of the cause is found. This process has a limitation when the source lines are more.

Cause Elimination is manifested by induction or deduction and introduces the concept of binary partitioning. Data related to the error occurrence are organized to isolate potential causes.

Alternatively, a list of all possible causes is developed and tests are conducted to eliminate each.

If initial tests indicate that a particular cause hypothesis shows promise the data are refined in an attempt to isolate the bug.

11.9 SUMMARY

1. A strategy for software testing must accommodate low-level tests that are necessary to verify that a small source code segment has been correctly implemented as well as high-level tests that validate major customer requirements.
2. Black Box Testing is also called as functional testing. In this testing, the tester just focuses on inputs and outputs of the software system without having any internal knowledge of the program. Black box testing is often used for validation.
3. White box testing is a testing technique that takes internal logic and structure of the code into account. White box testing is also called as structural testing or glass box testing or open box testing or unit testing.
4. In white box testing, the tester needs to have a look inside the source code and find out which part of the code is behaving inappropriately. White box testing is often used for verification.
5. *Cyclomatic complexity* is software metric that provides a quantitative measure of the logical complexity of a program.
6. Loops are fundamental to many algorithms and need thorough testing. There are four different classes of loops: simple, concatenated, nested, and unstructured.
7. Validation can be defined in many ways, but a simple definition is that validation succeeds when software functions in a manner that can be reasonable expected by customer.
8. Most software product builder's use a process called alpha beta testing to uncover errors that only the end user seems able to find.
9. System testing is the testing to make sure that by keeping the software in different environments (for example, Operating Systems) it still works.
10. Recovery testing is a system test that forces the software to fail in a variety of ways and verifies that recovery is properly performed.
11. Security testing attempts to verify that protection mechanisms built into a system will in fact protect it from improper penetration.
12. Stress testing executes a system in a manner that demands resources in abnormal quantity, frequency, or volume. The tester attempts to break the program.
13. Performance testing is designed to test run-time performance testing occurs throughout all steps in the testing process.
14. Debugging occurs as a consequence of successful testing. That is, when a test case uncovers an error, debugging is the process that results in the removal of the error. Debugging is not testing, but it always occurs as consequence of testing.

Software Metrics

Structure

12.1 INTRODUCTION

In unit 11, we have studied software testing strategies, now we will see software metrics, software metrics are used to assess the quality of the product or process used to build it. The metrics allow project managers to gain insight about the progress of software and the assess the quality of the various artifacts produced during software development. The software analysts can check whether the requirements are verifiable or not. The metrics allow management to obtain an estimate of cost and time for software development. The metrics can also be used to measure customer satisfaction. The software testers can measure the faults corrected in the system, and this decides when to stop testing. Hence, the software metrics are required to capture various software attributes at different phases of the software development.

Object-oriented (OO) concepts such as coupling, cohesion, inheritance and polymorphism can be measured using software metrics.

In this unit, we will study, software quality metrics, metrics for analysis model, metrics for design model, metrics for source code, metrics for testing and metrics for software maintenance.

Objectives

After studying this unit, you should be able to:

- explain software quality metrics
- describe function-based metrics
- list the characteristics of an object oriented design
- explain metrics for software maintenance

12.2 SOFTWARE QUALITY METRICS

Measurement of the various aspects of software quality is considered to be an effective tool for the support of control activities and the initiation of process improvements during the development and the maintenance phases. These measurements apply to the functional quality, productivity and organizational aspects of the project.

Among the software quality metrics available or still in the process of development, we can list metrics for:

- Quality of software development and maintenance activities
- Development teams' productivity
- Help desk and maintenance teams' productivity
- Software faults density
- Schedule deviations

Software quality metrics focus on quality aspects of product metrics, process metrics, and project metrics. Product metrics describe the characteristics of the product such as size, complexity, design features, performance and quality level. Process metrics can be used to improve software development and maintenance.

In general, Software quality metrics are more closely associated with process and product metrics than with project metrics. The project parameters such as the number of developers and their skill levels, the schedule, the size and the organization structure certainly affect the quality of the product.

Product, process and project metrics can be grouped into following three categories:

- Product quality metrics

  Mean time to failure

  Defect density

  Customer reported problems

  Customer satisfaction

- In – process quality metrics

  Phase-based defect removal pattern

Defect removal effectiveness

Defect density during formal system testing

Defect arrival pattern during system testing

- Maintenance quality metrics

Fix backlog, and backlog management index

Fix response time

Pattern delinquent fixes

Defective fixes

12.3 METRICS FOR ANALYSIS MODELS

Analysis model metrics examine the intent of predicting the "size" of the resultant system. Size is sometimes an indicator of design complexity and is almost always an indicator of increased coding, integration and testing effort. These metrics address various aspects of the analysis model and include:

12.3.1 FUNCTION – BASED METRICS

The function point metric, first proposed by Albrecht, can be used effectively as a means for measuring the functionality delivered by a system. Using historical data, the function point (FP) can then be used to:

1. Estimate the cost or effort required to design, code, and test the software.
2. Predict the number of errors that will be encountered during testing.
3. Forecast the number of components and/or the number of projected source lines in the implemented system.

Function points are derived using an empirical relationship based on countable (direct) measures of software's information domain and assessments of software complexity. Information domain values are defined in the following manner:

Number of external inputs (EIs): Each external input originates from a user or is transmitted from another application and provides distinct application-oriented data or control information. Inputs are often used to update internal logical files (ILFs). Inputs should be distinguished from inquiries, which are counted separately.

Number of external outputs (Eos): Each external output is derived within the application and provides information to the user. In this context external output refers to reports, screens, error messages and so on. Individual data items within a report are counted separately.

Number of external inquires (EQs): An external inquiry is defined as an online input that results in the generation of some immediate software response in the form of an on-line output (often retrieved from an ILF).

Number of internal logical files (ILFs): Each internal logical file is a logical grouping of data that resides within the applications boundary and is maintained via external inputs.

Number of external interface files (EIFs): Each external interface file is a logical grouping of data that resides external to the application but provides data that may be of use to the application.

12.3.2 METRICS FOR SPECIFICATION QUALITY

Davis and his colleagues propose a list of characteristics that can be used to assess the quality of the analysis model and the corresponding requirements specification, these include: specificity (lack of ambiguity), completeness, correctness, understandability, verifiability, internal and external consistency, achievability, concision, traceability, modifiability, precision and reusability. Although many of these characteristics appear to be qualitative in nature, Davis suggest that each can be represented using one or more metrics. For example, we assume that there are n_r requirements in a specification, such that

$$n_r = n_f + n_{nf}$$

where n_f is the number of functional requirements and n_{nf} is the number of non-functional (e.g., performance) requirements.

12.4 METRICS FOR DESIGN MODEL

It is inconceivable that the design of a new aircraft, a new computer chip, or a new office building would be conducted without defining design measures, determining metrics for various aspects of design quality, and using them to guide the manner in which the design evolves. And yet, the design of complex software-based systems often proceeds with virtually no measurement. The irony of this is that design metrics for software are available, but the vast majority of software engineers continue to be unaware of their existence.

Design metrics for computer software, like all other software metrics, are not perfect. Many experts argue that further experimentation is required before design measures can be used. And yet, design without measurement is an unacceptable alternative.

12.4.1 ARCHITECTURAL DESIGN METRICS

Architectural design metrics focus on characteristics of the program architecture with an emphasis on the architectural structure and the effectiveness of modules or components within the architecture. These metrics are "black box" in the sense that they do not require any knowledge of the inner workings of a particular software component.

Card and glass define three software design complexity measures: structural complexity, data complexity and system complexity.

For hierarchical architecture (e.g. call and return architectures), structural complexity of a module i is defined in the following manner:

$$S(i) = f^2_{out}(i)$$

where $f^2_{out}(i)$ is the fan-out of module i

Data complexity provides an indication of the complexity in the internal interface for a module i and is defined as

$$D(i) = v(i)/[f_{out}(i) + 1]$$

where $v(i)$ is the number of input and output variables that are passed to and from module i.

Finally, system complexity is defined as the sum of structural and data complexity, specified as

$$C(i) = S(i) + D(i)$$

As each of these complexity values increases, the overall architectural complexity of the system also increases. This leads to a greater likelihood that integration and testing effort will also increase.

12.4.2 METRICS FOR OBJECT-ORIENTED DESIGN

There is much about object-oriented (OO) design that is in which an experienced designer "knows" how to characterize an OO system so that it will effectively implement customer requirements. But, as an OO design model grows in size and complexity, a more objective view of the characteristics of the design can benefit both the experienced designer and the beginner.

Some of the characteristics of an object oriented design:

Size: Size is defined in terms of four views: population, volume, length and functionality. Population is measured by taking a static count of OO entities such as classes or operations. Volume measures are identical to population measures but are collected dynamically at a given instant of time. Length is a measure of a chain of interconnected design elements. Functionality metrics provide an indirect indication of the value delivered to the customer by an OO application.

Complexity: Like size, there are many differing views of software complexity. Complexity in terms of structural characteristics by examining how classes of an OO design are interrelated to one another.

Coupling: The physical connections between elements of the OO design (e.g., the number of collaborations between classes or the number of messages passed between objects) represent coupling within an OO system.

Sufficiency: A design component (e.g., a class) is sufficient if it fully reflects all properties of the application domain object that it is modeling – that is, that the abstraction (class) possesses the features required of it.

12.5 METRICS FOR SOURCE CODE

Halstead's theory of "software science" proposed the first analytical "laws" for computer software. Halstead assigned quantitative laws to the development of computer software, using a set of primitive measures that may be derived after code is generated or estimated once design is complete. The measures are:

n_1 = the number of distinct operators that appear in a program.

n_2 = the number of distinct operands that appear in a program.

N_1 = the total number of operator occurrences.

N_2 = the total number of operand occurrences.

Halstead uses these primitive measures to develop expressions for the overall program length, potential minimum volume for an algorithm, the actual volume, the program level, the language level and other features such as development effort, development time and even the projected number of faults in the software.

Halstead shows that length N can be estimated

$$N = n_1 \log_2 n_1 + n_2 \log_2 n_2$$

and program volume may be defined

$$V = N \log_2(n_1 + n_2)$$

V will vary with programming language and represents the volume of information (in bits) required to specify a program.

Theoretically, a minimum volume must exist for a particular algorithm. Halstead defines a volume ratio L as the ratio of volume of the most compact form of a program to the volume of the actual program. In actuality, L must always be less than 1. In terms of primitive measures, the volume ratio may be expressed as follows:

$$L = 2/n_1 \times n_2/N_2$$

12.6 METRICS FOR TESTING

The majority of metrics proposed focus on the process of testing, not the technical characteristics of the tests themselves. In general, testers must rely on analysis, design, and code metrics to guide them in the design and execution of test cases.

Function- based metrics can be used as a predictor for overall testing effort. Various project-level characteristics (e.g., testing effort and time, errors uncovered, number of test cases produced) for past projects can be collected and correlated with the number of function points produced by a project team. The team can then project "expected values" of these characteristics for the current project.

Architectural design metrics provide information on the ease or difficulty associated with integration testing and the need for specialized testing software (e.g. stubs and drivers). Cyclomatic complexity (a component-level design metric) lies at the core of basis path testing. Modules with high cyclomatic complexity are more likely to be error prone than modules whose cyclomatic complexity is lower.

12.6.1 HALSTEAD METRICS APPLIED TO TESTING

Testing effort can also be estimated using metrics derived from halstead measures. Using the definitions for program volume, V, and program level, PL, halstead effort, e, can be computed as

$$PL = 1/[(n1/2) \; x(N2/n2)]$$
$$e = V/PL$$

The percentage of overall testing effort to be allocated to a module k can be estimated using the following relationship:

$$\text{percentage of testing effort (k)} = e(k)/\Sigma e$$

where e(k) is computed for module k using above equation and the summation in the denominator of equation is the sum of halstead effort across all modules of the system.

12.6.2 METRICS FOR OBJECT-ORIENTED TESTING

Binder suggests a broad array of design metrics that have a direct influence on the "testability" of an OO system. The metrics consider aspects of encapsulation and inheritance. A sampling follows:

Lack of cohesion in methods (LCOM): The higher the value of LCOM, the more states must be tested to ensure that methods do not generate side effects.

Percent public and protected (PAP): This metric indicates the percentage of class attributes that are public or protected. High values for PAP increase the likelihood of side effects among classes because public and protected attributes lead to high potential for coupling. Tests must be designed to ensure that such side effects are uncovered.

Public access to data members (PAD): This metric indicates the number of classes (or methods) that can access another class attributes, a violation of encapsulation. High values for PAD to the potential for side effects among classes. Tests must be designed to ensure that such side effects are uncovered.

Number of root classes (NOR): This metric is a count of the distinct class hierarchies that are described in the design model. Test suits for each root class and the corresponding class hierarchy must be developed. As NOR increases, testing effort also increases.

Fan-in (FIN): When used in the OO context, fan-in for the inheritance hierarchy is an indication of multiple inheritance. FIN>1 indicates that a class inherits its attributes and operations from more than one root class. FIN>1 should be avoided when possible.

12.7 METRICS FOR SOFTWARE MAINTENANCE

When development of a software product is complete and it is released to the market, it enters the maintenance phase of its life cycle. During this phase the defect arrivals by time interval and customer problem calls (which may or may not be defects) by time interval are the de facto metrics. However, the number of defect or problem arrivals is largely determined by the development process before the maintenance phase. Not much can be done to alter the quality of the product during this phase. Therefore, these two de facto metrics, although important, do not reflect the quality of software maintenance. What can be done during the maintenance phase is to fix the defects as soon as possible and with excellent fix quality. Such actions, although still not able to improve the defect rate of the product, can improve customer satisfaction to a large extent. The following metrics are therefore very important:

- Fix backlog and backlog management index
- Fix response time and fix responsiveness
- Percent delinquent fixes
- Fix quality

12.7.1 FIX BACKLOG AND BACKLOG MANAGEMENT INDEX

Fix backlog is a workload statement for software maintenance. It is related to both the rate of defect arrivals and the rate at which fixes for reported problems become available. It is a simple count of reported problems that remain at the end of each month or each week. Using it in the format of a trend chart, this metric can provide meaningful information for managing the maintenance process. Another metric to manage the backlog of open, unresolved, problems is the backlog management index (BMI).

$$BMI = \frac{Number\ of\ problems\ closed\ during\ the\ month}{Number\ of\ problem\ arrivals\ during\ the\ month} \times 100$$

As a ratio of number of closed, or solved, problems to number of problem arrivals during the month, if BMI is larger than 100, it means the backlog is reduced. If BMI is less than 100, then the backlog increased. With enough data points, the techniques of control charting can be used to calculate the backlog management capability of the maintenance process. More investigation and analysis should be triggered when the value of BMI exceeds the control limits. Of course, the goal is always to strive for a BMI larger than 100. A BMI trend chart or control chart should be examined together with trend charts of defect arrivals, defects fixed (closed), and the number of problems in the backlog.

12.7.2 FIX RESPONSE TIME AND FIX RESPONSIVENESS

For many software development organizations, guidelines are established on the time limit within which the fixes should be available for the reported defects. Usually the criteria are set in accordance with the severity of the problems. For the critical situations in which the customers' businesses are at risk due to defects in the software product, software developers or the software change teams work around the clock to fix the problems. For less severe defects for which circumventions are available, the required fix response time is more relaxed. The fix response time metric is usually calculated as follows for all problems as well as by severity level:

Mean time of all problems from open to closed

If there are data points with extreme values, medians should be used instead of mean. Such cases could occur for less severe problems for which customers may be satisfied with the circumvention and didn't demand a fix. Therefore, the problem may remain open for a long time in the tracking report.

In general, short fix response time leads to customer satisfaction. However, there is a subtle difference between fix responsiveness and short fix response time. From the customer's perspective, the use of averages may mask individual differences. The important elements of fix responsiveness are customer expectations, the agreed-to fix time, and the ability to meet one's commitment to the customer. For example, John takes his car to the dealer for servicing in the early morning and needs it back by noon. If the dealer promises noon but does not get the car ready until 2 o'clock, John will not be a satisfied customer. On the other hand, Julia does not need her mini van back until she gets off from work, around 6 P.M. As long as the dealer finishes servicing her van by then, Julia is a satisfied customer. If the dealer leaves a timely phone message on her answering machine at work saying that her van is ready to pick up, Julia will be even more satisfied. This type of fix responsiveness process is indeed being practiced by automobile dealers who focus on customer satisfaction.

12.7.3 PERCENT DELINQUENT FIXES

The mean (or median) response time metric is a central tendency measure. A more sensitive metric is the percentage of delinquent fixes. For each fix, if the turnaround time greatly exceeds the required response time, then it is classified as delinquent:

$$\text{Percent delinquent fixes} = \frac{\text{Number of fixes that exceeded the response time criteria by severity level}}{\text{Number of fixes delivered in a specified time}} \times 100$$

This metric, however, is not a metric for real-time delinquent management because it is for closed problems only. Problems that are still open must be factored into the calculation for a real-time metric. Assuming the time unit is 1 week, we propose that the percent delinquent of problems in the active backlog be used. *Active backlog* refers to all opened problems for the week, which is the sum of the existing backlog at the beginning of the week and new problem arrivals during the week. In other words, it contains the total number of problems to be processed for the week – the total workload. The number of delinquent problems is checked at the end of the week.

It is important to note that the metric of percent delinquent fixes is a cohort metric. Its denominator refers to a cohort of problems (problems closed in a given period of time, or problems to be processed in a given week). The cohort concept is important because if it is operationalized as a cross-sectional measure, then invalid metrics will result. For example, we have seen practices in which at the end of each week the number of problems in backlog (problems still to be fixed) and the number of delinquent open problems were counted, and the percent delinquent problems was calculated. This cross-sectional counting approach neglects problems that were processed and closed before the end of the week, and will create a high delinquent index when significant improvement (reduction in problems backlog) is made.

12.7.4 FIX QUALITY

Fix quality or the number of defective fixes is another important quality metric for the maintenance phase. From the customer's perspective, it is bad enough to encounter functional defects when running a business on the software. It is even worse if the fixes turn out to be defective. A fix is defective if it did not fix the reported problem, or if it fixed the original problem but injected a new defect. For mission-critical software, defective fixes are detrimental to customer satisfaction.

The metric of percent defective fixes is simply the percentage of all fixes in a time interval (e.g., 1 month) that are defective. A defective fix can be recorded in two ways: Record it in the month it was discovered or record it in the month the fix was delivered. The first is a customer measure, the second is a process measure. The difference between the two dates is the latent period of the defective fix. It is meaningful to keep track of the latency data and other information such as the number of customers who were affected by the defective fix. Usually the longer the latency, the more customers are affected because there is more time for customers to apply that defective fix to their software system.

There is an argument against using percentage for defective fixes. If the number of defects, and therefore the fixes, is large, then the small value of the percentage metric will show an optimistic picture, although the number of defective fixes could be quite large. This metric, therefore, should be a straight count of the number of defective fixes. The quality goal for the maintenance process, of course, is zero defective fixes without delinquency.

12.8 SUMMARY

1. Measurement of the various aspects of software quality is considered to be an effective tool for the support of control activities and the initiation of process improvements during the development and the maintenance phases.
2. Software metrics can be classified into three categories: product metrics, process metrics, and project metrics.
3. The function point metric (FP), first proposed by Albrecht, can be used effectively as a means for measuring the functionality delivered by a system.
4. Architectural design metrics focus on characteristics of the program architecture with an emphasis on the architectural structure and the effectiveness of modules or components within the architecture.
5. Some of the characteristics of an object oriented design are size, complexity, coupling and many more.
6. The majority of metrics proposed focus on the process of testing, not the technical characteristics of the tests themselves.
7. Fix backlog is a workload statement for software maintenance. It is related to both the rate of defect arrivals and the rate at which fixes for reported problems become available.
8. The mean (or median) response time metric is a central tendency measure. A more sensitive metric is the percentage of delinquent fixes.
9. Fix quality or the number of defective fixes is a important quality metric for the maintenance phase.

13 Quality Management

Structure

13.1 INTRODUCTION

In unit 12, we have studied software metrics, now we will see quality management. It is general perception from the software development team is that the quality is something we need to worry after the coding has been completed and that the responsibility of quality assurance lies with the testing team. It is totally incorrect. Quality assurance is responsible of entire team and the quality assurance is an umbrella activity that is applied throughout the lifecycle of the project across all phases. It not only involves testing of the code that is developed, but also includes activities such as technical reviews, documentation, compliance etc.

In this unit, we will study, quality concepts, software quality assurance, software reviews, formal technical reviews and the ISO 9000 quality standards.

Objectives

After studying this unit, you should be able to:

- list the factors of quality
- describe the software quality assurance
- explain the software reviews
- describe IEEE 1028 generic process for formal reviews

13.2 QUALITY CONCEPTS

The term 'quality' is commonly quoted to describe good products available. Quality parameters can differentiate between different products as good and otherwise. Quality is a relative term and it is defined by users. It is based on the perception of a customer about the product which he/she is going to purchase. The term quality means different things to different people at different times and in different perspectives. For example, a quality product may be one which has no (minimum) defects and works exactly as the user expects.

Quality often used in a vague, blurred way. If someone talks about 'working on quality', they may simply mean activities designed to improve the organisation and its services. Quality is essentially about learning what you are doing well and doing it better. It also means finding out what you may need to change to make sure you meet the needs of your service users. Quality is about:

- Quality is conformance to product requirements and should be free.
- Quality is achieved through prevention of defects.
- Quality control is aimed at finding problems as early as possible and fixing them.
- Doing things right the first time is the performance standard which results in zero defects and saves the expenses of doing things over.
- Quality is what distinguishes a good company from a great one.
- Quality is meeting or exceeding our customer's needs and requirements.
- Software Quality is measureable.
- Quality is continuous improvement.
- The quality of a software product comes from the quality of the process used to create it.
- Quality is the Entire Company's Business.
- Quality network testing products help make our customers successful.
- Satisfying the stakeholders.

Some of the factors of quality are available and they are mentioned below:

- **Correctness** - Extent to which a program satisfies its specification and fulfills the client's objective.
- **Reliability** - Extent to which a program is supposed to perform its function with the required precision.
- **Efficiency** - Amount of computing and code required by a program to perform its function.
- **Integrity** - Extent to which access to software and data is denied to unauthorized users.
- **Usability**- Labor required to understand, operate, prepare input and interpret output of a program.
- **Maintainability**- Effort required to locate and fix an error in a program.
- **Flexibility**- Effort needed to modify an operational program.
- **Testability**- Effort required to test the programs for their functionality.

- **Portability-** Effort required to run the program from one platform to other or to different hardware.
- **Reusability-** Extent to which the program or it's parts can be used as building blocks or as prototypes for other programs.
- **Interoperability-** Effort required to couple one system to another.
- **Extensibility-** Effort required to add functionality without damaging the existing system.

13.3 SOFTWARE QUALITY ASSURANCE

Software quality assurance is defined as a planned and systematic approach to the evaluation of the quality and adherence to software product standards, processes and procedures. SQA includes the process of assuring that standards and procedures are established and are followed throughout the software acquisition life cycle. Compliance with agreed upon standards and procedures is evaluated through process monitoring, product evaluation and audits. Software development and control processes should include quality assurance approval points, where an SQA evaluation of the product may be done in relation to the applicable standards.

The software quality assurance group works with the software project during its early stages to establish plans, standards and procedures that will add value to the software project and satisfy the constraints of the project and the organization's policies. By participating in establishing the plans, standards and procedures, the software quality assurance group helps ensure they fit the project's needs and verifies that they will be usable for performing reviews and audits software work products throughout the life cycle and provides management with visibility as to whether the software project is adhering to its established plans, standards and procedures.

Software Quality Assurance (SQA) is a continuous activity carried throughout the project lifecycle. It comprises of:

1. An approach that determines the technique need to be adopted for managing the quality in the project.
2. Software engineering methodologies and tools.
3. Technical reviews that need to be applied throughout the software development processes.
4. Testing strategy for the project.
5. Documentation mechanism and effective ways of controlling the changes to the documents.
6. Procedure for software compliance when needed to be obtained.
7. Metrics gathering and reporting mechanisms.

In the broad sense the software quality assurance is comparable with similar practices followed in product manufacturing. However, there are some major changes as well between software project and product manufacturing in terms of quality assurance. One obvious reason for the difference is that that manufactured product is physical and can be seen and felt; hence the cost and benefit can be easily measured. The same does not apply to software product.

SQA runs through the entire life cycle of the project and is a complicated and complex process. The main aim of the SQA is to ensure that the highest quality is maintained for the computer programs that are developed. By definition quality is "conformance to explicitly and implicitly stated requirements for the software product". Hence the activity covered in the SQA tries to improve upon the processes that develop the software product.

In order to properly execute the software quality assurance processes, we need to have the data. The data that tells about the effectiveness of the current practices followed in the project. Hence the data need to defined, collected, evaluated, and analyzed. This statistical analysis helps the SQA to be more predictable and reliable.

The two major activities that determine the success of the SQA are the product evaluation and monitoring of the process. The project plan describes about the goals of the project and the activities to be carried out in order to achieve the goal. Now the SQA will help in ensuring that the activities and the procedures stated in the project plan are carried out correctly to develop the product properly and also the developed product is evaluated to confirm that the product is as per the specs and the goal of the project is met. Proper reviews of the plan and regular audits of the process are highly important for the success of the project.

Now let's look at the product evaluation. In SQA's context we define all the procedures and standards defined are also considered as the product along with the software product the needs to be generated. Hence the product evaluation ensures that the standards and procedures defined for the project are followed properly and follows the compliance as stated. Finally, the product evaluation will also assure that the software product developed is as per specified requirements through the different testing strategies.

Process monitoring on the other hand deals with the activities that are carried out during the project execution. Process monitoring is a SQA activity that ensures that appropriate steps to carry out the process are being followed. The process monitoring in SQA compares the actual steps that are carried out during the project execution against the documented steps to record and correct any deviation in the practice. For this purpose, the Audits are carried out regularly. The Audit looks at the process and product development in depth. The goal of the audit is to compare the actual practice followed in the process implementation against the established procedures and standards. Audits help to review management, technical, and compliance processes to obtain the status of the project and provide indication on the quality of the product being developed.

The goal of an SQA audit is to ensure that proper control mechanisms are being followed, that required documentation is maintained, and that the team's status reports accurately reflect the status of the work being carried out. The SQA product is an audit report to management consisting of findings and recommendations to bring the development into conformance with standards and/or procedures.

13.4 SOFTWARE REVIEWS

Software reviews are a "filter" for the software engineering process. That is, reviews are applied at various points during software development and serve to uncover errors and defects that can then be removed. Software reviews "purify" the software engineering activities that is analysis, design and coding. "Software reviews means viewing your software again".

A software review is a process or meeting during which a software product is examined by project managers, users, customers or other interested parties for comment or approval. The purpose of any review is to discover errors in the analysis, design, coding, testing and implementation phases of the software development cycle. The other purpose of a review is to see whether procedures are applied uniformly and in a manageable manner.

The reviews predominately are at three stages: first, requirement review, then design review and finally technical review. Every organization has review guidelines and there is a procedure for each review. The review is performed by an authorized person, review meetings are held, an issue list is made, and decisions and actions are taken to resolve them. The issues and the solutions are rechecked in the next meeting. Table 13.1 shows a reviews, participants and focus.

Table 13.1 Reviews, Participants and Focus

Review	Participants	Focus
Requirements	Customer, Project manager, users	Meeting the requirement and software specification.
Design	Project manager, system designer, solution architect, and customer	Architecture, performance, deliverables
Technical	Project manager, designer, solution architect	Quality, standards and deliverables

Objectives for Software Reviews

Review objectives are used:

- To ensure that the software elements conform to their specifications.
- To ensure that the development of the software element is being done as per plans, standards and guidelines applicable for the project.
- To ensure that the changes to the software elements are properly implemented and affect only those system areas identified by the change specification.

Varieties of Software Reviews

Software reviews may be divided into three categories:

- Software **peer** reviews are conducted by the author of the work product, or by one or more colleagues of the author, to evaluate the technical content and/or quality of the work.

- Software **management** reviews are conducted by management representatives to evaluate the status of work done and to make decisions regarding downstream activities.
- Software **audit** reviews are conducted by personnel external to the software project, to evaluate compliance with specifications, standards, contractual agreements or other criteria.

13.5 FORMAL TECHNICAL REVIEWS (FTR)

In section 13.4 we have already seen software review, in this section we will see formal technical reviews. As we know, a review can be defined as, a meeting at which the software element is presented to project personnel, managers, users, customers or other interested parties for comment or approval. A software review can be defined as a filter for the software-engineering process.

Formal Technical Review (FTR): A formal technical review is a software quality assurance activity performed by software-engineering practitioners to improve software product quality. The product is scrutinized for completeness, correctness, consistency, technical feasibility, efficiency and adherence to established standards and guidelines by the client organization.

The FTR serves as a training ground, enabling junior engineers to observe different approaches to software analysis, design and implementation. Each FTR is conducted as a meeting and will be successful only if it is properly planned, controlled and attended.

Objectives of a formal technical review

The various objectives of a formal technical review are as follows:

- To uncover errors in logic or implementation.
- To ensure that the software has been represented according to predefined standards.
- To ensure that the software under review meets the requirements.
- To make the project more manageable.

For the success of a formal technical review, the following are expected:

- The schedule of the meeting and its agenda reach the members well in advance.
- Members review the material and its distribution.
- The reviewer must review the material in advance.

The review meeting

The meeting should consist of two to five people and should be restricted to not more than two hours (preferably). The aim of the review is to review the product/work and the performance of people. When the product is ready, the producer (developer) informs the project leader about the completion of the product and requests for review. The project leader contacts the review leader for the review. The review leader asks the reviewer to perform an independent review of the product/work before the scheduled FTR.

IEEE 1028 Generic Process for Formal Reviews

IEEE Std.1028 defines a common set of activities for "formal" reviews. The sequence of activities is largely based on the software inspection process originally developed at IBM by Michal Fagan. Differing types of review may apply this structure with varying degrees of rigour, but all activities are mandatory for inspection, which are listed below:

1. **Entry Evaluation:** The review leader uses a standard checklist of entry criteria to ensure that optimum conditions exist for a successful review.
2. **Management Preparation:** Responsible management ensure that the review will be appropriately resourced with staff, time, materials and tools and will be conducted according to polices, standards, or other relevant criteria.
3. **Planning the Review**: The review leader identifies or confirms the objectives of the review, organizes a team of reviewers and ensures that the team is equipped with all necessary resources for conducting the review.
4. **Overview of Review Procedures**: The review leader, or some other qualified person, ensures that all reviewers understand the review goals, the review procedures, the materials available to them, and the procedure for conducting the review.
5. **Individual Preparation:** The reviewers individually prepare for group examination of the work under review, by examining it carefully for anomalies, the nature of which will vary with the type of review and its goals.
6. **Group Examination:** The reviewers meet at a planned time to pool the results of their preparation activity and arrive at a consensus regarding the status of the document being reviewed.
7. **Rework/Follow-Up:** The author of the work product undertakes whatever actions are necessary to repair defects or otherwise satisfy the requirements agreed to at the examination meeting. The review leader verifies that all action items are closed.
8. **Exit Evaluation:** The review leader verifies that all activities necessary for successful review have been accomplished, and that all outputs appropriate to the type of review have been finalized.

13.6　THE ISO 9000 QUALITY STANDARDS

The International Organization for Standardization is a group of worldwide federations of national standards bodies from some 100 countries. ISO is a Non-governmental organization established in 1947.

The ISO-9000 standard specifies quality-assurance elements in generic terms, which can be applied to any business, regardless of the product or services being offered. In order to register for one of the quality-assurance system models contained in the ISO-9000, third-party auditors examine an organizations quality system and operations for compliance to the standard and for effective operations. Upon successful audit, the organization receives a certificate from a registered body represented by the auditors. Thereafter, semi-annual audits ensure conformance to the standard.

The ISO-9000 standard views an organization as a set of interrelated processes. In order to pass the criteria for ISO-9000 compliance, the processes must address the identified areas, and document and practice them. When a process is documented, it is better understood, controlled, and improved. However, the ISO-9000 standard does not specify how an organization should implement its quality system. Therefore, the biggest challenge is to design and implement a Quality Assurance system that meets the standard and gels well with the products/services of the organization.

The ISO-9001 is a quality-assurance standard that is specific to software engineering. It specifies 20 standards with which an organization must comply for an effective implementation of the quality assurance system.

The ISO-9000 series of standards is a set of documents dealing with quality systems that can be used for quality assurance purposes. The ISO-9000 series is not just a software standard. It is a series of five related standards that are applicable to a wide variety of industrial activities, including design/development, production, installation, and servicing.

ISO-9000 Mission

The mission of an ISO is to promote the development of standardization and related activities to facilitate the international exchange of goods and services, and to develop cooperation in the spheres of intellectual, scientific, technological and economic activity. The ISO published its ISO-9000 standard in 1988. ISO-9000 consists of three standards for external quality assurance. There are ISO-9001, ISO-9002 and IS0-9003.

- **ISO-9001:** The ISO-9001 is an international quality-management system. The ISO-9001 is mainly related to the software industry. It lays down the standards for designing, developing, servicing and producing a standard quality of goods. It is also applicable to most software-development organizations.
- **ISO-9002:** The ISO-9002 is basically related to manufacturing only and is silent on designing issues. Examples of this category of industries include steel and car manufacturing industries that buy the product and plant designs from external sources and are involve in only manufacturing those products. Therefore, the ISO-9002 is not applicable to software – development organizations.
- **ISO-9003:** The ISO-9003 standard applies to the service industry. The organizations who are involved in only installation of products, services and testing of products are eligible for the ISO-9003 certification.

13.7 SUMMARY

1. The term 'quality' is commonly quoted to describe good products. Quality is achieved through prevention of defects.
2. Some of the factors of quality are correctness, reliability, efficiency, integrity, usability, maintainability, flexibility, testability, portability, reusability and interoperability
3. Software quality assurance is defined as a planned and systematic approach to the evaluation of the quality and adherence to software product standards, processes and procedures.
4. Software Quality Assurance (SQA) is a continuous activity carried throughout the project life-cycle.
5. The two major activities that determine the success of the SQA are the product evaluation and monitoring of the process.
6. A review can be defined as, a meeting at which the software element is presented to project personnel, managers, users, customers or other interested parties for comment or approval. A software review can be defined as a filter for the software-engineering process.
7. The ISO-9000 standard specifies quality-assurance elements in generic terms, which can be applied to any business, regardless of the product or services being offered.

Structure

14.1 Introduction
    Objectives
14.2 Project Planning
14.3 Project Scheduling
14.4 Project Staffing
14.5 People Capability Maturity Model (P-CMM)
14.6 Summary

14.1 INTRODUCTION

In unit 13, we have studied quality management, now we will see software project management. Project Management is the discipline of organizing and managing resources (e.g.,. people) in such a way that the project is completed within defined scope, quality, time and cost constraints. A project is a temporary and one-time endeavor undertaken to create a unique product or service, which brings about beneficial change or added value. The goal of software project management is to understand, plan, measure and control the project such that it is delivered on time and on budget. This involves gathering requirements, managing risk, monitoring and controlling progress, and following a software development process. Software project management requires trained and experienced Software Engineers in order to increase the likelihood of project success because software development for large projects is extremely complex and following strict engineering principles will help to reduce the risks associated with the project.

In this unit, we will study, project planning, project scheduling, project staffing and people capability maturity model.

Objectives

After studying this unit, you should be able to:

- explain project planning
- discuss various factors that delay project schedule
- describe project staffing
- explain the objectives of maturity model

14.2   PROJECT PLANNING

Project planning is a part of project management. Initially, the project scope is defined and the appropriate methods for completing the project are determined. Following this step, the durations for the various tasks necessary to complete the work are listed and grouped into a work breakdown structure. Then the necessary resources can be estimated and costs for each activity can be allocated to each resource, giving the total project cost. At this stage, the project plan may be optimized to achieve the appropriate balance between resource usage and project duration to comply with the project objectives. Once established and agreed, the plan becomes what is known as the baseline. Progress will be measured against the baseline throughout the life of the project. Analyzing progress compared to the baseline is known as earned value management.

Every project starts with initiation. In which project scope, pros and cons are discussed. Once the project initiation phase is completed, the project team, usually the project manager and the analysts in the early stages, must determine the scope of the effort necessary to accomplish the necessary tasks. There are many methods available for accomplishing this planning process; many of them use graphics of varying types, but all require the same basic information.

1. Project start date.
2. Project completion date.
3. Selection of the project methodology or project life cycle to be used.
4. Scope of the project in terms of the phases of the selected project methodology or project life cycle.
5. Identification or selection of the project review methods to be used.
6. Identification of any predetermined interim milestone or other critical dates which must be met.
7. A list of tasks, by project phase in the order in which they must be accomplished.
8. An estimate of the personnel necessary to accomplish each task.
9. An estimate of the personnel available to accomplish each task.
10. Skill level necessary to perform each task.
11. Task dependencies.
12. Which tasks can be performed in parallel?
13. Which tasks require the completion of other tasks before they can start?
14. Project control, or review points.
15. Project cost estimation and cost-benefit analysis.

14.3   PROJECT SCHEDULING

It is essential to perform project scheduling to effectively manage the tasks of the project. Project scheduling provides details, such as start date and end date of the project, milestones and tasks for the project. In addition, it specifies the resources (such as people, equipment and facilities) required to complete the project and the dependencies of tasks of the project on each another. An appropriate project schedule prepared according to project plan not only aims to complete the project on time but also helps to avoid the additional cost incurred when the project is delayed.

There are various factors that delay project schedule. The commonly noticed factors are:

- **Unrealistic Deadlines:** project schedule is affected when the time allocated for completing a project is impractical and not according to the effort required for it. Generally, this situation arises when the deadline is established by inexperienced individuals or without the help of project management team. Here, the project management team is constrained to work according to that deadline. The project is delayed if the deadline is not achieved.
- **Changing user Requirements:** sometimes, project schedule is affected when user requirements are changed after the project has started. This affects the project schedule, and thus more time is consumed both in revision of project plan and implementation of new user requirements.
- **Under-estimation of Resources:** if the estimation of the resources for the project is not done according to its requirement, the schedule is affected. This under-estimation of resources leads to delay in performing tasks of the project.
- **Lack of Consideration of Risks:** Risks should be considered during project planning and scheduling; otherwise it becomes difficult for project management team to prevent their effect during software development.
- **Lack of Proper Communication among Team Members:** sometimes, there is no proper communication among the project management team members to resolve the problems occurring during software development. This in turn makes it difficult for the project management team to understand and develop the software according to user requirements and schedule.
- **Difficulties of Team Members:** software projects can also be delayed due to unforeseen difficulties of the team members. For example, some of the team members may require leave for personal reasons.
- **Lack of Action by Project Management Team:** sometimes, project management team does not recognize that the project is getting delayed. Thus, they do not take the necessary action to speed up the software development process and complete it on time.

Generally, the task of assigning the end date is done by the project sponsor or the user. While preparing the project schedule, the project manager assists the project sponsor by providing information about the project scope, deliverables and resources. In addition, the project manager provides an estimate of the time to be consumed to complete project tasks. Preparing an accurate project schedule is fixed, the project manager is responsible for monitoring the progress of the project. If there is a need to revise the project schedule, the project manager communicates with the project management team members.

Principles of Project Scheduling

To carry out project scheduling appropriately, some principles are followed. These principles help the project management team to prepare the project schedule. The commonly followed principles are:

- **Compartmentalization:** This divides the project into several tasks. The purpose of compartmentalization is to make the project manageable. Thus, it becomes easier to prepare the project schedule according to these tasks.
- **Interdependency:** Determines the interdependency of one or more activities or tasks on each other. All the activities of the project are not independent. There are various activities that are performed sequentially, whereas some of the activities are executed together with other activities. On the other hand, some activities cannot begin until the activity on which they are dependent is complete.
- **Time allocation:** Determines the time to be allocated to each project management team member for performing specified activities. However, before allocating time, it is important to estimate the effort required by them to complete the assigned task. In addition, the project management team members should be assigned a start date and an end date according to the work to be conducted on full-time or part-time basis.
- **Effort validation:** Ensures that the efforts required to perform the assigned task are valid. In other words, it should verify that the task allocated to one or more project management team members is according to the effort required for each task. This is because every project management team has a defined number of team members. Hence the project manager should allocate the tasks according to the effort and time required to complete the task.
- **Defined Responsibilities:** Specify the roles and responsibilities of every project management team member. Hence, the task should be allocated according to the skills and abilities of team members to perform the assigned task.
- **Defined outcomes:** Specify the outcomes of every task performed by the project management team members. The outcome is achieved after completion of a task. Generally, the outcome of a task is in the form of a product and these products are combined in deliverables.
- **Defined Milestones:** Specify the milestones when work products are complete and reviewed for quality.

Milestones

Milestones are formal representations of the progress of a project. Generally, milestones are planned when deliverables are provided. Milestones describe the end-point when software process activity is completed. After completion of a milestone, its output is described in the form of document. This document comprises information about the completion of a phase of the project. These documents are used as a reference for the project management team only and are not delivered to the user.

It is difficult to keep in mind all the tasks being performed during software development. Hence, each task is recorded in documents, which describe the work being done in that phase. With the help of these documents, it becomes easy for the project manager to check the status of the project. In addition, milestones have several advantages:

- They avoid losing control of the project according to schedule.
- They help in completing the project according to allocated budget.
- They report status of the project to the management.

Figure 14.1 shows examples of milestones in requirements and design phases of the project. 'Milestone 1', 'Milestone 2', 'Milestone 3' represent the completion of tasks in requirements phase. Similarly, 'Milestone 4', 'Milestone 5', 'Milestone 6', and 'Milestone 7' represent completion of tasks in design phase. Each milestone represents the completion of a specific task. For example, "Milestone 1' represents completion of feasibility study and 'Milestone 2' represents completion of requirements definition. Similarly, in the design phase, 'Milestone 4' represents completion of architectural design and so on.

Requirements		Design	
	Feasibility Study		Architectural Design
Milestone 1		Milestone 4	
	Outline Requirements Definition		Interface Design
Milestone 2		Milestone 5	
	Design Study		Formal Specification
Milestone 3		Milestone 6	
	Requirements Specification		Detailed Design
		Milestone 7	
			Implementation

Figure 14.1 Milestones

In project scheduling, there are several aspects that are important to be considered. These include techniques of project scheduling, task network, and tracking the schedule. Techniques of project scheduling focus on checking the activities that are completed according to project schedule. In addition, these techniques describe the information about activities in graphical form so that it is easy for a project management team to understand the time and effort required for each activity. Task network focuses on how the entire software project can be broken into several manageable tasks, which are understandable by the project management team. Tracking the schedule focuses on finding ways to complete the project according to the schedule.

14.4 PROJECT STAFFING

The number of team members required in a project depends on the type of project and the effort and cost required for it. In addition, it is important to consider the individual tasks to be performed and the skills and experience required to carry out these tasks efficiently.

Staffing process involves the selection of persons having the right shills and qualifications. Previously, personnel departments did matters relating to staffing processes. Now the term Human Resources (HR) is widely used to refer to the jobs done previously by personnel departments. Previously HR department is concerned with the appointment of persons only. With the change in technology and the nature of work, the traditional roles played by different departments are changing. In tune with this change, the role of HR department is also continuously changing. They are now doing a lot of activities for the growth of the employees and the organization. HR department is engages in developing the skills of the employees. They create the right environment for the employees. Some other functions of HR department are employee information management, recruitment management, policy management, performance appraisal, training and development and payroll management. HR department defines the roles of each employee in an organization. Identify the skills needed and take steps for the motivation of employees.

For software projects, different positions available are large and include project mangers, system analysts, software architect, program developers, etc., in the software development project, each member of the team has a vital role to play. The person at the top of the hierarchy is the project manager. Traditional skills of project managers were limited to such skills like value analysis, critical path method, risk analysis and financial management. But now the situation has changed. Project managers must have both tangible and intangible skills. Softer skills are also necessary for a successful project manager. Project managers must be skilled in both technical and people management aspects. They must have strong communication and leadership abilities. They must also have good people skills. They must be skilled in managing resources as well as customers alike. Direct involvement with customers as well as different team members are necessary for the success of projects. They must be able to identify and hire talented people for the project. Project managers must be able to navigate the team members to success.

Success or failure of a project depends on the ability of project managers. Responsibility of the project managers is to make a suitable plan for the development of the software. They set business objectives for the project and assigns priorities. Project manager must be a good planner. Project manager must be able to estimate the time and effort required to complete different activities in the project and prepares a realistic schedule. A typical organization structure for a software project can be as shown in Figure 14.2. This is only given as an example structure. The structure can vary depending upon the several factors.

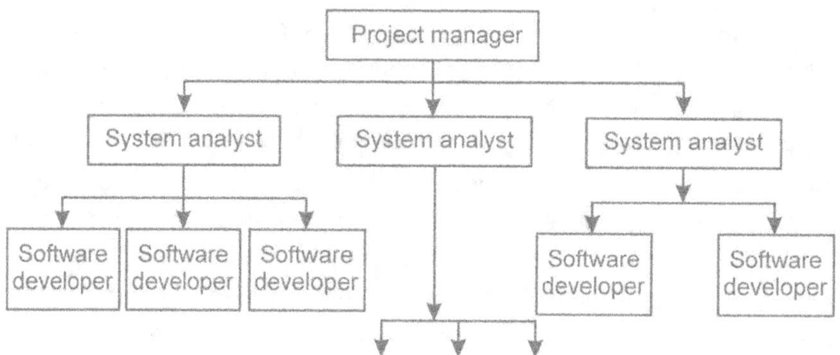

Figure 14.2 Typical Software Organization Structure

One of the main challenges involved in staffing process is the selection of the right persons and retaining them. This is essential for meeting the different business needs. This is challenging in the case of software projects. This is because of the fast technological changes taking place in the software development tools and techniques. Selection of wrong persons will create several adverse effects in the progress as well as in the development of the business. Several procedures ae followed by organizations to select the right person. This includes screening at different levels using different methods such as tests, interviews etc., to select the right person. The company must understand its manpower requirements. The number of persons required, their qualification and experience are decided before the recruitment process starts. Another challenging problem faced by software organization is the problem of retaining the skilled persons in the organization. This is very important as the technology is changing fast and it becomes very difficult to get the right skilled person in the new technology. Giving additional perks or incentives and other benefits are the techniques used by organization to retain skilled persons and to motivate them. In software projects, using the principles of the need hierarchy to retain employees is not found suitable to a certain extent. Now organization resort to new techniques such as career promotional plans, training on advanced techniques, compensation benefits, and performance-based incentives etc., to retain employees. Individuals in the IT field consider future growth potential and career prospects more important.

14.5 PEOPLE CAPABILITY MATURITY MODEL (P-CMM)

People are the assets of an organization. The capability of people is essential for the success of an organization. However, it is important that their skills ae developed so that the organization is able to get the best possible returns on its investments expended on the people. For this purpose, the people capability maturity model is used. The objectives of this maturity model are:

- Improving the capability of software organizations by increasing the capability of the staff.

- Ensuring that software development capability is a characteristic of the organization rather than of few individuals.
- Aligning the motivation of people along with the motivation of the organization.
- Helping retain people with extensive skills and knowledge.

P-CMM focuses on the development of capabilities of people who are involved in the project. This model is used in areas, staffing (including recruitment, selection and planning), managing performance, training, work environment, organizational and individual competence, and many more.

P-CMM is developed for increasing the productivity in the software development. It provides set of best practices, **procedures, and standard practices** to address the important aspects of the software development. The goal of the P-CMM is to define the characteristics of mature and capable processes in a way that can be measured across the other organizations in the industry. Any organization will grow in terms of maturity from one level to other level as it adopts to the processes as defined in the standards of Capability Maturity Model (CMM). Figure 14.3 shows various levels in CMM.

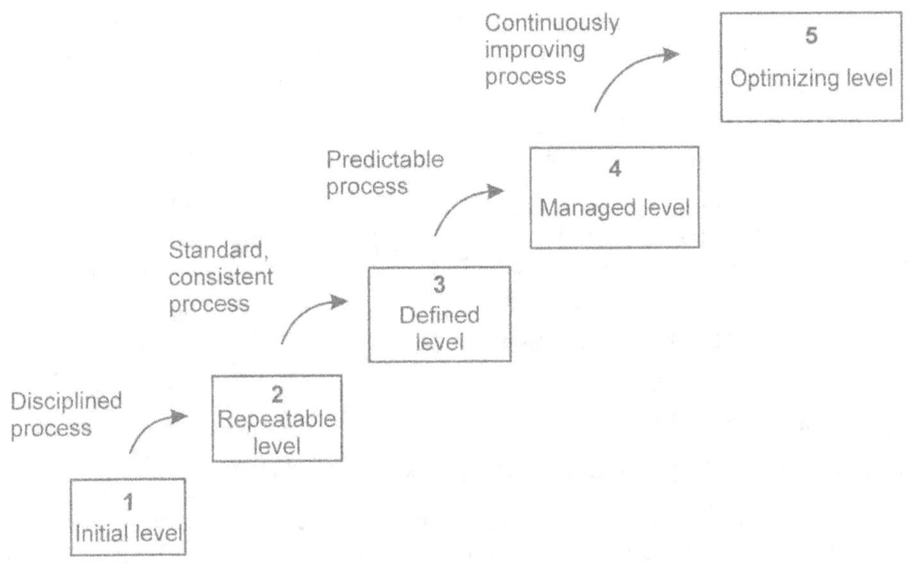

Figure 14.3 The CMM Model defines Five Levels of Organizational Maturity

1 **Initial level:** This is the first level of CMM which forms the basis for comparing with next higher levels of maturity. In this type of the organization, the result of the project depends on the resources and not on the practices. The success of the project depends on the personal approach taken by the project manager, his experience, and decisions. This means the project success is on the team which executed the project, and can be repeated only if the same set of resources is

available. If the resources leave the company, work will be severely affected. Accordingly the development process will be limited to coding and testing.

2   **Repeatable level:** In this level basic project management technologies are applied in the company. The project planning is applied and the standards and quality concepts are introduced and team tries to use these standards for their project implementation. At critical times though, team tends to roll back to initial level concentrating only on the code and testing.

3   **Defined level:** At this next level, the main target is to decrease the dependency of the company on the resources in the organization. At this level processes for software development and maintenance are introduced to the organization and the same will be documented and followed in practice for the projects. The quality team is also set up and quality team helps in transitioning to the organization to adapt to these new standards. Appropriate training will be provided by the quality department to help the organization to achieve this level. As the organization works on attaining this maturity level, the tendency of rolling back to previous level also decrease and the organization dependency on the resources is also avoided.

4   **Managed level:** At this level of maturity, quantitative analysis is applied for both software processes and the project performance as a whole for all the projects in the organization. Project management standards are improved based on the quantitative indices obtained across the organization. Also mature communication channel is set across the organization that leads to continuous process improvements based on the variations in indices and observations in the projects.

5   **Optimizing level:** At this highest level of maturity, the organization seeks continuous improvement for existing processes as well as evaluates the innovative approaches on newly introduced systems. As stated earlier organization seeks permanent improvement in its processes and tries to anticipate the possible errors and defects to achieve overall goal of decreasing the cost of software development.

Principles of People CMM

People CMM is based on several principles, as follows:

- People capability is a competitive issue. Competition arises when different organizations are performing the same task (such as software development). In such a case, the people of an organization are sources of strategy and skills, which in turn results in better performance of the organization.

- The people capability should be defined in relation to the business objectives of the organization.

- An organization should invest in improving the capabilities and skills of the people, as they are important for its success.

- The management should be responsible for enhancing the capability of the people in the organization.

- The improvement in the capability of people should be done as a process. This process should incorporate appropriate practices and procedures.
- The organization should be responsible for providing improvement opportunities so that people in the organization can take advantage of them.
- Since new technologies and organizational practices emerge rapidly, the organizations should continually improve their practices and develop the abilities of people.

14.6 SUMMARY

- Project planning is a part of project management. Initially, the project scope is defined and the appropriate methods for completing the project are determined.
- It is essential to perform project scheduling to effectively manage the tasks of the project. Project scheduling provides details, such as start date and end date of the project, milestones and tasks for the project.
- Some of the factors that delay project schedule are Unrealistic Deadlines, Changing user Requirements, Under-estimation of Resources, Lack of Consideration of Risks, Lack of Proper Communication among Team Members, Difficulties of Team Members, Lack of Action by Project Management Team.
- The common Principles of Project Scheduling are Compartmentalization, Interdependency, Time allocation, Effort validation, Defined Responsibilities, Defined outcomes and Defined Milestones.
- Milestones are formal representations of the progress of a project. Generally, milestones are planned when deliverables are provided.
- Staffing process involves the selection of persons having the right skills and qualifications.
- People are the assets of an organization. The capability of people is essential for the success of an organization.
- The CMM model defines five levels of organizational maturity, those are initial level, repeatable level, defined level, managed level and optimizing level.

Agile Programming

Structure

15.1 INTRODUCTION

In the previous units, you were given an overview of traditional predictive approaches to Software Development Life Cycle (SDLC). You were also provided an introduction to adaptive approaches to SDLC. You became familiar with the separation of design and construction in SDLC. You also learnt about unpredictability of requirements.

Project management skills are essential for managing the SDLC. An approach to project management, normally implemented in software development, is Agile programming. It allows teams to respond to the instability of software development through incremental and iterative work cycles, termed as sprints. Agile programming provides teams with frequent opportunities to evaluate the direction of a project during the complete development lifecycle. These evaluation opportunities are developed into the essential workflow of agile programming.

In this unit, you will become familiar with the different flavors of agile development. You will be given an overview on agile manifesto. You will also learn the different refactoring techniques and the limitations of the agile process.

Objectives

After studying this unit, you should be able to:

- describe the different flavors of agile development
- provide an overview of agile manifesto
- explain refactoring techniques
- analyze the limitations of the agile process

15.2 FLAVORS OF AGILE DEVELOPMENT

Projects are usually characterized by varying requirements. Agile programming involves iterations called sprints and can deal with these varying requirements. This has led to the increase in the popularity of agile forms of development. The waterfall model of development uses a single development strategy. This model is characterized by clear steps that are employed for developing software in successive stages. The waterfall model has been around for years and has been implemented in business practices. On the other hand, agile development does not represent a single development strategy. Agile includes an umbrella of choices for the development camps. Each camp present under the agile umbrella implements the overall agile development principles but distinguishes itself on method characteristics and fit to varying project situations.

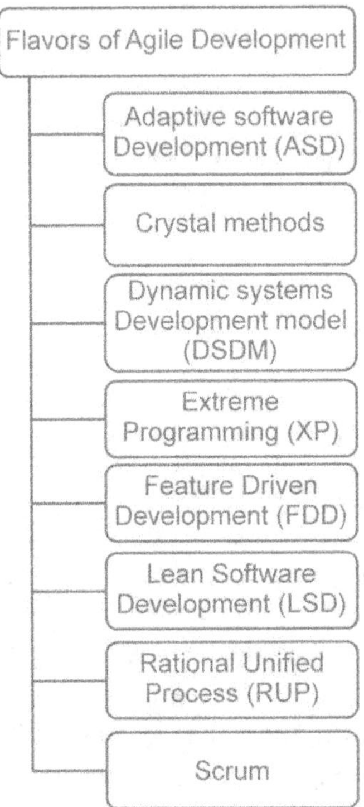

Figure 15.1 Major Flavors of Agile Development Adaptive Software Development (ASD)

Some major flavors of agile development as shown in Fig.15.1 are:

- Adaptive Software Development (ASD)
- Crystal methods
- Dynamic Systems Development Model (DSDM)
- Extreme Programming (XP)
- Feature Driven Development (FDD)

- Lean Software Development (LD)
- Rational Unified Process (RUP)
- Scrum

Let us now discuss these flavors in brief.

ASD involves an iterative strategy that enhances not just the software developed by the organization, but also improves an organization's processes. In ASD, you acquire key learning from the errors that were caused by false assumptions in the previous iteration. The lessons learnt can be used to modify the process for the next iteration.

Crystal Methods

Crystal is actually a group of methodologies that includes Crystal Orange, Crystal Light etc. Each methodology in the Crystal family is assigned the name of a color (Clear, Yellow, Orange, Orange Web, Red and Maroon) that corresponds to the geological crystal's hardness, and indicates the project's size and criticality. Since every team has different skills and every project has different requirements, the organization must follow a different process for each project.

There are seven key principles present in every Crystal implementation and they are:

1. Frequent delivery
2. Continual feedback
3. Constant communication
4. Safety
5. Focus
6. Access to users
7. Automated tests and integration

Let us now briefly discuss these principles.

Frequent delivery - Project owners or customers can anticipate deliverables from the teams every couple of months. In case of larger or more crucial projects, the deliverables may not enter the production level. However, stakeholders will see intermediate versions and they will be able to give a feedback.

Continual feedback - The entire project team meets regularly to discuss project activities. The team also meets with stakeholders on a regular basis to ensure the project is being carried out in the expected direction and to communicate any new issues that may impact the project.

Constant communication - In small projects, the whole team is expected to be in the same room. But, in larger projects the team is expected to be co-located in the same facility. Every project expects to have regular access to the persons defining the requirements.

Safety - Crystal is fairly unique in its focus on the safety part of software development and this is noticed in two forms. The first form is the safe zone where team members have to communicate the truth during the project without any fear of retaliation. This is applicable to most of the Agile methodologies. The second form of safety that only

Crystal identifies is that the purpose of every software project is not similar and that some software projects have an effect on the safety of their end users. For example, the importance of space shuttle system is much more when compared to a recipe organizer.

Focus - Team members must know the top two or three priority elements every member must be working on and must be given time to complete them without any disturbance.

Access to users - As seen in most of the agile methodologies, Crystal also expects that the project team must have access to one or more end-users of the system.

Automated tests and integration - Crystal has different capacities for verifying project functionality. There must be controls to support versioning, automated testing and frequent integration of system components.

Dynamic Systems Development Model (DSDM)

DSDM is one of the major agile methodologies available. It was initially developed as an extension to Rapid Application Development (RAD). There are three phases in DSDM and they are:

Pre-project phase

Project life-cycle phase

Post-project phase

The project life-cycle phase is again categorized into five stages and they include:

1. Feasibility study

Business study

Functional model iteration

Design and build iteration

Implementation

DSDM is developed based on nine principles and they are:

- Active use involvement is necessary.
- The team should be empowered to deliver.
- Frequent delivery is vital.
- The major criterion for acceptance is the delivery of functionality that meets the current business requirements.
- Iterative and incremental delivery is important.
- Any change made during the project lifecycle must be reversible.
- Requirements are baselined at a high level.
- Integrated testing during the entire project lifecycle is anticipated.
- Collaboration and mutual help between all stakeholders is necessary.

These nine principles make DSDM work much better.

Extreme Programming (XP)

XP focuses more on actual programming strategies than other mainstream agile methodologies. It gives greater importance to customer involvement. The XP practices are:

- **Test Driven Development (TDD)** - Here, unit tests are written prior to the code they test.
- **Continuous integration** - In this, each developer commits code daily and the build process automatically runs the unit tests.
- **Pair programming** - In this, two programmers (a driver who focuses on coding strategies and an observer) work together sharing resources like the keyboard, monitor etc.
- **Planning game** - It helps to quickly develop a rough plan and then improve it as the project continues. Both business and development teams meet to decide the aspects of the required system that will offer maximum value to the business.
- **Small releases** - This is a simple system containing a helpful set of features that is put into production phase initially and then updated frequently in short cycles.
- *Simple design* - This is constantly used to develop the application as long as it fulfills the current business requirements.
- **Refactoring** - It is the process of enhancing the code's structure while preserving its function.
- **Collective code ownership** - This practice states that all the code belongs to every team member; no single team member owns a piece of code and any member can make changes to the code base at any time.
- **Coding standards** - People involved in XP project use the same coding standards. This enables pair programming and sharing ownership of all codes.
- **Metaphor** - Every project contains a 'system of names' and description which enables to guide the development process and communication between all parties.

Feature Driven Development (FDD)

In FDD, a model of the domain under development is created in the beginning. Then, an iterative method of feature design and implementation starts. Features indicate an effective grouping of functionality to the customer. FDD is formed using the following five simple activities:

1. Develop the domain object model.
2. Create a feature list.
3. Plan by feature.
4. Design by feature.
5. Build by feature.

Lean Software Development (LD)

LD borrows principles from manufacturing processes developed by Toyota which emphasizes mainly on removal of waste and bureaucracy. The seven principles followed to achieve this are:

- *Remove waste* - Select only the most helpful features for a customer.

- **Strengthen learning** - Learn by doing and testing things rather than documenting.
- **_Decide as late as possible_** - Delay decisions to allow more facts to be collected and changes to occur.
- **_Deliver as fast as possible_** - The faster the software is delivered, the faster the feedback is received and included in the next release, gaining fast return on investment to the business.
- **_Empower the team_** - Make the team responsible and enhance motivation by including all members in the decision-making process.
- **_Develop integrity_** - Refactor on a regular basis to maintain a code that is flexible and compliant to modify.
- **_See the whole_** - Make sure that domain knowledge reaches the entire team for problems to be detected at any level of the system.

Rational Unified Process (RUP)

RUP is a collection of several practices from which organizations choose elements that match their common and individual project requirements. As a result, it is more a process framework rather than a process.

A RUP project includes a series of iterations that is divided into four different phases:

1. Inception
2. Elaboration
3. Construction
4. Transition

These phases occur sequentially and every phase concludes when a specified objective is accomplished. Let us now briefly discuss these phases.

Inception - During inception phase, the major objective is to develop a shared understanding of the scope of the new system and to define the candidate architecture.

Elaboration - During elaboration phase, the main objective is to increase the team's understanding of the system requirements and to validate the candidate architecture.

Construction - During construction phase, the development of the system is completed.

Transition - During transition phase, system testing is completed and the system is deployed for production.

Scrum

Scrum focuses on the management aspects of software development and gives lesser emphasis to engineering practices. It is relatively easy to learn and executes with little documentation.

The Scrum methodology has a series of 'sprints', usually lasting for two to four weeks, each sprint provides some functioning, potentially shippable software. The 'product backlog' drives the workload of these sprints. It comprises new features including bug fixes, technical debt, and anything that may contribute to the end deliverable. A product owner takes the help of the customer to prioritize the product backlog and works closely with the team through stand-up meetings and sprint retrospectives. The iterative feature of Scrum is that this cycle occurs repeatedly until the project is complete.

15.3 AGILE MANIFESTO

Although different developers prefer different flavors of agile, they realized that all flavors have some common principles. The agile Manifesto was formulated by 17 software developers who gathered in February 2001 in the Wasatch Mountains of Utah. It was formulated to find a common baseline for their perceptions of software development process and to develop the common elements previously implemented in various software organizations. The Agile Manifesto presents an alternative strategy to the software development process that had been implemented during the past 40 years, starting from the early phases of the development of complex software systems. Different agile methods apply the Agile Manifesto and some of them are:

- Scrum
- DSDM
- Extreme Programming
- Crystal
- Adaptive Software Development
- Feature-Driven Development

The Agile Manifesto is a statement of values of strongly held beliefs conveyed as preferences and not absolutes. All agile methodologies generally include the manifesto into their value system.

> **Manifesto for agile software development**
>
> "We are uncovering better ways of developing software by doing it and helping others to do it.
>
> Through this work we have come to value:
>
> Individuals and interactions over processes and tools
>
> Working software over comprehensive documentation
>
> Customer collaboration over contract negotiation
>
> Responding to change over following a plan
>
> *(Source: http://www.agilemanifesto.org/)*

Let us now discuss the values of the Agile Manifesto in brief:

Individuals and interactions over processes and tools

Individuals and interactions are very crucial for high-performing teams. Agile methods depend greatly on frequent inspect-and-adapt cycles for communication. These cycles may range between every few minutes with pair programming, every few hours with continuous integration and every day with a daily stand-up meeting. When individuals and teams are committed, they feel responsible to deliver output with high value. Agile methodologies help teams to be committed by supporting teams to take tasks from a prioritized work list, handle their own tasks, and concentrate on improving their work strategies.

Agile methodologies give more preference to individuals and interactions rather than to processes and tools to develop highly-productive teams. All agile methodologies try to improve communication and collaboration through recurrent inspect-and-adapt cycles. These cycles function only when agile leaders support the positive conflict that is required to develop a solid foundation of truth, transparency, faith, respect, and commitment for their Agile teams.

Working software over comprehensive documentation

In agile projects, the working software is considered to be the final quantification of the project's status. Producing a working software has to be the main objective of a team. If the team feels that the amount of documentation done is taking too much of their time, then it is necessary to reduce the documentation produced. The major drawback of comprehensive documentation is that it is a poor communication tool for assisting developers to understand the customer's requirements. It is also a poor communication means for explaining to a team of developers how to develop a product. It is a poor interpreter of what the product will do when it is completed. Documentation is basically a transient artifact, trying to maintain a record of decisions and communicate intent.

In more traditional environments, people are assigned the role of creating some kind of a requirements document, design document, or a project charter. Many people assume that the presence of the artifact is the only thing that is needed to develop software and the document becomes an end in itself. The document is not deliverable; it is only a record of an agreement that allows us to track the project. Documentation is used to record what has been created, rather than to predict what must be created. Documentation does not help you to decrease risk or confirm assumptions.

Customer collaboration over contract negotiation

This principle plays a major role in changing the insight of the customer's role in software development. It motivates Agile software developers to base their work on ongoing and daily contact with the customer. Such a close contact helps customers to manage effectively with the changes that characterize software projects. This principle also specifies a conceptual change regarding the nature and formulation of software product contracts.

Collaboration involves the customer in the development segment. However, most of the customers are not prepared for the responsibilities and many organizations consider customer proximity as countercultural. It is more often difficult to make contract negotiations adaptive. Mentoring and coaching the customer's performance in close collaboration or within the framework of a contract may become an important project task.

Responding to change over following a plan

This principle motivates Agile software developers to establish a process that efficiently manages the changes introduced during development, without compromising the high quality of the developed product. The basis for this principle is the recognition that customers cannot predict all their requirements in the beginning and hence a process must be established wherein the requirements gradually recognized by the customer can be shared with the team members. Agile software development enables the introduction of changes in the developed product which have evolved from a better understanding of the software requirements, without essentially increasing the cost of development.

Not implementing plan-driven strategies indicates putting a higher priority on satisfying customers. This implies dynamically responding to requirements that vary with experience rather than implementing a project plan.

After the development of Agile Manifesto, a set of agile principles was proposed. The 12 major principles of agile software are:

- Satisfying the customers with early and continuous delivery of valuable software is agile software's major priority.
- Welcoming varying requirements, even during the later phases of development. Agile processes also support change for the customer's competitive benefit.
- Delivering working software often, with a shorter timescale is preferred.
- Involving business people and developers in development of agile process and making them work together everyday during the project.
- Developing projects around motivated individuals and also providing those individuals the environment and the support they require, and trusting them to get the work done.
- Considering face-to-face conversation as the most proficient and useful way of conveying information to a development team.
- Considering working software as the major measure of progress.
- Supporting sustainable growth by ensuring that the sponsors, developers, and customers maintain a steady pace indefinitely.
- Providing constant attention to technical excellence and improving agility with good design.
- Simplifying, which is the art of maximizing the amount of work performed, is very crucial.
- Formulating best architectures, requirements, and designs from self-organizing teams.
- Planning done by the team at regular intervals on how to become more productive, then tuning and modifying its behavior accordingly.

These 12 principles help organizations to implement their projects effectively by practicing agile methods.

15.4 REFACTORING TECHNIQUES

The process of clarifying and simplifying the design of already existing code, without varying its behavior is known as refactoring. Agile teams maintain and extend their code from iteration to iteration without continuous refactoring and this is difficult to handle because un-refactored code can rot. The code rot can be in many forms such as harmful dependencies between classes or packages, bad allotment of class responsibilities, numerous responsibilities per method or class, duplicate code, and several other uncertainties and clutters. Each time the code is modified without refactoring it, the rot aggravates and spreads. The code rot becomes time consuming and excessively shortens the lifespan of useful systems. Refactoring code helps in avoiding code rot. It helps in the easy maintenance and extension of the code. However, we can safely refactor the code only if we have extensive unit test suites. If we are unable to execute the tests after every step in a refactoring, we have to face the risk of introducing bugs. When performing true Test-Driven Development (TDD), wherein the design develops continuously, then you cannot avoid regular refactoring.

In 1999, Martin Fowler explained refactoring programming technique as a disciplined method to restructure code. The crucial idea is that you make minor changes to your code to enhance your design, making it simpler to understand and to modify. Refactoring allows the users to develop their code in stages by adopting an iterative and incremental approach to programming. A major aspect of refactoring is that it maintains the behavioral semantics of your code, from a black box perspective. For example, Rename Method possibly from getPersons() to getPeople(). Even though this change looks simple, you need to change every single invocation of this function throughout the application code to invoke the new name. You can ensure that you have refactored the code accurately only if it continues to work as before.

It is necessary to remember that when you are refactoring, you need not add functionality. Refactoring indicates that you are enhancing the existing code and adding functionality implies that you are adding new code. You can refactor your existing code prior to adding new functionality. Hence, you must understand that refactoring and including new functionality are two different but complementary tasks.

Database refactoring

A simple change made to a database schema that enhances its design while retaining both its behavioral and informational semantics is database refactoring. A database schema contains both structural aspects like table and view definitions and functional aspects like stored procedures and triggers. Database refactoring is theoretically more complicated than code refactoring. In code refactoring, only behavioral semantics is supported. But in database refactoring, informational semantics is also supported.

Split Column is one of the database refactorings described in "A Catalog of Database Refactorings". In Split Column, a single table column is replaced with two or more other columns. For example, you are working on the 'Person table' in your database and you identify that the 'FirstDate' column is being used for two different reasons – when the person is a customer this column saves their birth date and when the person is an employee it saves their employment date as HireDate. The problem here is that your application must now support people who can be both a customer and an employee. Prior to implementing this new requirement, the database schema must be fixed by replacing the FirstDate column with BirthDate and HireDate columns. To maintain the behavioral semantics of the database schema, you must update all source codes that access the FirstDate column to work with two new columns. To maintain the informational semantics, you must create a migration script that loops through the table, verifies the type, and then copies the existing date into the suitable column.

There are two major reasons for using database refactoring and they are:

- **Fix existing legacy databases carefully -** Legacy databases do not fix themselves. Hence, from a technical perspective, database refactoring is a safer and simpler method to eventually improve data, database and quality.
- **Support evolutionary development -** Some of the modern software development processes including XP, RUP, and AUP (Agile Unified Process) work in an evolutionary way if not in agile manner. Data professionals must implement these techniques, including database refactoring, which allow them to work in such a manner.

Refactoring has two major benefits and they are:

- It maintains an application that is well designed and facilitates the "design as you go" principle.
- It helps to refactor a larger module or class into something much better instead of rewriting them.

Some of the basic refactoring techniques include:

- **Rename a type/class/function/variable -** All developers or teams have coding standards – both formally and informally defined and you need to apply them to your code. If there is a function ReadData and a complementary function DataWrite – you must rename one, such that they are consistent. If you need to change multiple identifiers, change only one at each step, and then compile and run. You must use unique names because when you forget to rename in one place, then the compiler can detect it.
- **Reformat a function to conform to your coding standards -** Ensure that your code is readable. If it is difficult to understand a working code, do not discard it. Instead spend some time in making the code readable.
- **Turn a code sequence into a function -** When the complexity of a process goes beyond acceptable levels or when you observe that similar functionality is applied at different places, make it a function.
- **Move functionality shared by several classes to a common base class or a helper class -** This can break down the level of complication of a single class back to a reasonable level.
- **Separate independent functionality into different classes/ functions -** If a class is very big and requires multiple files, then refactors logical functions of the class into partial classes.

In this manner, a base class is introduced only if required and early design decisions are often intentionally unchangeable.

15.5 LIMITATIONS OF THE AGILE PROCESS

Many software professionals frequently use agile and this has made it very popular. But, well qualified and skilled IT professionals acknowledge that there are some limitations to the agile process. The limitations of the agile process are:

- Restricted support for distributed development environments

- Limited support for subcontracting
- Limited support for developing reusable artifacts
- Limited support for development with large teams involved
- Restricted support for building safety-critical software
- Limited support for development of large and complex software

Let us now discuss these limitations in detail.

Restricted support for distributed development environments

Development environments wherein team members and customers are physically distributed may be unable to hold face-to-face communication required by agile processes. In such circumstances, one can at least approximate face-to-face communication by using technologies like video-conferencing. However, these technologies are costly and are not as effective as expected.

Limited support for subcontracting

Outsourcing of software development tasks to subcontractors is more often based on contracts that exactly specify what is needed of the subcontractor. Subcontracted tasks must be well-defined for the subcontractors to bid for the contract. During the development of a bid, a subcontractor will usually create a plan that includes a process, objectives and deliverables in adequate detail to decide a cost estimate. The process may be an iterative and incremental strategy, but the subcontractors may need to make the process predictive by indicating the number of iterations and the deliverables of every iteration to compete. It is possible to design a contract that provides some degree of flexibility to the subcontractor in the manner adopted to develop the product within specified time and cost constraints. This is definitely possible if the subcontractor has a good track record and the contracting company can trust the subcontractor to develop a product that fulfills the contracting company's requirements. A contract that supports agile development in the subcontractor environment must include the following two parts:

- *Fixed part -* This part defines the following:
  o The framework that specifies how the subcontractor will include changes into the product, for example, cost and time-based criteria for accepting or rejecting changes to the variable part of the contract.
  o The activities that the subcontractor must perform, for example, quality assurance activities.
  o The requirements that must be considered fixed.
  o The deliverables those are mandatory.
- *Variable part -* This part describes the requirements and deliverables that can change within the boundaries defined in the fixed part. This part can develop within the constraints described in the fixed part. When the contract is signed, an explanation of prioritized deliverables and requirements must be incorporated.

Limited support for developing reusable artifacts

Agile processes like XP emphasize developing software products that solve a specific issue. The development of generalized solutions and other forms of reusable software (like design frameworks) is best handled in projects that are mainly concerned with the development of reusable artifacts. This separation of the product-specific development from the reusable artifact development environment is a major feature of the reuse-oriented framework known as the 'Experience Factory'. The researchers at the University of Maryland at College Park developed the Experience Factory. The extensive applicability of a reusable artifact means that the process used to develop the artifact must focus on quality control because the impact of low quality (especially severe errors) is as extensive as the number of applications that reuse the artifact. On the other hand, timely development of reusable artifacts is required. While there appears to be a case for applying agile processes to the development of reusable artifacts, it is unclear how agile processes can be correctly adapted.

Limited support for development with large teams involved

Agile processes support process 'management-in-the-small'. Here, control, coordination and communication methods used are relevant to small and medium sized teams. With larger teams involved, the number of communication lines that must be maintained can minimize the efficiency of practices like informal face-to-face communications and review meetings. Large teams need less agile approaches to handle the issues particular to 'management-in-the-large'. Traditional software engineering approaches that focus more on documentation, change control, and architecture-centric development are more relevant here. This does not mean that agile practices are not relevant in such environments. The teams may get opportunities to use agile practices. However, the degree of agility possible may be less than that noticed in smaller projects.

Restricted support for building safety-critical software

Software whose failure can directly injure human beings or lead to severe economic damage is safety-critical software. The current agile processes promote some quality control methods like pair programming and informal reviews. But, these methods have not proven to be sufficient to ensure users that the product is safe.

Formal specification, severe test coverage, and other formal analysis and assessment strategies incorporated in software engineering strategies provide better, but also more expensive mechanisms to handle the development of safety- or business-critical software. Some agile practices may also provide benefits to the development of such software. For example:

- Test-first strategies need one to define unit tests prior to writing code.

- The early production of working code promoted by the incremental, iterative process structure of agile processes supports tentative development of critical software wherein requirements are not well-defined.

- Pair-programming might be a useful supplement to formal reviews.

Hence, it is considered that agile and formal software development are not incompatible, but may be combined when required. Formal strategies may be used in an agile way to deal with critical pieces of software to improve quality and confidence.

Limited support for development of large and complex software

The assumption that code refactoring eliminates the requirement to design for change may not hold for large complex systems. In such software, there might be important architectural aspects that are difficult to change because of the crucial role that they play in the core services offered by the system. In such cases, the cost of changing these aspects may be very high. As a result, it requires extra efforts to expect such changes at an early stage. Relying on code refactoring may also be problematic for such systems. Strict code refactoring can be expensive and error-prone because of the complexity and size of such software. Models can play a very crucial role here, mainly if tools exist for creating important portions of the code from the models. This view of models as the central object for developing systems is at the heart of the Object Management Group's (OMG) Model-Driven Architecture (MDA) approach. There are some systems wherein it is not possible to develop the software incrementally because functionality of such systems is tightly coupled and integrated. In these systems, an iterative approach, wherein code is created in the iteration can still be used. But, the code created in the iteration will contain all the pieces in different states of incompleteness. Hence, empirical data comparing the efficiency and limitations of agile and non-agile approaches may significantly improve our understanding of the true benefits and limitations of agile processes.

15.6 SUMMARY

Let us recapitulate the important concepts discussed in this unit:

- There has been increase in popularity of agile forms of development because of varying needs of project.
- Some of the major flavors of agile development are Adaptive Software Development (ASD), Crystal methods, Dynamic Systems Development Model (DSDM), and Extreme Programming (XP).
- Seventeen software developers gathered in February 2001 in the Wasatch Mountains of Utah and developed the Agile Manifesto.
- All agile methodologies normally include the manifesto into their value system.
- Agile software's major goal is to satisfy the customers with early and continuous delivery of valuable software.
- The method of clarifying and simplifying the design of already existing code, without varying its behavior, is known as refactoring.
- Refactoring allows the users to develop their code in stages by adopting an iterative and incremental approach to programming.
- Refactoring helps to maintain an application that is well designed and facilitates the 'design as you go' principle.

- Agile methodologies support process 'management-in-the-small' in which control, coordination and communication methods used are applicable to small to medium-sized teams.
- It is noted that agile and formal software development are not incompatible, but are combined when necessary.

15.7 GLOSSARY

Black box: A device, system or an object which can be viewed solely in terms of its input, output and transfer characteristics without any knowledge of its internal workings.

Counterculture: A culture, mainly of young people, with values or lifestyles in opposition to those of the established culture.

Database schema: It is a collection of meta-data that describes the relations in a database.

Legacy database: A database system that was inherited by a team from previous project owners.

Waterfall model: A sequential software development model wherein development is noticed as flowing steadily downwards (like a waterfall) through several phases.

15.8 CASE STUDY

Effective Soft: The Agile Case Study

Agile methodology is mainly advantageous for projects whose structure and features vary during the development process. Link Stock solution was a project that was successfully implemented with agile project management strategies.

Problem

A big medical company was applying the link exchange method for advertising their website. A special team of SEO specialists was looking for relative websites in the Internet to exchange links with. There was a growth in link base and it required close attention as every link had to be verified for validity on a regular basis and the members manually performed the verification. The marketing manager realized that the posting process and link verification could be optimized.

Solution

The company marketing manager recommended creating a special solution that would stock the links and verify them on a regular basis. The company approached Effective Soft. The Effective Soft project manager opted to work on agile methods because the requirements of the project were not completely clear at the beginning. After some duration, the customer was presented the project sprint-release. The customers then presented their new requirements and ideas.

Contd...

The agile principles that were used in implementing the project are:

* Face-to-face communication was opted for written documentation.

* The team was placed in the same office to enable better team work.

* The customer actively participated in developing process.

* There was mutual trust and respect between the developers and the clients.

In a short period of time, the first version of the Link Stock solution was ready for use. More features and functionalities were included in the subsequent iterations. The final solution allowed:

* Combining all the old bases into one new base

* Verifying automatically the link validity

* Providing different access levels

* Optimizing work process

Discussion Questions:

1.   What was the major problem that the big medical company faced?

     (Hint: Growth in link base)

2.   What did the company marketing manager recommend?

     (Hint: Creating a special solution)

16 Extreme Programming

Structure

16.1   INTRODUCTION

In the previous unit we studied the flavors of agile development and agile manifesto. We also studied the techniques of refactoring and limitations of agile process. Agile processes are widely used across many Information Technology (IT) organizations. Extreme Programming (XP) is one of the most popular and widely used agile processes.

XP is successful as it aims at customer satisfaction. It empowers the developers to be flexible and respond to the requirements of the customer, even after the software development life cycle is complete. XP gives importance to teamwork and make developers, managers, and customers equal partners in the development process.

This unit familiarizes you with the concept of XP. We will also study the values that XP imparts into a development project and how XP helps in assuming sufficiency.

Objectives

After studying this unit, you should be able to:

* describe the XP equation

- list XP values
- explain assuming time sufficiency and resource sufficiency

16.2 XP EQUATION

Extreme Programming (XP) is a powerful, well-organized and supple software development methodology. It focuses on coding inside each software development life cycle (SDLC) stage.

XP is not just a programming method, but a culture that aims at developing the program in the best possible way. It is more about understanding the capability of the development team, and planning and developing the software to meet the customer requirements. Thus, XP is about writing efficient code to optimize efficiency.

XP addresses the need to accomplish technical superiority in a development process and helps to retain good relationship among the team members and with the customer. XP believes that in order to develop efficient software, it is important to control the process of program development at every stage of the development life cycle by taking the team and customer into confidence. Therefore, XP is a style of software development that focuses on efficient application of programming techniques, clear communication, and teamwork which allows you to develop highly efficient software.

Figure 16.1 depicts a typical XP cycle.

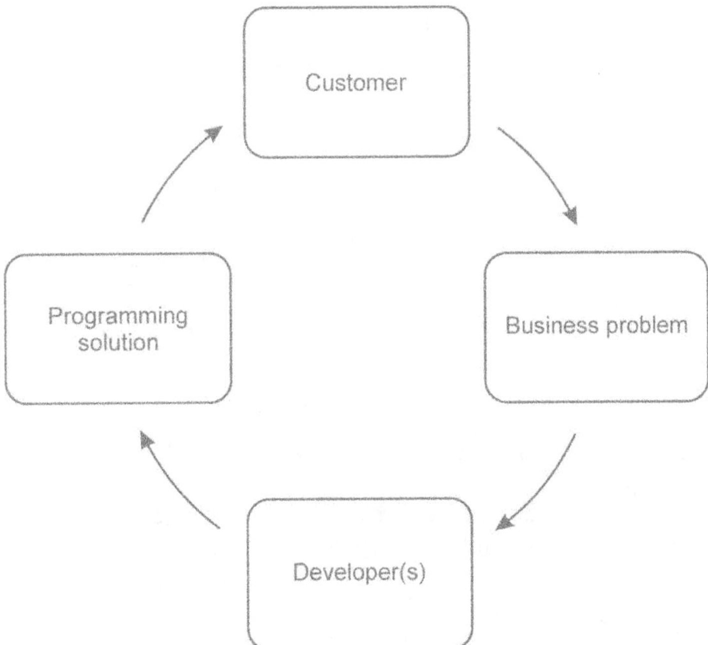

Figure 16.1 XP Cycle

As shown in the figure 16.1, a customer approaches the developer(s) with a problem. This problem of the customer is related to the customer's business. The role of the developer(s) is to provide an efficient programming solution to overcome the problem. To find a solution to the problem, the developer(s) analyzes the problem and comes up with a programming solution, develops software and gives it to the customer. The customer implements the software and approaches the developer(s) again for further optimization or modification based on the performance of the software. The cycle goes on till the software is developed and it resolves the problems of the customer effectively.

Figure 16.2 depicts the parameters that need to be analyzed while developing programming solution using XP.

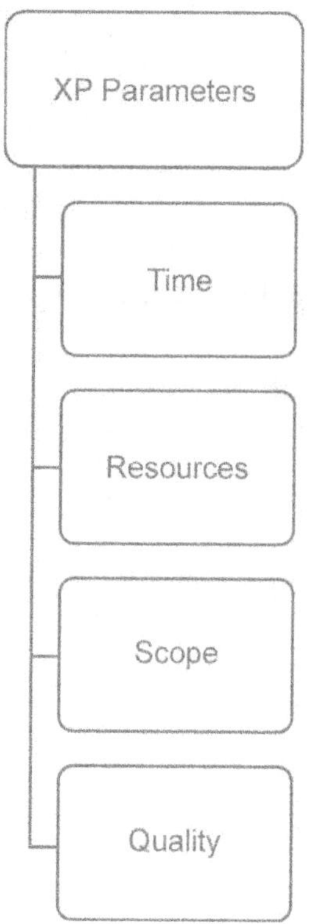

Figure 16.2 XP Parameters

As shown in figure 16.2 the four parameters that you need to analyze while developing software using XP are:

- Time
- Resources
- Scope
- Quality

Let us now discuss these parameters in detail.

Time

Time refers to the duration taken by the developers to deliver the programming solution to the customer. This is the most critical parameter in the development life cycle. According to XP, if more time is spent on development, then the resultant solution is more efficient. However, a reasonable timeline must be defined for delivering the solution within every cycle and to complete the entire development process.

Resources

Resources includes the managers, developers, subject matter experts (SMEs) (for example, if there is a requirement in the field of mechanical engineering, an expert from that field should be present to give specific inputs during the development process), software testers, technical writers etc. The resources are needed to develop and deliver the solution. Careful planning must be done to assess the number and type of resources required to deliver the solution within the given time. We can quicken the process by employing greater number of resources in the development team. However, if the number of resources exceeds the requirement, then it may decrease the overall efficiency of the team. For example, a company has 10 developers and the project that they are working on requires only five developers to complete the project in a month. The company decides to use two more developers to complete the software development in 20 days. Now, totally seven developers work on the project to finish it in 20 days. However, even though the other three developers have no work to do for 20 days, the company still has to pay them. This is a loss to the company. This decreases the efficiency of the company. Therefore, careful resource planning and management has to be done to deliver the solution efficiently.

Scope

Scope refers to the boundaries of the project. This defines what the project must accomplish and the resources required for achieving the objectives. The time required and resources available to the team directly influence the scope of work. Any increase in scope may require more time and resources allotted to the team or else the quality of the solution decreases.

Quality

Quality is the most complex parameter to define and also to manage. It can be defined as the compliance of the software to the customer's requirement or efficiency of the software in overcoming the customer's problem. Usually the customer defines the quality desired in the form of requirements and software quality is determined by the ability of the software to meet those requirements. As we discussed in scope, quality can be directly or indirectly affected by time and resources. Hence, the three parameters must be planned and managed efficiently to obtain high quality or develop efficient software. Different projects might have different quality needs and may change over time. The company must be able to change and familiarize itself according to the varying quality needs of its customers.

Many projects concentrate on time and resources assuming that quality can be achieved as it is remains constant. However, it is not always true. If the customer asks for a new feature then the quality parameter can vary. This has a direct impact on the scope, resulting in a decrease in the quality if you do not handle time and resources carefully.

Therefore, XP suggests that the acceptable level of quality has to be agreed as a team involving the customer, manager and developers. After agreeing on the quality, the next important point that has to be discussed and finalized is the scope. It includes what will be delivered? When will it be delivered? How will it be delivered? Usually the customer sets the priorities for these questions. The team has to work based on the priorities defined by the customers.

According to XP, scope has to be adjusted regularly based on the progress of the project. Therefore, people responsible for taking the business decision must have a clear idea of the work progress status of the development cycle. This helps both the customer and the team to make fine adjustments in the scope.

Effective and efficient coordination among the team members is necessary. As a XP practitioner, you have to maintain regular and rapid feedback system within the team. Along with this, sufficient resource must be present in the team to carry out communication and adjust the scope as required.

Activity 1:

Assume that you are an XP practitioner. Your project manager has asked you to prepare a report on the important parameters that you have to monitor and assess before you begin a new project. What are the important points that you will mention in your report and why?

16.3 XP VALUES

As a developer you choose XP not only to develop an efficient program, but also to develop the program in an efficient way. XP enables you to achieve efficiency by making the entire process systematic and simple. As programmers, you should design a simple program; constantly communicate with your fellow programmers and your valued customers. You must also get feedback from customers and fellow programmers by testing your software from the initial stage of the software development life cycle. You should deliver the system to the customers on time and implement changes suggested by your customers at the earliest. You must ensure that you respect every small success and unique contributions done by each and every member of the team. These practices build courage in you and help you to respond to changing requirements and technology courageously. There are four essential values of XP that you need to follow while developing software. Figure 16.3 depicts the four values of XP that help to improve a software development project.

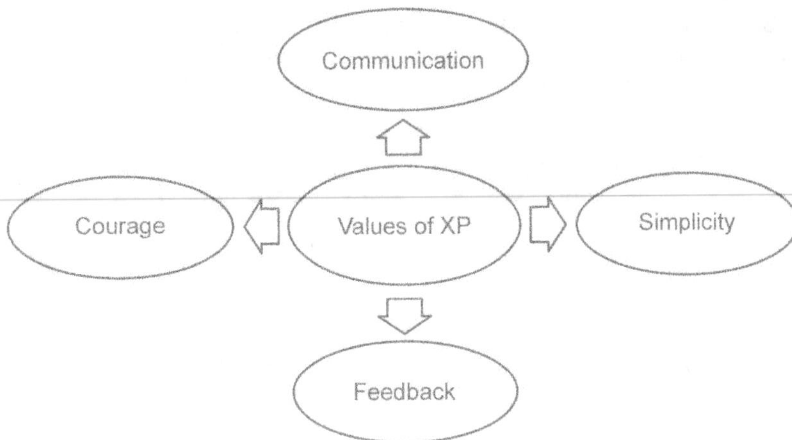

Figure 16.3 Values of XP

As shown in figure 16.3 the four values of XP that you need to adopt while developing software as an extreme programmer are:

- Communication
- Simplicity
- Feedback
- Courage

Let us now discuss them in brief.

Communication

In any project or development activity, communication is the key player. XP regards communication as the most important characteristic of software development activity. XP stresses the need for establishing and maintaining a communication channel or network for the flow of correct information. All those who are involved in the project - customer, management and developers must be connected to each other efficiently.

Communication not only helps to manage the project but also to manage the resources and improve the quality of the team. The role of management is very crucial in any project. The management must ensure that they keep the communication always open to everyone in the team. A company's management cannot function without proper communication with its developers and customers. Therefore, communication is very essential to successfully complete a project within a specified time frame and achieve the expected results.

XP usually favors face-to-face communication rather than communicating through phone, e-mails, etc. The most important form of communication in XP is oral face-to-face communication. However, written formal documentation is also used for communication in XP projects. Creating project documentation before, during and after the project is one form of written communication. Another important form of written communication is the Gantt diagram of the project. The Gantt diagram is a communication tool used to capture the progress of the project using graphic representation. It is also a good method of communication among the persons involved in a project. Figure 16.4 shows a Gantt diagram.

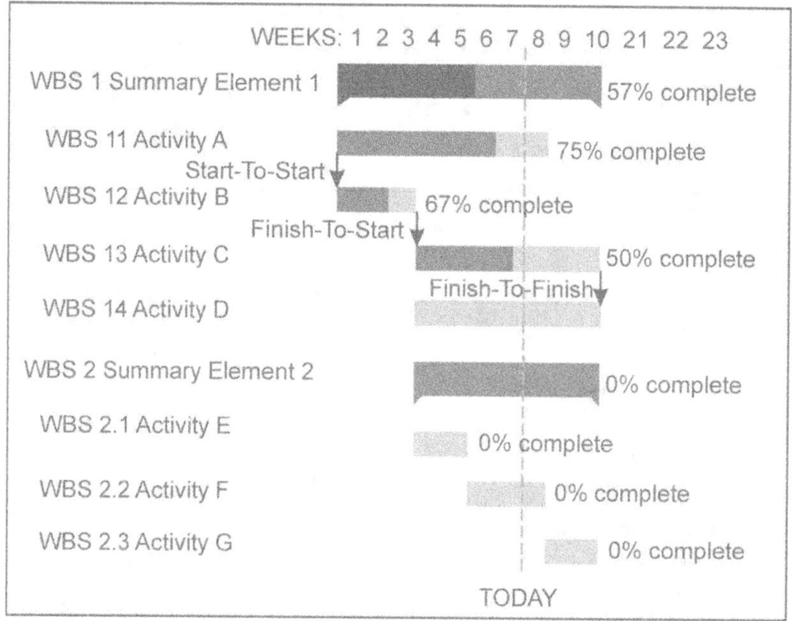

(Source: Reproduced from http://en.wikipedia.org/wiki/Gantt_chart)

Figure 16.4 A Gantt Diagram

As seen in figure 16.4, the Gantt diagram depicts the different activities of the project. It also shows the amount of work completed.

The more effectively a team can communicate with each other, the more is the chance of executing the project successfully. Therefore, teams that communicate often in an open and honest environment are able to make effective decisions and resolve the problems quickly. Thus, value of communication is very high in XP.

Simplicity

Usually, addressing a problem in the simplest way possible is the most preferred choice of any developer, as writing complex and lengthy codes decreases the efficiency of the program. Therefore, you as an extreme programmer must focus on developing or writing codes that are less complex. If you write a simple code now, it is easy to modify it in the future. If you write a complicated set of codes, it will be difficult to reuse or modify it in the future.

In a business environment, while working with customers, the requirements change often. These changes sometimes are significantly huge. Customer usually raises the request for change not during the initial stages of the development, but in the later stages of the development cycle. If you write a complex code, and if the customer asks for modifications, then there are chances that you may have to rewrite the entire code. This is not economical as it requires significant amount of time and resources.

Thus, the cost to modify the software will be high. If you had simplified the code that you had written in the initial stages, then cost incurred to modify the same in the later stages of the development life cycle is significantly less. At the same time, finding and resolving a software bug in highly complex software is very costly.

You must keep in mind that simplicity does not means that you have to develop simple software. It means that you have to adopt a simple approach that helps you to define and solve problem of a complex system in a simple way. Defining the problem and its solution is the most important aspect of any development activity. If you can simplify this, your coding process becomes simplified. If you make this complicated, you might develop the software, but modifying or reusing the same may become difficult.

As an extreme programmer you have to simplify not only the code but also the whole process. It is essential for the programmer to simplify the code developed, to document of the process, to design process, effective communication method etc. Simplicity also compels the team to develop what is needed to meet the requirements.

Feedback

Any team can work efficiently if an effective feedback system exists within the team. Continuous feedback is one of the values that govern XP. Usually, continuous feedback about the status of the project is very helpful to the development team as it reduces the cost that the company has to spend on unnecessary modifications.

Feedback is not the responsibility of one or two individuals in a team. It is a collective responsibility. Everyone involved in a project must ask for and give feedback about the status of the project and the results generated at each stage. Feedback can be in the form of communication among developers, managers and customers. Communication between any two members of the team can happen through a third person, who is also a member of the team. For example, customer requests the developer to provide information about a particular feature of the software sent to them. Instead of the developer, the manager communicates the information. Usually, the methods and techniques used to collect feedback may vary from project to project.

Feedback also means tracking and measuring the development life cycle to control the project. This is an indirect control on developing the code, where the code complexity and time spent is regularly monitored and assessed. This helps to take corrective actions to prevent situations where the code complexity is high or time spent on a particular task is more. For example, you check a portion of code that has been written by a developer. You realize that the code is too complex and can be simplified. You discuss with the developer to implement your suggestion to simplify the codes. Here, getting information from the developer and giving suggestion to the developer is known as feedback. Therefore, feedback is not just communication, but it also deals with tracking the issues and taking preventive measures at regular intervals of time during a development cycle.

Feedback is essential to keep the team on the right track. Therefore, an extreme programmer must ensure that feedback is obtained regularly. Feedbacks are collected not only by interacting with individuals, but also from automation of tests, progress charts, etc. This helps the XP development team to keep a track on the project target and ensures that the software being developed is of high quality. It also gives the customer or project stakeholders the confidence that your team will deliver what they need.

Courage

One has to have courage to exhibit leadership quality in a team. XP empowers developers to self-organize and estimate their work themselves. The team members must be honest and transparent when they estimate their work.

You need courage to try something new. You must be innovative and come up with new solutions to address the problem. You can do this only if you have enough courage to convey your ideas and opinion to the team. Your idea might be correct or completely wrong, but you must share it with the team and get a feedback. This attitude helps the team to think about different ways of solving a problem. Usually one or two ideas are best suited to resolve the problem, but sharing and discussing the ideas indicates that the team is working together with a focus to meet the desired requirements.

You also need courage when you are asked to refactor the software in depth. Usually you need courage to take up a task when you are given an impossible deadline to finish it. You have to respect the deadline and meet it without eliminating the features that you had planned to include. You may choose to eliminate the features that are unnecessary, but not the most important.

You, as a developer, must have courage to speak to the project stakeholder that you are not going to completely adhere to the defined schedule due to certain issues. This helps the team to analyze the issues and find ways to resolve them during the initial stages of the life cycle. Any issues related to the project, must be informed to the customer at the earliest if required.

Thus, XP stresses on the fact that individuals of the team must be courageous enough to speak and do the right thing for completing the project within the defined timelines with desired quality.

Activity 2:

You are the project leader of a ten member team of developers in a company. The team is developing software using XP. List the different feedback you have to provide to the different stakeholders of the project.

16.4   ASSUMING SUFFICIENCY

Developing software involves managing time and resources. The project stakeholders i.e., developers, managers and customers compete with each other to get the best possible results. For example, managers and customers compete with each other to obtain the best bargain regarding the development cost, time, etc. Developers and managers compete with each other to bargain project closure time, resources required, salary etc. However, XP makes you think differently. As an extreme programmer you have to ask a question, "Given sufficient time and resource, how am I going to develop software?"

16.4.1 SUFFICIENT TIME AND RESOURCES

Let us now learn what is sufficient time and resource.

Sufficient time

XP provides developers sufficient time to develop the software. Instead of struggling hard to meet an impractical deadline, you must work at your normal speed. At the same time the amount of work that you can do is also fixed, as you cannot overwork to meet a deadline. This is due to the reason that an impractical deadline might affect the quality of the outputs. Therefore, you must adjust the scope of the work to manage the schedule for a given deadline.

Sufficient time also means that you must ensure that any new modification to the software must require less time to implement and be inexpensive. That means, customer can request for change by quoting less cost, but you must be in a position to make changes to the code easily. Various XP practices can be adopted to develop a flexible code within a given time duration.

XP concentrates on producing high quality software using the time and resource available. Therefore, first you must assess your project and estimate accurately the amount of work that needs to be done and work that you can actually do. Even the customer must be able to identify the most important features or components of the software that they need on high priority. Along with this, you must be in a position to change the schedule and modify the software as the customer's requirement changes. However, sometimes it may be difficult to complete the desired work within a given schedule. But, XP helps you to identify such issues at the earliest, so that you can inform the customer and revise the schedule to a reasonable extent.

Usually XP projects have short development cycles. They have less time duration between an action (writing codes) and its analysis (testing the codes). However, XP provides many opportunities for you to judge the current progress of the project and make necessary modifications to the software according to the customer requirements. Therefore, a project starts generating results quickly. This again shows whether you are on the right track. Also in XP, you have sufficient time for developing software, if you make the best utilization of the time you have.

Sufficient Resources

In XP, it is important to have sufficient development resources for carrying out a project. The number of developers in the team defines the amount of work that the team can do. Therefore, the scope has to be adjusted to execute the project with the available resources.

Usually, developers give time estimation for very small tasks. As a developer you must improve your estimation by evaluating them to the actual time spent on the tasks. After gaining little experience, you will be able to estimate and plan the work efficiently. The same can also be used for planning the whole project. Your estimates help managers and customer to plan a resource budget for scheduling the complete project.

Resources vary with time, the more experience you gain the more control you have on your estimates. As you learn more about the problem you solve, you can develop new techniques and refine your skills. Therefore, as the code evolves, it will be easier for you to add new features and solve the most important problems of the customer with the available resources.

16.4.2 CONSTANT CHANGE OF COST

XP tries to make sure that the costs of changes dose not vary with time. That means, the cost of adding a feature to the software today must be same as adding the same feature to the software next year. This has a lot of significance, as you can develop the software only with the necessary features today and add other features later. Adding a new feature is regarded as upgrading the existing software. At the same time, you can add any necessary features to the software in the future easily without worrying about cost and time spent on it. Thus, XP helps you to invest time and resources to develop software that is necessary to produce the desired result quickly.

In XP, the continuous customer feedback helps you to reduce the cost of modifications done to the software. Usually, the customer receives a working version of the software at the earliest, within a few weeks after the start of the project. Based on the customer feedback, the development team improves or modifies the software. Thus, development becomes a refinement process. Every release will have new features along with the improved old features. The development team adds new features as they release the software to the customer for obtaining feedback. This also helps the customer to check whether the request made in the previous feedback was addressed. XP ensures that changes due to the business requirements are reflected in the code and is delivered to the customer quickly.

XP helps the customer to adjust the schedule to match their business needs. At the same time the customer can also change the project's priorities at any point of the development cycle. Therefore, you, as a developer, must constantly refine your understanding of the software and business problem.

XP helps you to develop flexible and maintainable software by stressing on simplicity and verification capability. This thorough testing gives team the assurance that the code meets customer needs. Therefore, any future changes will not affect the existing code and developers can improve the code with small and measured changes. Thus, you get freedom to address new requirements confidently without spending too much time and money on it.

16.4.3 DEVELOPER EFFECTIVENESS

To develop good software you need good developers. The development of software becomes effective only if the development team has developers who are efficient, have broad knowledge and are productive.

XP practices form a system of checks and balances. (Refer unit 17 for XP practices). For example, in a team two developers develop a code, two members review every line of the code. Two members of the team evaluate each solution or idea that is implemented in the form of code i.e., ideas flow freely within the team and each idea is analyzed and evaluated at least by two team members separately. At the same time only those ideas or solutions are implemented that makes the project simpler, highly maintainable and highly accurate.

During the coding process, XP sets up several feedback networks loops for communication and trouble shooting. Regular and thorough tests provide immediate status of the project and help to assess the project. This helps the team to analyze the project and take necessary measures to meet the project requirements. This shows that XP makes the entire process, design and implementation open for changes and improvement as per requirement. Therefore, you can expect your project to evolve and deliver highly efficient results over a short period of time. As changes happen, you are exposed to different challenges. This helps you to learn from your mistakes. Thus you can build valuable experience which you can use in future projects.

XP also helps you to overcome several barriers that can hinder the development process. Customer trusts the technical decisions of the developers and in turn the developers trust and respect the business decisions of customers. XP tries to avoid overwork and frustration for developers by making the customer to agree for adjusting the scope of the project without altering the time. Mutual respect, valuing honesty, improved communication and working closely as a team are the major elements of XP that helps you to succeed as a team.

16.4.4 FREEDOM TO EXPERIMENT

According to XP, the whole team (i.e., developers, managers and customers) has the freedom to experiment. This has a significant impact on every issue, regardless of its magnitude. XP can be successful only if the team starts thinking about and searching new, better ways of developing the software. This is done only if you start experimenting. XP believes that there is no reward without risk.

XP encourages and believes that teams have the liberty to remove barriers that hinder the project. For example, each member of a large team was working in an office in separate cubicles. The team thought that they could improve their productivity by removing the physical barriers so, they sat in an open area to collaborate with each other and thus increase productivity Therefore, if you can overcome the problem and show that the change has a positive impact, you may find it easier to remove further barriers.

XP usually does not wait for a perfect solution to reduce the risk. If the solution is good enough then you can go ahead and implement the same. The objective is to focus in the right direction and make necessary changes as you proceed. For example, you can develop significantly efficient code initially. The code can be optimized later. But, while developing the code for the first time you must ensure that the code is simple and can be modified easily later.

During the initial stage, any XP project requires a considerable investment of time and resources. The project begins to deliver usable software within a few weeks of time. This can be delivered to the customer and the team can immediately make modifications to the software and obtain a better solution based on customer feedback. The team can also stop the project if the customer is satisfied with the software performance. This experimental nature of XP makes it unique.

As an extreme programmer, XP gives your team all the rights to change the culture of the team or to experiment. However, each team member must remember that the primary goal of every programmer is to develop effective software that meets customer requirement.

16.5 SUMMARY

Let us recapitulate the important concepts discussed in this unit:

- XP is an intense, disciplined and agile software development methodology focusing on coding within each software development life cycle (SDLC) stage.
- The four parameters that XP focuses on in a development project are:
  o Time
  o Resources
  o Scope
  o Quality
- Communication within the team is the most essential value that XP emphasizes in a development project.
- XP stresses on imparting simplicity in the development of software.
- Feedback is very essential in an XP project as it helps to identify and eliminate the issues at the earliest.
- In a XP project, the programmers must have the courage to take up tasks and perform them with confidence, as it yields better results.
- XP provides sufficient time and resources to each developer to develop software of high quality.
- Constant change of cost is monitored and effectively controlled by XP in a project.
- XP helps to continuously improve the developer's effectiveness as only an effective developer can deliver quality software.
- XP gives developer an opportunity to experiment with their work, come up with suggestion and ideas for developing efficient software in an effective way.

16.6 GLOSSARY

Bugs: A problem or an error in a computer program that can cause the computer system to crash.

Cubicles: A small compartment, as for work or study.

Productivity: the rate at which the company produces goods which are proportional to the number of people and the amount of materials used.

Refactor: a technique to rewrite an existing source code to alter the internal structure to enhance readability, reusability or structure without changing the external behavior.

16.7 CASE STUDY

Developing Software for Rudresh Motors

Rudresh Motors Pvt. Ltd. is an automobile dealer in Bangalore. They are one of Bangalore's biggest automobile dealers. They have six showrooms in Bangalore and four showrooms in other parts of Karnataka. They have recently opened two showrooms in Chennai and one showroom in Hyderabad. They also sell automobile spare parts in the showroom and it is one their major business verticals.

Issue

Rudresh Motors approached GSL Software Services Pvt. Ltd. for automating their entire business process. This included automating receiving and replying to customer orders, workforce maintenance, demand prediction, tracking the stock, communicating and coordinating between other distribution centers, communicating with the suppliers, registering complaints, tracking sales records, etc.

Approach

GSL took the task of delivering a solution to automate the business process of Rudresh Motors. Rudresh Motors wanted GSL to complete the project within six months as the demand for the automobiles would increase after six months as it was the beginning of three month long festive season.

The business solution that Rudresh Motors wanted was diverse. The software was expected to have many components or features that dealt with many business aspects of Rudresh Motors. For example, the software had to track stocks in the warehouse. In case the stock was less, it had to generate a report that would be sent to the supplier to refill the stock. The software had to keep a record of the employees' work related activities and generate performance report of each employee on a weekly basis. The software had to collect information from the sales executives and generate the demand forecast for the next two months. The software had to track customer complaints and generate a report on the same.

Keeping all these things in mind, the project manger of GSL decides to use XP for developing the software. The features required were diverse and the team of developers was developing software with such diverse features for the first time.

GSL began the project with a team of six developers who were working five days a week for eight hours a day. The manager decided to come up with this team size after careful planning, keeping in mind that the project has to be delivered in six months.

The team of developers was in constant touch with the members of Rudresh Motors to understand how they do their business. This helped the developers to precisely know how they carried out their tasks. The developing team did not deliver the entire product at once. The project manager of GSL spoke to the

Manager of Rudresh Motor and decided that they would release the software in patches every week. Another team of developers with a team size of three members would be deployed in one of the showrooms and implement the software patch. The employees can use the software and give feedback to the development team in the showroom. Based on the feedback, the patch would be modified if required.

This was a great success. The team did not wait till the entire software was ready to test it in the showroom. They were able to test every feature that they developed as and when it was developed.

Result

The team of developers working at GSL was able to develop and optimize the software efficiency based on the feedback that they collected from Rudresh Motor's employees. As they developed the software block by block, in the form of patches, trouble shooting was very easy and the development process was quickened. Against all odds, the team completed the project within the scheduled time of six months.

Discussion Questions:

1. Why did Rudresh Motors approach GSL Software Services?
2. How did GSL help Rudresh Motors?

E-References for case study:

- http://www.techopedia.com/definition/3791/extreme-programming-xp - Retrieved on February 15, 2012.
- http://www.extremeprogramming.org/rules.html - Retrieved on February 16, 2012.
- http://www.software-testing-tips.com/xp-extreme-programming-in-practice - Retrieved on February 16, 2012.
- http://en.wikipedia.org/wiki/Gantt_chart - Retrieved on February 29, 2012.

Extreme Programming Practices

Structure

17.1 INTRODUCTION

In the previous unit, you studied about Extreme Programming (XP). You also studied the XP values and the significance of time and resource for an XP practitioner. As a development model, the XP empowers the developers and stakeholders, associated with the project, to successfully carry out the project and develop efficient software. However, just like any other programming model, even in the XP, you must follow certain practices to utilize the model to its fullest capacity.

The 12 practices of XP are classified into three groups namely, coding, developer, and business practices. These practices will help you to achieve higher productivity and quality.

This unit will familiarize you with coding practices of XP. You will also study the developer and business practices of XP.

Objectives

After studying this unit, you should be able to:

- list the coding practices of XP
- describe developer practices of XP
- explain the business practices of XP

17.2 CODING PRACTICES

Writing the code is the most important part while developing any software. Some projects may use existing codes. However, in most of the projects the codes are written from scratch. The coding practices of XP can be broadly classified in to four types. Figure 17.1 depicts the four coding practices.

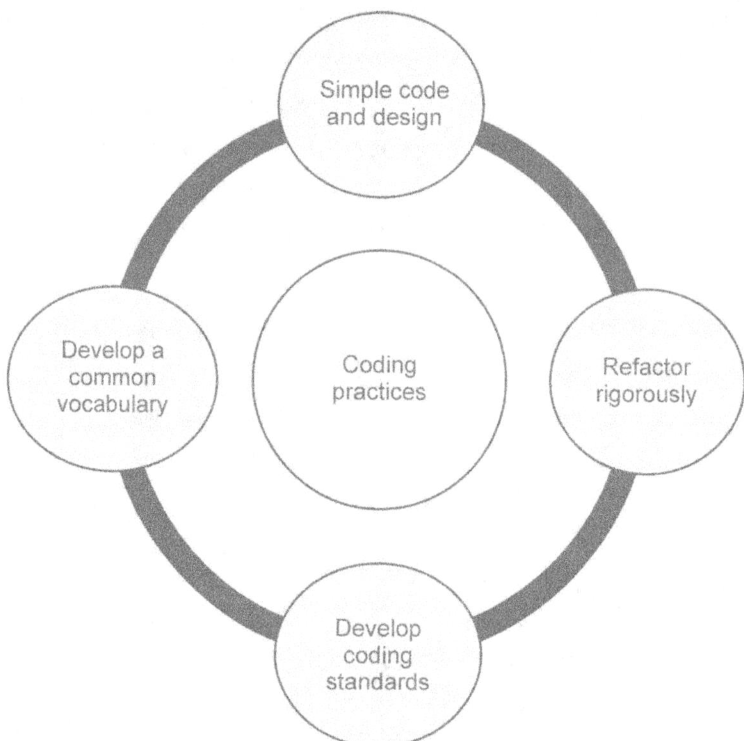

Figure 17.1 Practices of Coding

As shown in the figure 17.1, the four XP practices of coding are:

- Simple code and design
- Refactor rigorously
- Develop coding standard
- Develop a common vocabulary

All the four coding practices work together to develop, deliver, and maintain code efficiently.

17.2.1 SIMPLE CODE AND DESIGN

It is essential to produce software that is easy to modify. Hence, you must code and design simplistically. XP has three rules that govern simplicity. They are:

- Design the simplest software possible that could meet the requirements.
- Add only those features that are essential to meet the requirements.
- Avoid redundancy of codes through refactoring.

Simplicity makes your software highly flexible. Simple designs are easier to understand and explain. At the same time, simple codes are easier to test, maintain and modify.

With XP you spend comparatively less time to develop the design and allow the design to evolve as the software is being developed. This is different from traditional development models. Traditional models require you to develop the design first, because modifying the design at a later stage of the development cycle is difficult. But, XP requires you to work in very small and simple steps, with continuous testing to verify whether or not you are on the right track. Using this method, you can identify mistakes and make changes quickly.

Adding unnecessary or unrequested feature wastes time and resources of the project. You cannot guess that a customer may ask for a feature to add. This is a gamble. Therefore, you must add only those features that the customer has requested. Unnecessary features make the system complicated.

Adding an unrequested feature may undermine the customer's authority over the project. You can make recommendations to the customer and add other features only after you finish developing the software with the required features. Therefore, you must not worry about the future needs and address the current needs of the customer first.

XP's simple design supports:

- ***Collective code ownership*** - Everyone associated with the project must be familiar with the code design to a certain extent. The code must be designed so that it does not require only a specialized group of people to analyze it.
- ***Refactoring*** - Simple design makes it easy to identify smaller changes and implement them.
- ***Testing*** - Simple codes are easier to test or debug.
  As an XP practitioner, you must remember that for a simple design it is very important to have a good flow of communication between all the members of the

team (which are developers, managers and the customer) to identify the necessary features and schedule. The entire team must believe they can adapt to any changes in the project requirement. Most importantly, the team must have the ability to recognize and adopt simplicity, or must have the willingness to try and achieve simplicity.

17.2.2 REFACTOR RIGOROUSLY

Refactoring is carried out mainly to optimize the existing software design or code. While refactoring, you as a developer must try to improve the design of the software without changing its behavior. Refactoring is also done to make the code simple and flexible and in turn, reduce redundancy.

The XP practitioners refactor the code regularly. After the code has been tested, you can refactor the code by eliminating the redundant codes. You must break long and complex methods (and functions) into comparatively short and simple methods (and functions) without changing its actual behavior. You, as a developer, must judge whether or not refactoring is required, and to what extent it has to be used.

The XP approach of allowing the design to evolve as the project progresses may produce undesired or inefficient code if you do not test it regularly. Therefore, regular testing and refactoring is essential in XP. Testing must be done after refactoring to ensure that the behavior of the code has not changed.

Every refactoring has a goal. Usually these goals are small and incremental, and build on each other. Usually breaking a long and complex method into smaller methods may create new opportunity for further simplification.

Refactoring to delete similar codes in each task or blocks of codes of the software is common. This helps to avoid duplication of codes in each task or block. For example, consider that you are developing a gaming software that has three games in one package. Each game has a money counting application. Instead of repeating the code that counts the money in each game code block, you can write the code used for counting the money only once and call the block of code whenever it is required during the game.

Regular refactoring requires discipline. You must never postpone the refactoring work because it can decrease the efficiency of your development activity. You must refactor rigorously. The smaller the code block, the more efficiently you can refactor. If you start refactoring as soon as you finish a small block of code you can refactor efficiently.

17.2.3 DEVELOP CODING STANDARDS

In XP, you must develop standards to communicate ideas clearly in the form of codes. Codes must be communicated in a proper form within a project because the entire project revolves around it.

Coding standards are usually conventions that describe the best practices for coding. They are developed by gathering inputs from the team. They also evolve with the project. For example, the coding standards followed in the beginning of the project may be changed at a later stage. This change is based on the usefulness of a coding standard during a particular stage of the project. You must allow your coding standards to evolve with the project as they will help you to invent new and better standards to provide clarity about the coding done.

Usually, the best coding standards serve as guidelines for coding. They must not be used as commandments as they are the shared values of the project team. Therefore, coding standards are changed or suspended according to the requirements. A good developer knows when to break the rules or protocols professionally without affecting the team's integrity.

Usually coding standards support:

- *Refactoring -* It is easier to check and implement potential refactoring when all the codes written follow a common style.
- *Pair programming -* Developers can concentrate on the intent of the code rather than style or manner in which the code has to be written.
- *Collective code ownership -* All the members of the project team contribute to the standardization.

Any coding standard requires the development team to work together. The developers must set aside their individual habits and preferences, and work together to obtain consistency in coding across the team. This helps the team to communicate the codes effectively among the other developers. At the same time, the coding standards must be reviewed periodically to ensure that the existing standards of coding communicate the shared values and intent of the code effectively. In case of any inconsistencies, modifications can be made to the standards after discussing it with the team. Thus, coding standards helps the team to ensure that all the new codes developed adhere to the standards and in turn makes refactoring or future modifications easy and simple.

17.2.4 DEVELOP COMMON VOCABULARY

Using coding standard practice, you can communicate ideas clearly through codes. However, with the help of a common vocabulary, you can communicate ideas about the code clearly. Therefore, you must develop a common vocabulary to describe the project as it evolves.

The vocabulary must describe the main components of the project. For example, assume that you are using a message delivery system in your project. You must explain how it works and how to use it to send a message. The description must be expressive and clear because it will be given to the customer. The vocabulary must build a clear picture of what is being explained in the reader's mind. Even a reader who is unaware of the software component must be able to understand the component after reading the description.

You must regularly review the vocabulary to check whether or not it describes the project accurately. This is due to the fact that as the project progresses, the project changes and vocabulary must also be changed to describe the current state of the project. Simplicity and clarity must be maintained in the description you write.

Like good writing, your vocabulary must be as concise as possible, yet cover the entire subject. Describe only the feature that exists in few words clearly and completely.

A common vocabulary supports collective code ownership as all the developers of the team know the vocabulary and have a clear picture of the project. It allows technical and business users to communicate using a common language. Therefore, you must develop a simple design that can be described clearly.

> **Activity 1:**
>
> Your XP team manager finds out that the team is facing repeated setbacks due to issues related to the actual coding process. He plans to review the coding practices of the team to overcome the shortcomings of the team. He asks you to join him in the review process. How do you think you can scale up the team performance using the XP coding practices?

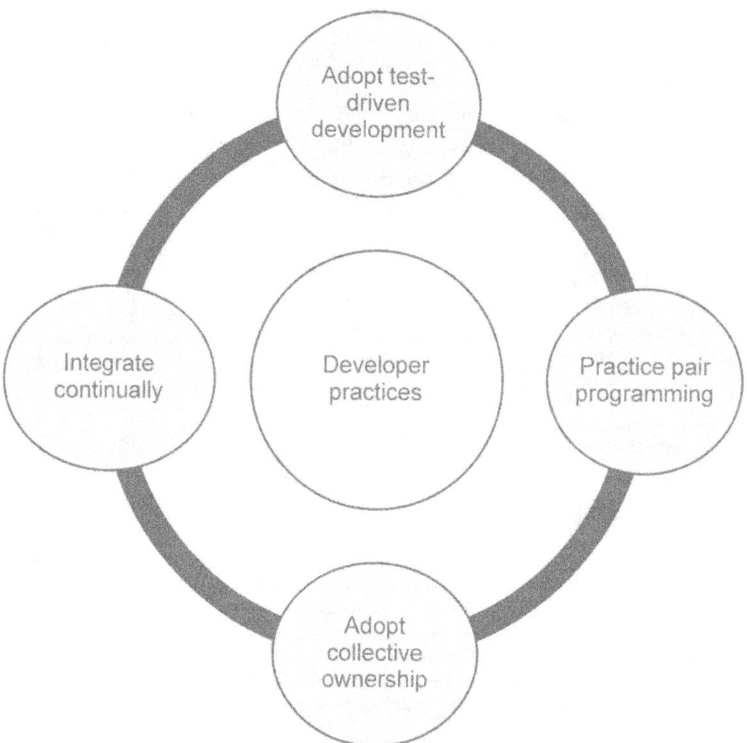

Figure 17.2 XP's Developer Practices

17.3 DEVELOPER PRACTICES

Developers must work together regardless of the size of the project. If the team is able to work smoothly, then they can deliver high quality software. As everyone in the team contributes to the project, XP dedicates several practices to improve the teamwork. These practices strengthen the good programming practices of the team. They also help to nurture and guide the less experienced developers of the team. Thus, XP developer practices help to keep everyone in the team on track.

Figure 17.2 depicts XP's developer practices.

As shown in the figure the four developer practices of XP are:

- Adopt test-driven development
- Practice pair programming
- Adopt collective ownership
- Integrate continually

Let us now discuss these practices.

17.3.1 ADOPT TEST-DRIVEN DEVELOPMENT

The main reason for adopting test-driven development practice is to prove that the code developed works based on the requirement. XP emphasizes the need for testing every code as and when it is developed. You must test the code to check if the code actually does what it is intended to do and if anything can make the code to behave erratically. Usually traditional testing is carried out by writing test cases to check the conditions under which the software fails. But XP also writes test cases to find out if the software passes the test.

In XP, the development of a feature is said to be finished only when it passes the test. Therefore, test your code or feature whenever you get an opportunity to run a test. This gives the developer the confidence about the code. Also, you must run a test before and after refactoring your code. You must remember that finding a bug in few lines of code is easy, but finding the bug in a code with hundreds of lines is difficult.

Many automated testing tools or frameworks are available for testing. Using a good testing framework helps to save lot of time and resources. It also gives an accurate feedback about the status of the project any time. Manual testing may fail to identify or overlook certain bugs, but it does not happen in automated testing.

A good test must try to explore one issue at a time. When a code fails the test, you must have sufficient information to track the test to identify and debug the software. Therefore, you must use simple tests as they enable easy debugging when compared to complex tests.

Usually tests are of two types:

- *Unit test -* This test is carried out to find out the behavior of the individual pieces or functions of the software.
- *Acceptance test -* This test is carried out to verify that the software features match the business requirements and expectations of the customer.

Every unique piece of code requires its own test case. The test case probes the limits of expected and unexpected use of the codes. It also serves as a guide for any future changes. Usually a well written unit test also tells you how to use the code.

The acceptance test case is written based on the customer's requirements. You must work with the customer to write automated acceptance tests to prove to the customer that all the requirements are met successfully. Only when the software passes the acceptance test, the development is complete.

Test-driven development supports refactoring to improve the software efficiency. It helps developers to ensure that the system is kept in good condition during every release. It also serves as a benchmark for future development.

Any test-driven development method requires positive peer pressure to help developers to overcome the initial setbacks of test-driven development method and continue testing even if it seems difficult. At the same time, it is also essential to clearly communicate with the customer and obtain the test cases from the customer for acceptance tests.

17.3.2 PRACTICE PAIR PROGRAMMING

Pair programming aims to spread knowledge, experience, and ideas in a team. In pair programming, two developers work together to perform a single task. Usually, both the developers interact with each other and decide the best possible solution or method, and implement the same together.

The developers must discuss with each other about the sequence of steps to be accomplished, test to be performed, refactoring of the codes, etc. Usually, this reinforces good programming habits, because each developer tries to exert positive peer pressure on the other. It also helps to avoid the temptation of skipping the tests, refactoring or simplifying.

When two individuals work together to develop, test, refactor and simplify the code, the codes developed will have fewer bugs and will fit into the team's coding standards efficiently.

Pairing happens informally by exploring the possibility of combination of developers. However, pairing can be uncomfortable sometimes. But, it is of great help as it helps to break the monotony at the work place. For example, it decreases the feeling of individual code ownership as the responsibility is shared by two individuals. Usually some developers prefer to carry out refactoring individually. However, most developers prefer pair programming.

Pairing can also be an investment for continual training. Developers, who are new to the project, or with less experience, benefit when they work in pairs with experienced developers. The new developers can learn from their experienced counterparts. You also get an opportunity to explain your assumptions, goals, and ideas about the project to your partner, and your partner has the opportunity to ask questions that help to explore the new possibilities in the project.

Pair programming requires facilities where the two developers are allowed to sit and work together at one workstation. Managers must be willing to try pair programming to produce efficient codes with less overall effort. The team must have coding standards that help the developers to code following a common style.

17.3.3 ADOPT COLLECTIVE OWNERSHIP

The main goal of collective ownership is to share the code's responsibility with the whole team. According to this practice, the entire codebase is shared with the whole team. A developer is free to make modifications to any piece of code to complete the task. Therefore, the developer can write the necessary code, write the appropriate tests, and run the required tests to check the correctness of the code. At the same time all the relevant details are made available to other developers.

Collective code ownership makes the team more flexible. For example, if one of the developers is on leave, another developer in the team can complete the task. Collective code ownership helps a team member to read any section of the code and refactor it if it requires improvements.

Collective code ownership requires teamwork and frequent, small integrations. A pair of developers develops a new feature and immediately release it to the other developers so that the entire team can work on it. Thus, no one owns the code and everyone in the team contributes to maintaining the code.

Collective code ownership promotes large scale refactoring. It supports pair programming. However, it requires coding standards to ensure that the code style remains the same across the team. It also requires comprehensive testing to ensure that the risky changes are detected and fixed quickly. It is essential to have frequent integration and shared vocabulary to effectively adopt and follow collective coding.

17.3.4 INTEGRATE CONTINUALLY

Integrating continually helps you to reduce the impact of bugs and large scale refactoring by adding a new feature to the software as soon as the old features are completed. It is essential to carry out the tests to verify that the new feature fits into the software efficiently. If errors or bugs are detected, make necessary changes or debug it and perform the test again to verify the behavior of the software. Test the codes regularly as and when you integrate a new feature to the software.

Continual integrations help to keep everyone on the same line. Pairs can divide the tasks into small pieces, develop it and integrate them as soon as they are developed. This helps them to stay close to the main source code and avoid the problem that they may face to integrate large blocks of codes that are created.

Integrations must be simple -- add the codes, test, and release. As it must be quick, you can also automate the process of integration. Automation helps to bring in flexibility. You will be integrated often and the team must not be kept waiting till you complete integration. Therefore, automating the integration helps to quicken the process.

Continual integration also helps you to avoid the temptation to postpone the work. You must integrate the codes developed regularly or else it will decrease the productivity of the entire team. Small and frequent integrations have fewer bugs or errors compared to large integrations.

Continual integration supports practices such as refactoring and releasing regularly. However, with continual integration you must have a collective source code repository to hold the master source code. You must also conduct comprehensive testing to judge the condition of the software regularly. The planning game and working at a sustainable pace practices are essential for continual integration.

> **Activity 2:**
>
> The team leader of a development project plans to adopt XP for his project and conveys this plan of action to his team, manager and the customer. After getting a formal approval he decides to implement it. However, he learns that he must chart out the practices that would help his team of developers to develop the code efficiently. If you are one of his team members and he asks you to prepare a note on the developer practice, what are the important things you will discuss in the note? Give your reasons.

17.4 BUSINESS PRACTICES

Developing a software project is not just about coding, but it is coding to meet the business requirements of the customer. This must happen within a finite time limit defined by the customer. Even the quality is defined by the customer.

XP helps to minimize the risks by improving the communication between the customer and developers. The customer can regularly observe the project status and guide the project by giving feedback regularly as and when it is required.

XP also divides the project based along business and technical lines to enable the customer and developer to make decisions efficiently.

Figure 17.3 depicts the business practices of XP.

As shown in figure 17.3, the business practices of XP are:

- Add a customer to the team
- Play the planning game
- Release regularly
- Work at a sustainable pace

Let us now discuss these practices briefly.

17.4.1 ADD A CUSTOMER TO THE TEAM

Adding a customer to the team helps the development team to address the business concerns of the customer directly and accurately. This is because the customer also plays an active role in the team.

The customer is also a part of the development team. The customer provides the actual business perspective of the use of the software. This helps the development team to know what must be developed. Regular, reliable, and rapid communication between the technical and business members of the team improves confidence and reduces misunderstandings. This helps the developers to produce the desired results more quickly.

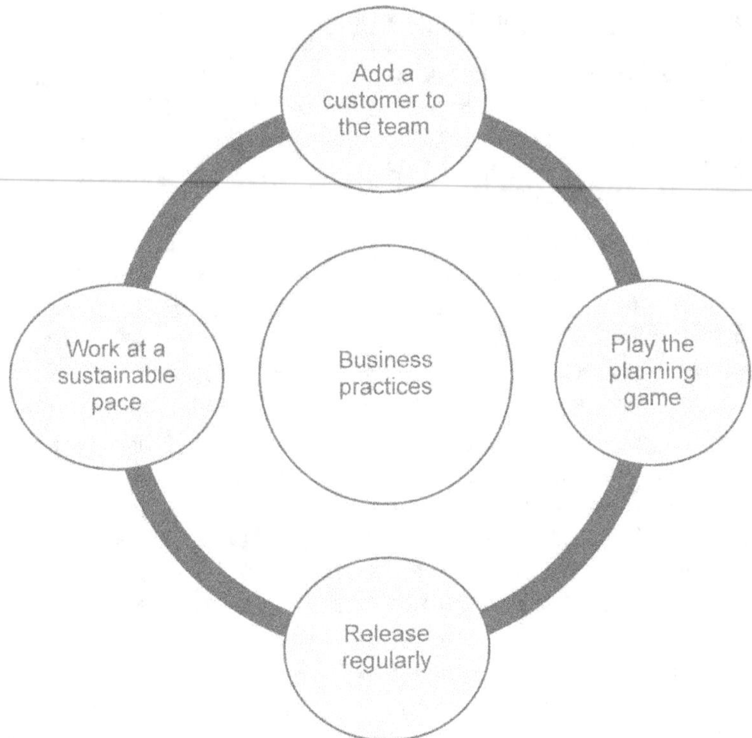

Figure 17.3 Business Practices

XP requires the customer to work closely with the developers. The customer may not spend a lot of time with the team, but must spend significant time with the team till the first few releases. The customer writes the description of the features required with the business concept to the developer. The customer checks the behavior of the software during the initial releases and gives the feedback. Therefore, including the customer from the beginning of the project will help the team to prevent bugs and large-scale rework.

The customer gives the business perspective of the project to the team and also defines the scope of the project. (Refer to Unit 16 for more about project scope). This helps the developer to stick to a regular schedule and avoid overwork. It also helps the developer to discuss with the customer and ignore the features that are not required currently in the software. The software that fulfills the customer's most important needs is delivered on time. However, remember that it is the customer who must decide the level of importance of features.

The customer in the team sets the project goals and schedule. Hence, close communication with the customer is very important. The acceptance tests are written by the customer and feedback is given to the developers after every release.

You must convince the customer to join the team, and investment must be made to have a robust and flexible communication system. A common vocabulary must be developed to make communication effective between the developer and customer.

17.4.2 PLAY THE PLANNING GAME

The goal of the planning game is to schedule the most important work. The customer must develop a refined schedule for the project. XP uses the term 'planning game' for the process that defines the project schedule based on the priority in which the features are developed and released. It describes the order in which the features are developed and implemented.

XP schedules are based around the iteration, which is one entire development cycle, that is, design, develop, test, and implement. For example, the customer requests features and the team develops the code, tests and delivers them. This is the first iteration. Based on the customer feedback the refactoring or debugging is carried out and delivered after testing the modified software. This is the second iteration. The process continues till the code meets the customer's requirements.

The planning decisions are divided into business and technical decisions. The business people make business decisions. They decide the allocation of the resources, set priority for developing the features, define the business value and risk of each feature, etc. The technical decisions are made by technical people. They decide on the technologies to be chosen to develop and implement the software, the technical risks that each feature has, the time required to develop and implement each feature, etc.

Usually, the planning game happens at the start of each release or iteration. The customer writes the story card and sends it to the developer when making the request for developing a feature. The story card is a description about the features. Each story card describes only one feature. It describes the behavior, use and significance of the feature. With the help of the story card, the developer estimates the time required and complexity of the feature. The developer estimates an imaginary time called 'ideal hour'. An ideal hour represents the amount of time required to develop and implement the feature. This helps the customer and developer to define the schedule and scope of the project.

Next, the developer produces task cards for each story card. The task card describes the development tasks necessary to implement the feature. The tasks must be explained in detail and must specify the time needed to complete each task.

Usually a planning game supports a simple design as only the features that the customer schedules are delivered first. It simplifies the acceptance test as the story card identifies what the customer wants. The planning game requires active customer involvement in writing story cards and setting priorities. It also requires mutual respect between customer and developer for the priorities that are set.

17.4.3 RELEASE REGULARLY

At the end of every iteration, the software is released or delivered to the customer. In XP, iterations and feedback time is short, that is, around one to four weeks. This helps to release the software, receive the feedback, work on the feedback, and re-release the software at the earliest. This helps the team to achieve the desired result quickly and the customer starts getting the return on the investment made in the project.

As the developers work on the customer feedback and quickly re-release the software, the customer can know the status of the software and its correctness in meeting the requirements. Regular releases also help to find and fix bugs and deliver the software to the customer. The customer can sometimes report a bug and carry out other tests as the customer knows that the bug will be fixed by the developer in the next iteration.

Usually, regular and small releases are simple and require less time. You can receive useful feedback if you release the work done in a few weeks when compared to work done in a year. XP emphasizes automated releases to ensure a smooth process.

Regular release allows the customer to know that their business priorities are met. They can also ensure that immediate action is taken if their requirements are not met. It will be easy for the team to adjust the estimates and practices accordingly.

Regular release also gives the customer the final option of stopping the project any time the initial investment has been recovered.

17.4.4 WORK AT A SUSTAINABLE PACE

Everyone has a natural level of productivity and this varies from person to person. XP assumes that an individual has a limited amount of physical, mental and creative energy. Every hour of work done by an individual drains a certain amount of the individual's energy. Recreational activities replenish the energy reserves of an individual. However, pushing one's limits may be counter-productive.

The choices made by your team may become habits, especially the number of hours worked. If you overwork to complete the iteration quickly, instead of reducing the scope, you may deliver poor quality. Therefore, you must adjust your work pace based on the schedule. Do not promise the customer more than what you can actually deliver.

It is a good practice to adjust the scope when you realize that you have more tasks to finish in the time remaining or scheduled time. In such a situation, you can shuffle tasks between developers who have time or expertise to complete the task. If this does not work, then you must inform the customer about the delay.

Try to keep the number of working hours and iteration length a constant. As the software has to go through regular releases and as the customer adjusts the schedule, there is always a scope for implementing the changes in the next iteration.

Sometimes, change of scope is not the best solution to adjust the schedule. In case you work late often to complete a task, evaluate your actions and fix the situation by changing the practices you follow for development.

You can keep your productivity high only when you work at a sustainable pace. A tired developer is always tempted to take shortcuts, susceptible to lapses in judgment, and can commit errors due to fatigue. You must take regular breaks throughout the day to recharge your energy. Recreational activities also play a crucial role in recharging your energy. When planning for iteration, plan for time to recharge your energy levels.

Working at a sustainable pace helps you to avoid working overtime. It also helps you to decide to work only on a reasonable number of projects that the team can handle. By removing the obstacles to production such as long meetings, excessive documentation, etc., you can concentrate on the more important tasks. Practices such as pair programming, collective code ownership, and test-driven development help to build technical credibility and enable the team to work efficiently.

Working at a sustainable pace can be made easier by an effective planning game and regular releases. You can always have the customer with the team to make scope changes.

17.5 SUMMARY

Let us recapitulate the important concepts discussed in this unit:

- XP practices of coding are simple code and design, refactor rigorously, develop coding standard, and develop common vocabulary.
- The objective of a simple code and design practice is to produce software that can be modified easily according to the requirements.
- Rigorous refactoring is carried out to make the code simple, reduce redundancy, and make the code flexible. Thus, it optimizes the software design or code.
- Developing coding standards helps to communicate ideas clearly in the form of codes.
- Developing common vocabulary enables the description of the project in a simple, clear and concise manner as it evolves. This helps to improve the communication within the team.
- Adopt test-driven development, practice pair programming, adopt collective ownership, and integrate continually are XP developer practices.
- Adopt test-driven development practice to prove to the customer that the code works according to the requirements.
- By practicing pair programming, the development team can share knowledge, experience and ideas in the team.
- Collective code ownership ensures that the whole team is responsible for the code. This promotes the idea that everyone owns the code.
- By integrating continually, you can add new features to the software during development. It makes coding simple.
- The XP business practices are classified as add a customer to the team, play the planning game, release regularly, and work at a sustainable pace.
- A customer added to a team will be involved actively in the development process. The customer gives the actual business perspective of the software and its uses to the developers.

- The planning game describes the schedule for developing the features based on priority. The customer defines the priority. The developer delivers the features based on the priority in every iteration.
- The software is released to the customer after every iteration. The iterations are of short periods and occur regularly.
- XP stresses that the work must happen at a sustainable pace and the team must not overwork as it will affect the quality of the work done by the team.

18 | XP Events

Structure

18.1   INTRODUCTION

In the previous unit, you studied the 12 practices of XP which are classified into three groups namely, coding, developer and business practices. These practices help you to achieve higher productivity and quality.

In XP projects, developers work in pairs to enhance the quality of the software. All developers are responsible for the entire system in XP projects. In a XP project, the whole team has to collectively work together to carry out the project that might stretch for few months or years. To ease the burden of the project's length the XP project is broken into iterations. Each iteration represents a small cycle of the development process. XP emphasizes coding in small iterations and working towards short release cycles. In XP, software is deployed in many releases which are made of one or more iterations. The software reaches the final release stage when all the iterations have passed the acceptance test.

This unit familiarizes you with iteration planning in XP projects. We will also study the significance of release in the XP development process.

Objectives

After studying this unit, you should be able to:
- describe iteration planning

- explain the significance of iteration
- define software release

18.2 ITERATION PLANNING

The primary purpose of any project remains the same i.e., to develop the most efficient software for the customer. Usually the customer requirements change over time, and every iteration offers a chance to adjust the schedule to match those requirements. Therefore, iteration planning is very crucial for any project.

A single development cycle is called iteration. Iteration planning meetings help to bring the customer and the developers together and agree upon the project requirements and schedule the iteration. During iteration planning meetings, the customer plays an important role. The customer defines the priorities for the features that have to be implemented and delivered during the iteration.

Every iteration begins with an iteration planning meeting. Usually the meeting does not take more than one day. Some teams prefer that the meetings are less than a day. All the team members, including the customer attend the meeting. You just need a comfortable room and a whiteboard to conduct the meeting. The meeting proceeds in the following sequence:

1. Read out the stories for the current iteration.
2. List out all the tasks that must be done for each story on the whiteboard.
3. Add any necessary technical tasks that need to be done.
4. Estimate tasks. Developers propose estimates based on their individual velocity.
5. Ask the customer to modify or remove some stories if any story is not completely signed up by the developer.
6. Inform the customer to add stories if extra time is available during the iteration.

18.2.1 STORIES AND TASKS

The customers convey their requirements of a desired feature as a story card. A story card informs the developer the customer's specification. Based on the inputs the customer provides, the developers estimate the schedule to develop the required software (or software feature). As developers also contribute in iteration planning, we can consider it developer driven.

The customer has to prepare for the iteration planning session by giving more details about the stories. This can be done in the following ways:

- The customer can briefly explain the story. As this is simple and verbal, it is effective.
- The customer can present a written description of the story details. This can be of few pages, and it mainly tries to corroborate all the important aspect of the story.
- The customer can provide an acceptance test for the story.

The discussion between the customer and developer results in the production of task cards. A task is characterized by the total effort it needs i.e., actual number of person days required to implement the story card. Usually a task is assigned to one team member or pair of developers for developing the code.

Figure 18.1 depicts a sample story card.

Customer Story and Task Card

Date: _______________   FUNC. Test

Type of Activity:
New: ________   Fix: ________   Enhance: _________

Story Number: _____________   Priority: User: _________   Tech: _______

Prior Reference: __________________   Risk: _________________

Tech Estimate: __________________

Task Description:

Notes:

Task Tracking:

Date	Status	To Do	Comments

Figure 18.1 Story Card Sample

The business changes can affect the pending stories as the project progresses. The customer re-evaluates their business requirements when necessary. This affects the tasks as when the stories change, even the tasks also change. Therefore, you have to evaluate the tasks that may have changed after planning the iteration.

Usually stories are written along with acceptance tests to check whether the story has been implemented correctly. The acceptance test is written on a card called index card. Each story will have one acceptance test, but sometime one acceptance test will be written for more than one story or one story may have more than one acceptance test. However, the story and its respective acceptance test have to be implemented in the same iteration.

The developer estimates the time to complete each story. This is done by assigning each story a number of story points or milestones. Therefore, every iteration has number of story points that are implemented one after the other through the course of the iteration. These story points determine the project velocity. At the end of each iteration, the customer and the developer have to identify the number of story points actually implemented. This helps to plan for the next iteration.

18.2.2 ESTIMATES AND SCHEDULES

The customer and the developers estimate the time required for each story and task. Story estimates help the customer to schedule stories for an iteration. Task estimates help developers to schedule tasks for the iteration.

Time estimations are simple guesses by the developers. However, an honest approach is made to measure the ideal time required for developing the required software or completing an iteration. This helps to measure the time for performing the actual work. However, it ignores other interruptions such as meetings, holidays, etc. However, the time includes the time taken for testing, refactoring, and integration.

It is very important to distinguish estimates and actual time. As we have learnt in previous unit, XP prefers to adjust the schedule by adjusting the project's scope, and resources.

The customer sets iteration priorities based on story estimates. The customer sets the priority for the stories sent to the developer based on the following requirements:

- What are the most valuable stories at present?
- How much work can be accomplished in the current iteration?

In any project, the customer's main goal is to maximize the return on the investment in the project. Therefore, the customer's estimates revolve around the returns on investments made in the project.

A story has business and technical risks. An ideal story must focus on lowering the costs and increasing the returns. The returns can be in the form of adding an important new feature or overcoming a high business or technical risk successfully. You must choose high risk stories during the initial stage of the project, as easier stories can be taken up at the end when you have less time or fewer resources.

The customer first selects a story and then estimates the ideal hour required to implement the story. The shorter the story the easier they fit into an iteration. The once that do not fit into an iteration are taken up in the next iteration as every iteration has a fixed length i.e., one or two weeks. Therefore, it becomes very important for the customer to know how much work the team can do before planning the iteration.

XP uses a principle called "Yesterday's Weather", where you predict the future by examining the recent past. That means you have to plan the current iteration by examining the previous iterations. This is because it is assumed that today's performance will be almost similar to yesterday's performance. Also it does not need expensive and sophisticated techniques to analyze and plan the iteration. For example, a team had implemented a story which was estimated to be completed in 20 ideal hours, but the team took 40 real hours to complete the iteration. Therefore, we can assume that they will need the same time for the next iteration which requires the same amount of work to implement a similar story.

The team's velocity is determined by taking a ratio of estimated and actual work of the team. A development team works with its own velocity. If the estimated implementation time for a story is 10 ideal hours and the team takes 20 real hours to implement it, then the velocity of the team is 0.5. The velocity of the project is a direct indication of the project's health.

Velocity can increase suddenly when developers come up with new, shorter ways of accomplishing the tasks or when they use new techniques to increase the productivity. A decrease in the velocity indicates that there is a communication failure, decrease in team's morale, or difficulties in understanding a story.

Iteration planning can be either parallel or sequential. However, the whole team must work together. That is, in parallel planning, when the developers are creating task cards, the customer writes stories or clarifies doubts. In sequential planning, the customer writes the story only after the completion of an iteration.

Sometimes, after you start the project you realize that your estimates are inaccurate. In such a situation, you must contact the customer, raise a request for modifying the scope of the iteration, and get it done at the earliest. However, you can continue with your current story and let the customer re-schedule the other or future stories. Any newly added story must be given high priority and delayed story must be of least priority. You can always re-evaluate the priority for the next iteration after discussing with the customer.

18.2.3 FIRST ITERATION

A new project begins and evolves quickly. Therefore, XP recommends that the developers start learning about the project as soon as possible. For every new project, the first iteration is very special as it does not involve any code or feedback.

During the first iteration, small tasks are chosen to lay the basic architecture to the project. It is a good practice to ensure that the iteration planned is of a normal size and is delivered on time. You must add enough functionality during the first iteration as it helps to start the next iteration easily. For example, consider a simulation project, where in the first iteration you write enough code that allows the player to buy an entrance ticket, walk around the park, and buy a balloon and candy. This gives a basic foundation for the project. Later, in the successive iterations, you can add other functionalities.

The main purpose of first iteration is to gather and analyze actual data. This data can be the amount of work that a developer can do, the velocity with which the developer works, and the changing needs of the customer after receiving the working software. Outlining the software structure enables you to explore all the elements of the software that you must develop over a period of time. These elements work as a single entity to form a software package. This helps you to identify the risks and eliminate them during the early stages of the project. For example, during the first iteration, you identify that the operating system that you have chosen and the database you are using are not compatible. You can then take necessary action to make the correction. Developing an outline also helps you to adjust the source control system, platform used to build the software, release process plan, etc., before they become too complex to change.

For the first iteration, many XP teams choose an arbitrary velocity and schedule the work. Other teams start the project with zero velocity and ask the customer for the next most important story during the end of the current iteration. Therefore, you have to choose and start the story that is very important.

Activity 1:

Mohan, a project manager in a reputed IT company, is planning to carry out his next project using XP. He interacts with the customer to discuss about using XP for the project and discusses the same with the management also. Both the customer and Mohan agree to go ahead with XP. Mohan gets from the approval of the company's management also. What are the important things that Mohan as a project manager must take care of while planning the iterations for the project? Explain the key things that Mohan and his team must keep in mind while they take up the first iteration.

18.3 ITERATION DEVELOPMENT

Iteration can be defined as a procedure in which repetition of a sequence of operations yields results successively closer to a desired result. The customer prepares the project schedule with the help of stories and iterations. Developers make use of tasks to plan the schedule. Similar to team's velocity, the developers work according to their velocity during every iteration. For example, in the current iteration if you have implemented a task in 10 hours, then you can schedule the next iteration for 10 hours to complete a similar task. The velocity of a developer considers time spent in meetings, planning, and pairing with other developers. This velocity is called actual velocity, unlike ideal velocity where these parameters are not considered. Usually, ideal velocity of a team or developer is used as the reference velocity, based on which the actual velocity of a team or developer is planned.

You have to take up the most important and risky task during the first few iterations. Therefore, you have to invest more resource and time on the most difficult or riskiest task and keep the easier tasks for the end. This usually helps you to spend a significant amount of time and resource on implementing, integrating, and testing the tasks that are complex or difficult. This also helps to reduce the stress that the team experiences at the end of the project. Usually, as the project deadline approaches, the team often works under pressure.

Choosing the right task and working on just one task are important. In some projects, the team prefers to distribute the tasks to developers during iteration planning, and the developers estimate the time required for the implementation of the task. However, in some projects the entire team estimates the time required for each task assigned to individual developers or developer pairs of the team. A sign off is taken from each developer or pair on the estimates for the tasks assigned to them. In other teams, each developer chooses one task at the start of an iteration. The remaining task cards can be chosen by the developer as soon as they finish their current task.

A developer spends significant amount of time in pairing with another developer. Similarly the developer must spend time in pairing with the task i.e., understanding the task. As the tasks are short, frequently forming and reforming the developer pair is easy. You can also break and form a new pair during the middle of the task. For example, if you are finding it difficult to code a section, you can change your partner to get a fresh, experienced or knowledgeable partner. Pairing must not happen forcefully, it must happen naturally by choice.

The team has to meet regularly during the iteration to discuss the goals and progress of the project. When the meeting happens, all the team members assemble at one place and discuss. The team members stand throughout to ensure that the meeting is short. Aspects like, what was done yesterday, what will be done today and issues that the pair or team is facing are discussed and analyzed in the meeting.

Developing a flexible iteration improves the efficiency of the development process. It is good practice to keep the iteration length constant throughout the project as it ensures the reliability of measuring the project progress and planning.

Just-in-time iteration planning is preferred by many XP development teams. It means that the iteration is planned just before the start of the iteration. This helps the development team to plan the iterations according to the current requirements of the customer.

One has to take iteration deadlines seriously and keep a track of the work progress during an iteration. In case the team is finding it difficult to meet the deadline, then a meeting can be called to re-estimate the schedule. The customer, management and developers must be aware of the re-estimation. A sign off must be taken from the customer on the re-estimated schedule. This helps to establish transparency within the team and improves communication.

At the end of every iteration, the code developed is tested. You must get a sign off from the customer which confirms that the iteration is complete. Some organizations have a formal document to record the customer sign off. The customer can see the test results before signing off the closure of the iteration. If the customer discovers that the story is not according to the requirements or some defects are present, then the customer can delay the sign off. These defects or errors are usually taken up in the next iteration. Thus errors or defects that are taken up in the next iteration reduce the velocity of the team according to the workload planned for the next iteration.

18.4 RELEASING

Software release means handing over the software to the customer at the end of an iteration. In XP, release usually happens as planned unlike in traditional development models. Developers feel satisfied during a software release as they have achieved what they had aimed for in the current iteration. The team can relax, discuss about the previous iteration and prepare for the next iteration after they release the software.

Customers can directly use the released software if it meets their business requirements. Or, the customer can request the developer to re-work on the defects in the next iteration and re-release the software at specific milestones as and when a portion of the software or feature is completed. This method is suited for commercial software which is released once in a quarter or year. Usually, an iteration takes a minimum of three weeks. Therefore, short iterations help you to plan and deliver important features first.

Short iteration means frequent releases in short duration. This has a direct impact on how the development team works. In order to keep the variations simple you must ensure that the changes are small. However, this is against XP goal as XP supports changes in large scale. Therefore, you need to balance the iteration duration and changes done during the iteration of a XP project.

In many projects, it is believed that the more frequent you release, the chances of variations are less. However, releasing the software everyday is not feasible. Therefore, it is a good practice to release the software once in two to three weeks. This helps you to decrease the possible difference between the shortcomings of previous and current code.

Frequent releases help the team to learn from the mistakes committed in the current and previous iteration, and to prepare for the next iteration. The developers must have the time to think and analyze the things that went well, things that can be improved, things that can be experimented in the next iteration, etc. The entire team must come together to analyze and make changes in their practices after discussion.

One of the drawbacks of frequent releases is that it makes it difficult for the team to meet the long-term goals. Therefore, it is very important for the customer to set milestones while setting the priorities of the stories. Both, the developers and customer have to analyze and schedule the releases according to the business requirements of the customer.

A feedback loop between implementing story and delivering the feature to the end user is developed by frequent releases. Therefore, it is very important to keep the loop as short as possible. This helps the customer to collect the information from the end user who actually uses the software and make necessary changes in the new stories. The development team must be able to understand and address the feedback given by the customer. This helps the development team to add value to the software and meet the business requirements of the customer. Any project that grows by reacting and adjusting to changes efficiently is considered a healthy project.

A release plan is drafted for the overall project after a release plan meeting. Later, the release plan is used to create an iteration plan for each developer. A set of rules are used for release planning. These rules allow everyone involved in the project to make their own decisions. Usually these rules define a method to negotiate a schedule that the team can commit to.

Release planning meeting is very important for the development team as it helps them to estimate the ideal hours required for each story. During release planning the customer decides what stories are the most important ones or to be completed first. Usually, a detailed plan for individual iterations is done just before the start of each iteration during release planning. The release planning meeting is also called as planning game. (Refer to Unit 17 for more details about the planning game.)

After you finalize the release plan, if the management is not happy with it then, you must not change the estimates for the stories. Instead negotiate an acceptable release plan after discussing with the developers, customers and managers. The main idea behind the release plan is that a project can be quantified based on the following variables:

- *Scope -* This defines the quantity of the work to be done.
- *Resource -* This defines the resources available.
- *Time -* This defines the schedule for the project release.
- *Quality -* This specifies how good and how well tested the software will be.

During the course of the project, if any of these variables are changed then it affects the other variables. Therefore, it is very important to plan the release by taking into consideration all these variables.

Activity 2:

Imagine that you are the team leader of a XP project team. Before you start your project you have to plan the iteration releases. Your project manager wants you to explain the project variables that might be affected by your release plan to the customer. Prepare a note that you can present to the customer regarding the significance of release plan with respect to project variables.

18.5 SUMMARY

Let us recapitulate the important concepts discussed in this unit:

- The customer and the developer participate in meetings for iteration planning to agree upon the requirements of the project and schedule the iteration.
- The customer writes the story to inform the business requirements or software features to the developer. Based on the story card, developers write task cards to carry out the development process.
- Estimations help the customer and the developers to schedule the iteration. They give the ideal time required to develop the software for an iteration.
- The first iteration is always important for any development team. The first iteration lays a basic foundation for the rest of the project.

- Developing a flexible iteration improves the efficiency of the development process.
- The customer prepares the project schedule with the help of stories and iteration.
- It is essential to get a sign off from the customer after releasing the software to confirm that the iteration is complete.
- Software release means handing over the software to the customer at the end of an iteration.
- Releasing the software frequently helps the team to learn from the mistakes committed in the current iteration and to prepare for the next iteration.
- Release planning meeting is very important for the development team as it helps them to estimate the ideal hours required for each story.
- A release plan is drafted for the overall project after a release plan meeting.

18.6 GLOSSARY

Acceptance test: A test that confirms that a story is complete by matching a user action scenario with a desired outcome.

Ideal hours: The planned hours required to complete a task.

Milestones: A scheduled event signifying the completion of a major deliverable or a set of related deliverables.

Sign-off: To express approval formally or conclusively.

19 Extreme Programming Artifacts

Structure

19.1 INTRODUCTION

In the previous chapter, you learnt the various events of Extreme Programming (XP). You are now familiar with iteration planning. You also learnt the aspects of releasing software in XP.

You now know that stories and tasks are an integral part of XP. XP was conceived, designed and developed to address the needs of constant changing and vague requirements of clients who are interested in obtaining what they want and can spend time and share their knowledge with the developers. XP makes use of artifacts such as story cards and task cards to describe the coding that has to be done. The XP developers can share these artifacts with the customers and obtain their feedback.

In this chapter, we shall be learning about XP artifacts like story cards and task cards. We will also discuss how working in a bullpen-like room can help developers in developing software quickly.

Objectives

After studying this unit, you should be able to:

- create story cards and task cards
- describe the importance of a bullpen sitting arrangement in XP

19.2 STORY CARDS

User stories describe the functionality that is required by the user. Story cards are the cards which are used by the customers to write the details of the user story or of a feature. Each story card describes one feature which is desired in a story form. It describes the details of the story like priority of the feature, estimate to complete the job, risks involved and methods of monitoring.

There are three main phases in creation of a story card. They are:

1. *Exploration* - During this phase, the customer analyzes and summarizes the needs in the system.
2. *Commitment* - During this phase, all the subsets of the feature requested are finalized along with their estimated time.
3. *Steering* - During this phase, the plan is updated based on the learnings of the exploration and the commitment phase.

There are many iterations involved in the development of a story card. Story cards follow the Spiral Model of Software Development Life Cycle (SDLC). Figure 19.1 depicts a sample story card.

Story Tag: Doc Book to HTML   Release: Book   Priority: 1

Author: Joanne   On: 2/21/02   Accepted: 3/17/02

Description: Make the DOC BOOK files readable and printable

Considerations: HTML has some drawbacks: Estimate: 4.1
    °Printed version is not production quality
    °Footnotes can't appear at end of page

Who	Task	Est.	Done
Rob	Simple tags: <chapter>,<title>,<para>	/	2/24
Rob	Asymmetrical tags: <attractive>	/	3/3
Rob	Contextually related tags: <title>	/	3/11
Rob	Statefull output < footnote>	/	3/14
Joanne	Acceptence Test Print the first chapter	/	3/17

Figure 19.1 A Sample Story Card

There are two stakeholders involved in the planning of any software – the Development team and the Business team. The Development team includes people who are responsible for designing, creating, testing and implementing the system. The Business team includes people who make the decisions about what the system is supposed to do.

The Business team who wants to create custom-made software prioritise the process. The Business team needs to decide the requirements and the priority of the features released.

The end users of the software systems are the customers who actually use them. When the process of exploration or requirement gathering is being done the customer is already very comfortable using the old system. Hence, the customer gets confused in separating the new requirements and specifying the old features that need to be retained. Use of XP methodology in software development helps both users as well as developers. Users can propose changes even after the initial release of the system and it is not difficult for developers to include the features or make the necessary changes.

Let us now discuss the different phases of creation of the story card.

19.2.1 EXPLORATION PHASE

The purpose of the exploration phase is to find the requirements of the users in terms of features and functionalities. Exploration phase has the following three steps:

1. **Write a story -** The Business team starts writing a story describing an action the system needs to do. The stories are written on cards with a name (generally the name of the feature or unit) and a short paragraph describing the purpose of the story.

2. **Estimate a story -** The Development team estimates the duration to implement the story after designing, coding and testing. If the Development team cannot estimate the story, it can ask the Business team to clarify or divide the story into smaller sections. While estimating the story, a developer has to determine the time they require to implement the story assuming that there are no interruptions during implementation. In XP, this is called as Ideal Engineering Time (IET). Before a commitment of a schedule is done, one has to measure the ratio between ideal time for the development and the calendar time (includes the holidays, meeting time etc.).

3. **Split a story -** In case, the Development team cannot estimate a complete story at a time, or if the Business team realizes that one part of a story is more important than the rest, then the Business team can split a story into two or more stories.

The exploration phase can take a few weeks to complete and depends on how familiar the Development team is with the technology required.

19.2.2 COMMITMENT PHASE

The purpose of the commitment phase is to enable the Business team to choose the scope and date of the next release, and the Development team to confidently commit to delivering it.

The commitment phase has the following four steps:

1. **Sort by value** - In this step, the Business team sorts the stories into the following three categories:
   - Those which are mandatory for the system to function
   - Those that are not very necessary but which increase business value
   - Those that would enhance the look and feel
2. **Sort by risk** - In this step, the Development team sorts the stories into the following three categories:
   - Those that can be estimated accurately
   - Those that can be estimate approximately
   - Those that cannot be estimated
3. **Set velocity -** In this step, the Development team informs the Business team how fast the team can program in IET per calendar month.
4. **Choose scope -** In this step, the Business team chooses the set of story cards, for the release. It is done by priortizing the features needed and then calculating the dates for completing implementation based on the estimate provided in the story card. This way, the final date of release is also estimated after adding the number of iterations needed and the duration of iteration.

Commitment phase basically gives the final estimate of the software after including all the risks, time and iterations required.

19.2.3 STEERING PHASE

The purpose of the steering phase is to update the project plan based on what is learnt by the Development and Business teams simultaneously during the exploration and commitment phase. The steering phase has the following four steps:

1. **Iteration -** In the beginning of every iteration (every one to three weeks), the Business team picks an iteration of the most valuable story (set of stories) to be implemented. The stories selected for the first iteration must be chosen so that the Development team can create a prototype of the system.
2. **Recovery -** In this step, if the Development team realizes that it has overestimated its pace, it can ask the Business team to determine the most valuable set of stories to retain in the current release based on the new pace and estimates.
3. **New story -** Here, if the Business team realizes it needs a new story during the middle of the development of a release, it can create another story card. The Development team estimates the story, and then the Business team removes stories having equivalent estimate from the remaining plan and inserts the new story card.

4. **Re-estimate -** In this step, if the Development team feels that the plan no longer provides an accurate map of development, it can re-estimate all of the remaining stories and set the pace again.

The planning methodology discussed gives the customer the capability of steering development.

Activity 1:
A university has a database of students which has the details of the student and the course they are taking. The university regularly arranges seminars. A student can enroll in a seminar only if it is relevant to their course. Create a story card for this.

19.3 TASK CARDS

We have discussed how story cards are an important tool used by the customers to convey their requirements. Task cards are the planning tools of the developers. The tasks are the actual steps required to implement a story.

Engineering Task Card   B/W   Small talk/Future

Based on Conversation to/REB:AMA   NEW

STORY NUMBER: X923   SOFTWARE ENGINEER: ______   TASK ESTIMATE: ________

TASK DISCRIPTION

Composite Bin Regular Needs to be Displayed on GUI, we have the hidden bin for Regular Base(Lost Time) to Display NOT the auto gen, bin but the BIN that composites the Auto Pay the lost Time. There is a separate composite bin started that needs to be completed

SOFTWARE ENGINEER'S NOTES:

TASK TRACKING:

Date	Done	To Do	Comments

Figure 19.2 A Sample Task Card

Task cards are the cards created for the individual programmers for smaller units of a story. The steps followed to create a task card are similar to that of a story card. But, here the story is broken into smaller units and the time estimated to complete the tasks is also less.

Figure 19.2 depicts a task card. As you can see it is similar to the story card but has details only for the programmer.

As in a story card, the development of a task card too involves the following phases:

- Exploration phase
- Commitment phase
- Steering phase

Let us now discuss the different phases involved in the creation of a task card.

19.3.1 EXPLORATION PHASE

The purpose of the exploration phase is to convert story cards to task cards. This phase has the following three steps:

1. **Create a task -** In this step, the task cards are created from the story cards by the developers. Generally the tasks are smaller than the complete story because developers cannot implement a complete story in a couple of days. Sometimes one task may support several stories. Sometimes a task may not directly relate to any particular story. For example, migrating to a new version of system software may have smaller task cards.
2. **Split a task or combine a few tasks -** In this step, we break down tasks into smaller tasks or combine tasks. If we cannot estimate a task, we must break it down into smaller tasks. We can combine tasks that take less time to get completed.
3. **Estimate a task -** In this step, the Development team estimates the duration for the task to be implemented. While estimating the task, a developer has to determine the time they require to implement the task if there are no interruptions.

The exploration phase thus converts the customer requirements to different tasks.

19.3.2 COMMITMENT PHASE

During the commitment phase the development team takes the responsibility of the task cards on an individual basis and estimates the delivery of the task.

The commitment phase involves the following steps:

1. **Accept a task -** In this step, a programmer accepts responsibility for the development of a task.
2. **Estimate a task -** In this step, the programmer responsible for the task estimates the number of ideal engineering days required to implement each task. Programmers can get help from another programmer who is more familiar with the

code and can help them to modify the code to make the features more stable. The development team has to determine a threshold for the number of days a task can take to implement. Tasks that take more time than this threshold have to be split into smaller tasks.

3. **Set load factors** - In this step, each programmer chooses the load factor for the iteration. The percentage of time the programmers spend actually developing and the time they spend helping other programmers or talking with the customer, and going to meetings are added up to obtain the load factor. It is important to ensure that the programmers are not overloaded either by doing their own work or in helping their team members or in meetings etc.

4. **Balance the tasks** - In this step, the programmers add up their task estimates and multiply it by their load factor. Programmers who turn out to be overcommitted must delegate some tasks to other programmers. If the whole team is overloaded or overcommitted, then either by increasing the time frame or resources, the team has to balance the work load.

This phase involves the assignment of responsibilities and assessment of costs and schedule.

19.3.3 STEERING PHASE

During the steering phase, the developers implement the tasks. The steering phase has the following four steps:

1. **Implement a task** - Developer takes a task card and then finds a partner to code and write the test cases. After the task is successfully tested, it is integrated and released for testing by the customer.

2. **Record progress** - In this step, the progress of the software is recorded by one member of the team. This can be done by asking each programmer how long they have spent on each of their tasks and how many days are left for the completion of the task.

3. **Recovery** - In this step, the programmers who are assigned too many tasks should ask for help by:
   - reducing the scope of some tasks
   - requesting the customer to reduce the scope of some stories
   - discarding non-essential tasks
   - getting more or better help
   - asking the customer to defer some stories to a later iteration

4. **Verify story** - The story is verified by running functional tests on them. Real time test cases are brought to life during implementation and they can be added to the functional test suite.

The main difference between iteration planning and release planning is that stakeholders can tolerate fewer changes in the iteration schedule than in the commitment schedule.

In iteration planning, programmers sign up for the tasks before they estimate. It is the collective responsibility of the team to give estimations for the stories. Individual programmers accept responsibilities for individual tasks. Therefore, they must estimate the tasks themselves.

During iteration planning, some tasks can arise which can make the system more stable but are not part of the features or stories. But if there is the need to strengthen the tools for integration and it is not a minor development, then it can be combined with the normal design changes. This then becomes a task in its own right. Therefore, this is scheduled and prioritized with all the other tasks.

If we want rapid feedback on the progress of the project, we must question the stakeholders. This will enable us to get an idea, halfway through the iteration, if we are on schedule or not. This provides us enough time to react locally to problems and to make changes without the customer's approval.

The individuals responsible for delivery must also be responsible for estimating it. This can be successful as long as the programmers sign up for tasks before they estimate.

We want a process that does not generate so much pressure that people do inappropriate things. We need a process to meet the needs of a short-term plan.

> **Activity 2:**
> One of the tasks in inventory management is updating the inventory database when supplies are received. Create a task card for this.

19.4 BULLPENS

Apart from story cards and task cards, XP makes use of bullpens to make programming more effective. A bullpen has small individual cubicles around the walls, and tables with high-speed machines located in the middle. Such an arrangement facilitates XP practices such as pair programming.

If the facility provided to the developers during the project is not in accordance with the requirements it is very likely that the project will not succeed. It is very important that the development team is provided with a good working environment.

It is observed that when people are working in close proximity and the proper atmosphere is maintained, the output obtained is better and according to requirements.

There are many conflicting constraints in providing proper facilities. The facility planners are mostly judged on how flexibility is retained in the plan at reduced costs. The people using the facilities want to work closely with the rest of the team and also retain their own privacy.

XP is a software development discipline where the members of the team need to be in close proximity and there should be easy access to each other's time. Hence sitting together in the same room is better for the team where there is access to the hardware, software, and the persons who are going to be the part of development team.

Normal office layouts do not work well for XP. In Pair-Programming, two people need to sit side-by-side and program. The cubicles must not have high walls and computers kept in the corner. The walls between cubicles should be medium sized or they must be eliminated entirely. At the same time, it is essential to separate one team from other teams.

The best setup for XP is the open bullpen, which has small cubicles around the office space. The team members can keep their personal items in these cubicles and spend time here when they do not want to be interrupted. The other members of the team respect the 'virtual' privacy of someone sitting in the cubicle.

All the biggest and fastest development machines can be located in the center of the office space. Everyone can see what is happening around them, and each pair can draw from the energy of the other pairs who are also developing at the same time.

The most effective way to keep yourself fresh while you are developing is to step away from your cubicle for some time. A pleasant place where employees can sit, relax and have refreshments can enable them to refocus on their work.

The XP attitude gives greater importance to the team's attitude when the management's attitude toward facilities is at odds with the team's attitude. If the computers are incorrectly placed, they are moved. The changes are done to suit the developers. For example, the lights are dimmed and phone bells are made pleasant if they are a disturbance to the developers.

Many offices have old style desks which provide space for only one person to sit. In XP, two programmers need to sit in one cubicle and use one computer together. Therefore they need a bigger space to sit. In such situations, the developers have to make the facilitator understand the importance of a proper physical environment.

When the physical environment is in control of the developer's team, it gives a powerful message to the team members. They are not going to let irrational and opposing interests of the organization to get in their way of success. Taking control of the physical environment where the team needs to spend most of the time is the first step toward taking control over their overall performance. A change in existing facility depends only on constant experimentation (the feedback they get at work). This is needed as the organization spends lots of money in facilitating people at work place, so that they can work in peace and be productive.

19.5 SUMMARY

Let us now recapitulate the important points discussed in the unit:

- User stories describe the functionality that is desired by the user of a system. Story Cards are the cards which are used by the customers to write the details of the user story or a feature.

- There are three major steps in the process of the story card creation. They are:

Exploration - During this phase, the customer analyzes and summarizes the needs in the system.

Commitment - During this phase, all the subsets of the feature requested are finalized along with their estimated time.

Steering - During this phase, the plan is updated based on the learnings of the exploration and the commitment phase.

- Task cards are the cards created for the individual programmers for smaller units of a story.
- The development of a task card involves the following phases:
- **Exploration phase -** The purpose of this phase is to convert the story cards to task cards.
- **Commitment phase -** In this phase, the development team takes the responsibility of the task cards on an individual basis and estimates the delivery of the task.

  Steering phase - During this phase, the developers implement the tasks.
- XP makes use of bullpens to make programming more effective. A bullpen has small individual cubicles around the walls, and tables with high-speed machines located in the middle.

19.6 GLOSSARY

Commitment schedule: The commitment schedule is the date of release of iteration. It can be modified through re-estimation and recovery.

Customer: A team member from the business side for identifying the stories the system has to satisfy, the stories that are needed first and the stories that can be deferred.

Exploration: The phase of development in which the customer communicates what the system should do.

Functional test: A test written from the perspective of the customer which tests the functional aspects of the feature.

Ideal programming time: The measure of estimation using which a programmer defines timelines to complete a task.

Iteration: A period of one to four-weeks in which the unit test is done for any task and if needed, the changes are incorporated in the stories to be redesigned. The complete process is repeated till its success and completion.

Load factor: The measured ratio between ideal programming time and the calendar time (work days).

Pair programming: A programming technique in which two people program with one keyboard, one mouse, and one monitor. In XP, the pairs typically change a couple of times a day.

Programmer: A role in the team for someone who analyzes, designs, tests, programs, and integrates.

Recovery: A planning move where the customer preserves the completion date of a release by reducing the scope of the release in response to increased estimates or decreased team speed.

Re-estimation: A planning move where the team re-estimates all the stories remaining in the release.

Release: A pile of stories that together makes business sense.

Story: A thing the customer wants the system to do. Stories should be estimable at between one to five ideal programming weeks. Stories should be testable.

Task: Small units of program which are derived from stories. These must be estimable at between one to three ideal programming days.

Test case: An automated set of inputs and outputs for the system. Each test case should leave the system the way it found it, so tests can run independently of each other.

Unit test: A test written from the perspective of the programmer.

19.7   CASE STUDY

Extreme Programming in Workshare

Workshare specializes in the domain of technical document change management. As its products are unique and as its marketplace is constantly changing, it needed flexible design and functional specifications. Its engineering team faced the following problems:

- Development was not driven by functional requirements.
- Programming knowledge was not shared.
- Quality was not being built in the code.

Workshare required a methodology to quickly deploy software, improve inter-departmental communication, be scalable, and fit into its culture and philosophy. Therefore, Workshare decided to adopt Extreme Programming (XP).

Workshare has a department within Engineering for dealing with the needs of its external customers. This department sometimes assumes the role of the customer in the XP process. The Product Management group interfaces with all functional areas in Workshare. Its responsibilities include:

- Product direction
- Collating stories of all sources

Contd...

- Determining the stories to be used for the next release
- Prioritizing the stories
- Developing acceptance tests for the stories along with the Quality Assurance (QA) team

Each customer was responsible for their XP story. The customers had to be constantly available to the Engineering team. If the customer was not available, then Product Management department had to take the responsibility for answering any queries. The customers controlled the design, new features and priorities. They also decided which defects can adversely affect the output and determine the priority for fixes.

Customers defined scope with user stories at the planning meeting. They wrote each story on a separate index card. The customer had to write the story in simple English. The story had to briefly describe the feature that the customer wanted. This story card was then used as a notation by the programmers. Customers also had to define the functional tests for the system. The customer could write these tests on the index card of the story.

Workshare used a tracking system called Blue Sky. This tracking system was designed to meet the needs of its Engineering department. It enabled the Engineering department to monitor the progress of each project from release planning to the individual tasks that made up a story. As all the data were stored and updated continuously, it could be analyzed easily.

Over a period of two years, Workshare's development department saw a drastic improvement in its defect rate. It reduced its defect rate by about 80%. Now it spends only 14% of its efforts on defects and 86% on new development.

Discussion Questions:
1. What were the problems faced by Workshare's Engineering department?
   (Hint: Non-sharing of programming knowledge, poor quality)
2. How did the customers of Workshare specify their requirements after it adopted XP?
   (Hint: Stories, index cards)

20 Roles in Extreme Programming

Structure

20.1 INTRODUCTION

In the previous unit you became familiar with the artifacts of Extreme Programming (XP) like story cards and task cards. You learnt the three major steps in the process of story card creation, which are exploration, commitment, and steering. You also learnt how working in a bullpen-like room can help developers in developing software quickly.

XP projects have many roles, each with unique rights and responsibilities. Amongst all, the customers and developers play an important role in XP projects. XP helps to improve the communication between the developers and customers by distributing the work between the two. Communication between the developers and customers is vital for the accomplishment of any work.

In this unit, you will study the rights and responsibilities of the customers and developers in relation to XP. You will also learn about supplementary roles which are not part of the core team but are required for the execution of the project.

Objectives

After studying this unit, you should be able to:

- analyze the importance of customer rights and responsibilities in XP

- provide an overview of developer rights and responsibilities in XP
- explain supplementary roles in XP

20.2 CUSTOMER'S ROLES

The customers play a primary role in XP. They drive the project and define its goals. When a project is defined clearly by the customer there are more chances that it will succeed. It is not easy to be an XP customer. XP customers need to have certain skills. These skills include writing good stories and an attitude that can bring in success.

The customers make the business decisions. The customer's rights and responsibilities stem from their business knowledge. They have the right to define the goals and features of the project. They are supposed to answer questions such as the following:

1. What should a feature do?
2. How will we know when it is done?
3. How much time and money can we spend?
4. When shall we start working on it?

The customers work closely with the developers to define the features required. They also write story cards to describe and schedule the desired features. This answers the first question.

The customers create and run the acceptance tests. They do this by taking the help of developers. That is, the customers take the help of the developers to ascertain that the features are complete. This answers the second question.

The customers take part in the planning game to schedule stories for the next iteration. This answers the third and fourth question.

The customers also act as an end user. They can act either as a direct end user or as a proxy for an end user. In an organization, for an in-house project, the customers may be the end users. In other situations, they act as a proxy for the end users. By acting as an end user they identify the features needed by the users from their perspective.

The customers are the one who represent the business interests of a project. Their goal is to increase their Return on Investment (ROI) and develop a software with the most valuable features, by using the available resources.

The XP customers should be able to analyze the business problems that have to be solved, even as they change over a period of time. The business problems may include the following:

- Is a story that was created earlier more valuable or less valuable now?

- Is it possible to delay, defer, or simplify a story?

The customers should be able to evaluate projects at any time. That is, they must check which features are complete and which are not. They should also check how well the completed features conform to the stories.

The customers should analyze and understand the technical implications of a story that can affect its values and its risk.

Customers are always referred by XP as a single person. The customers should speak with one voice irrespective of them being a proxy for an actual investor or for the end users who are far-off. The customers hold a position that gives them the authority to say what needs to be done.

20.2.1 CUSTOMER RIGHTS

XP grants various rights to the customers. The customers have a right to:

- increase their investments by selecting stories to schedule in the current iteration. This is because XP schedules are centered on the iteration. Iteration here refers to a snapshot of the complete development cycle. That is, the customers request the features and the project team plans them. This plan is then implemented, tested and delivered, which takes some weeks before the iteration resumes again.
- ascertain the feature to be implemented by choosing story cards in the iteration planning meeting. The planning game occurs at the beginning of every release. Story cards are used by the customers to request for features to be implemented in their projects.
- modify the scope of a project in order to deal with any changes in the schedule. This can be done by selecting stories to add or remove from iterations in case the estimates prove to be incorrect.
- evaluate the progress of the project by running an acceptance test. The acceptance test can be run by the customers any time based on their story cards. This enables the customer to provide a quick feedback on the team's current progress.
- terminate the project at any time without losing their investments. The customer can keep the software product in a releasable state and schedule the most worthwhile features continually.
- plan on a large scale with costs.
- define development priorities on a weekly basis.
- drive the project by providing user requirements and quality control.

20.2.2 CUSTOMER RESPONSIBILITIES

In XP, customers have some responsibilities also. The customers have to:

- rely on the developers' technical decisions. This is because the developers have technical knowledge which needs to be respected and trusted.
- analyze risks accurately by weighing the stories against one another.

- schedule the most valuable stories that can suit the next iteration by selecting stories with maximum value.
  - provide the developers with stories that are precise. This helps the developers to produce correct estimates and accurate task cards.
  - work with the developers or the project team.
  - offer guidance and receive accurate and quick feedback.
  - respond to the day-to-day questions of developers on required functionality.
  - coordinate releases with the demands of the outside world.
  - support the team by taking up certain implicit responsibilities such as having good contact with the stakeholders of the project, particularly with the end users, clients or the financiers of the project.
  - maintain confidence of the development team and the business.

Customers are said to be best not only when they actually make use of the system being developed, but also when they have a certain perspective on the problem to be solved. The customers need to learn and understand how to write stories. They should also be able to decide which information to include and which to exclude.

It is essential for a customer to learn to write functional tests. In case of a customer who is working for an application with a mathematical basis, working for a few hours with a spread sheet is sufficient to create the data for a test case. Customers who are working on programs with a formulaic basis also need to know about functional tests. It is the responsibility of the customers to work closely with the project team to identify the functionalities to be tested and the type of tests that are redundant. The customers may even assist the project team to choose, write, and run the tests. Testing the system helps customers to gain confidence about the working of the system.

20.3 DEVELOPER'S ROLES

While the customers know what to program the developers know how to program. Hence, the developers are considered to be the heart of XP. They convert the customer's stories into working code. To elaborate, XP developers analyze, design, test, program, and integrate the system. They prepare an estimate of the complexity of all stories, and track the pace at which they can deliver the final product to the customers.

The role of the developers in planning and implementing features is based on the knowledge and understanding of the technical issues. In fact, if the developers can decide the short term and long term priorities of the project there would not be any requirement for technical people on the project.

Developers are solely responsible for creating and maintaining the system as it evolves. They are liable to answer questions such as:

- How they would implement a story?
- How long would it take to implement it?
- What kind of risks could be involved?

The developers work with the customers as a team to understand their need and decide the steps to implement. They understand the customers' need by understanding their stories and thereby decide its implementation.

Next, the developers form an estimate of the amount of work to be done for every story. The developers estimate this depending on the implementation decisions and their previous experience of working on such projects. These estimates assist the customer to schedule the work for the subsequent iteration by answering the question of "How long?"

During the creation of task cards from the story cards or during the implementation of tasks in the programming cycle, the developers might recognize features that are based on some other feature. They might also find risky features that make use of new technology or are otherwise complicated. These issues are communicated by the developers to the customers, who consider them while creating the schedules. In fact, these risks are uncommon and simplification of the process usually reduces them.

When we compare an XP developer with a developer who is working within other software development disciplines, we find that both of them spend their time working on programs, enhancing them or making them simpler and faster. However, the role of developers is just not this; their focus is quite different. The job of an XP developer does not only involve developing a program, but also involves communicating with other people. Although a program can be executed, if there are a few critical components of communication left to be done, the process of developing a program cannot be considered as complete. Therefore, the developers are expected to write tests that explain the critical aspect of the software. The developers might also have to break down the program into smaller parts, or combine the various parts that are very small into larger parts. The XP developers are also expected to find a system of names that reflects their intention accurately.

XP developers need to have certain skills that are not always essential in other styles of development. They are as follows:

- The XP developers need to have the ability to pair program. Pair programming is a software development technique wherein two programmers work together at one workstation. Other software development teams use this technique only some time, but an XP software development team always makes use of this technique.
- The XP developers need to possess good communication skill. This is because the developers need to communicate and coordinate with the customers and other developers to be successful.
- The developers need to possess the habit of simplicity. When the customers ask the developers to do certain work they need to analyze and tell which of those tasks and how much of those tasks are necessary. Simplicity extends even to the code written by the developers. Obviously the developers can perform a job in a better way if they have more tools in their tool box. However, it is essential to have some tools that the developers know when not to use, rather than know everything and risk using too many solutions.
- The developers need skills that are technically oriented. That is, they should be able to write reasonably good programs.

- The developers should have the ability to refactor. Refactoring is a skill that requires as much depth and subtlety as programming.
- The developers should be able to perform unit tests of the code.

Amongst all the above mentioned skills, the XP developer's major skill is to write good programs, because this helps in delivering the business value.

20.3.1 DEVELOPER RIGHTS

The various developer rights that are recognized by XP are as follows:
- Develop code to meet the customer's requirement, by concentrating on testing, refactoring, and customer communication.
- Work on a schedule that is sensible and predictable, by allotting only an amount of work that can reasonably be accomplished.
- Form an estimate of the tasks by giving authority over technical decisions to the developers.
- Avoid making business decisions, by allowing the customers to make decisions related to the business.
- Report the progress of the allocated tasks to the customers.
- Produce superior quality work at all times.
- Get information on what is the most important task to be performed next.
- Ask business-oriented questions whenever the need arises.
- Ask for and receive assistance from customers, peers, and superiors.
- Accept the responsibilities instead of someone else assigning it.

20.3.2 DEVELOPER RESPONSIBILITIES

The various customer responsibilities that are recognized by XP are as follows:
- Implement only what is essential, to have a project that is simple and valuable for the customer.
- Follow the guidelines laid out for the team to maintain a system that is simple, well-tested and agile.
- Write every production code in pairs as described in Pair Programming. This leads to increase in speed and cross-training, in support of ownership of the shared code and rapid progress.
- Follow a single coding standard. This could be a standard created by one of the developers in a team or a standard adopted from elsewhere. It is possible to make everybody's code look alike by having good communication among the team members.
- Communicate with the customers constantly, to assist them in making accurate scheduling decisions and to understand their concerns if any.
- Program the system such that it can be released in small units, so that the customers can provide the best possible feedback on the tasks accomplished.
- Maintain an integrated system at all times. This helps to have a good version always.

Thus, we can conclude that in XP, the programmers get to do what they are best at, that is, programming, while providing the customers with what they need most, that is, business value.

20.4 SUPPLEMENTARY ROLES

There are a few other roles in XP apart from the customers and developers. Even though they are not part of the core team, they are essential for the execution of the project. They are:

- Tracker
- Coach

20.4.1 TRACKER

A tracker is a person who keeps track of the schedule. A tracker can be a manager or a trusted developer. XP keeps track of certain metrics that include team velocity. This is the ratio of ideal time estimated for accomplishing a task to the actual time spent implementing them. The tracker also includes other data such as change in velocity, overtime worked, and the ratio of passing tests to failing tests.

It is the responsibility of the tracker to prepare good estimates of the tasks. Preparing good estimates is a matter of practice and feedback. The tracker has to make estimates to a great extent and notice how reality conforms to the estimates. Giving feedback is essential because the team can work on the feedback and improve their performance.

The tracker should also be able to keep an eye on the final outcome. Halfway through an iteration, the tracker should be able to tell the team whether they will accomplish the task if they follow the current schedule or if they need to modify it. After a couple of iterations into a commitment schedule, the tracker should also be able to tell the team whether they are going to make the next release without making big changes.

The tracker acts as a team historian. The tracker keeps a record of the functional test scores and the defects reported. It is the job of the tracker to keep track of who accepted responsibility for each task, and what test cases were added on each defects.

The data presented by the tracker helps in calculating the progress and finding the rate of progress. They help in ascertaining if the project is on schedule for iteration. They can also show behavioral changes that may affect the schedule.

In order to measure velocity within the iteration, the tracker needs to ask each developer about the tasks accomplished by them every day or two. This has to be done in an informal and comfortable way as possible. The developers need to be honest while giving out their work details and at the same time the tracker needs to be non-judgemental. The XP team adjusts to the flow of work when there is regular tracking of progress.

20.4.2 COACH

A coach is a person who is highly respected and has experience in guiding and mentoring the team. Having a coach can be helpful when adopting XP.

It could be difficult to apply XP consistently. An XP team requires certain skills that may take some time to develop. Also there are certain occasional obstacles and subtleties that need the guidance of a master. Thus, a coach's main quality is experience.

The coach helps the XP team to understand the XP practices and software development methodologies either by teaching the team, working along with the team or by being an intermediary. It is the responsibility of the coach to make suggestions with reference to how a practice is implemented, offer ideas to solve technical problems, or act as a mediator between the team and management. The responsibility of the coach is also to ensure that the team works smoothly and harmoniously towards achieving their goal.

Coaching is mainly focused on the technical execution of the process. An ideal coach should be a good communicator, technically skilled and confident. A coach can be a person who has worked on other projects as a lead developer or system architect. The role of a coach is not to make decisions, but instead it is to help everybody else make good decisions.

The coach is not expected to take responsibility of all the development tasks, instead they are expected to take up the following job responsibilities:

- Act as a development partner, especially for new developers or for technical tasks that are difficult.
- Encourage small scale refactoring by looking into long term refactoring to address parts of these goals.
- Assist developers with tasks such as testing, formatting, and refactoring.
- Give details of the process to the top level managers.
- Ensure that the project stays 'Extreme' by mentoring the team efficiently.
- Formulate a vision of the goal and convey it to other developers, for them to work towards it.
- Select methodologies that are suitable and adapt it in the business.
- Keep the team on track with respect to XP.
- Act as a mediator between the XP developer and the management.

Therefore, we can conclude that the role of a coach is very essential for an XP team.

Activity 1:

Assume you are the coach of an XP project at RSD Software Inc. This project deals with the development of a simple chat room application using client server architecture. This application will manage only a single room of six members. Every client will be able to type messages that would be echoed to all the connected clients. What do you think would be your responsibilities as a coach in this project?

(Hint: Refer section 20.4 for detailed guidelines)

20.5 SUMMARY

Let us recapitulate the important concepts discussed in this unit:

- The XP customers drive and define the goals of a project, and make business decisions.
- XP customers need skills such as story writing and an attitude that can bring in success.
- The XP customer evaluates the project.
- Some of the rights of the XP customer include increasing their Return on Investment (ROI) by selecting stories to schedule in the current iteration, modify the scope of a project, evaluate the progress of a project by running an acceptance test, and terminating a project at any given time without losing the investments.
- Some of the responsibilities of XP customers involve analyzing the risks in a project by weighing the stories against another, scheduling the most valuable stories that are suitable for next iteration, and coordinating releases with the demands of the outside world.
- The developer's role to plan and implement features depends on the knowledge and understanding of technical issues. An XP developer has to communicate with other people apart from developing programs.
- Some of the rights of XP developers include developing code to meet the needs of the customer, working on a schedule that is predictable and sensible, produce superior quality work at all times, and report the progress of the tasks to the customers.
- Some of the responsibilities of XP developers include following a single coding standard, follow the guidelines, and communicate with customers constantly.
- A person who keeps track of the schedule is known as tracker. A manager or a trusted developer can take up the role of a tracker. A tracker prepares estimates of tasks. Tracker keeps record of functional test scores.
- A coach in XP guides and mentors a team.
- The coach assists the team in understanding XP practices and software development methodologies. A coach acts as a mediator between the XP developer and management, selects methodologies suitable for a business, formulates a vision of the goal, and makes sure that the project stays 'Extreme'.
- Coaching is primarily focused on technical execution of a process.

20.6 GLOSSARY

Refactoring: Restructure or rewrite source code to improve internal consistency and readability without changing its function.

Story card: A very high-level definition of a requirement, containing just enough information so that the developers can produce a reasonable estimate of the effort to implement it.

Task card: Developers primary planning tool. Act as a detailed plan for the iteration.

Coding XP Style

21.1 INTRODUCTION

In the previous unit, you learnt the rights and responsibilities of the customers and developers in Extreme Programming (XP). You became familiar with the supplementary roles, which are not part of the core team but are required for the execution of an XP project.

XP is a system development approach which is meant to improve software quality and meet changing customer requirements. The goal of XP is to produce superior software more productively. As XP recommends frequent releases in short development cycles, it tries to reduce the cost of meeting the changing requirements. XP developers keep in mind the goal of flexibility through simplicity by following the principles of XP.

In this unit, you will learn how XP coding functionality can be balanced with simplicity. You will learn the importance of implementing only the required features. You will also analyze how to eliminate repetition in XP coding style.

Objectives

After studying this unit, you should be able to:

- explain how functionality is balanced with simplicity in XP
- implement only the required features while coding
- analyze how to eliminate repetition while coding in XP style

21.2 BALANCE FUNCTIONALITY WITH SIMPLICITY

XP mainly concentrates on simplicity. Concentrating on simple designs reduces the risk of spending more time and resources for designing a complex feature that the customer may not want. Focusing on identifying a simple solution for the current problem minimizes the cost of changes in the future.

According to traditional theory of software engineering, it is very expensive to make any changes over the lifetime of a project. As the project moves on to the design phase, it is hard to make a change. Once the project moves on to the coding phase, it is harder to make a change. There are several reasons for this. One reason is that if you want to make any changes in the coding phase, you have to modify the code. If the design is not simple, a single change may affect other parts of the system. Over time, as more and more programmers modify the system, it becomes difficult to keep track of the modifications made and their impact on the system.

Most software designers would agree with simplicity of design as a basic software principle. According to XP, simplicity means the following:

- A code that runs all the tests.
- A code that has no duplication.
- A code that defines the programmer's purpose clearly.
- A code that has minimal classes and methods.

XP advocates argue that coding is the core part of system development process. Ideally, coding must be as simple as possible while passing all tests. Subsequent tests make the code behave according to the necessary requirements. Frequent refactoring of the code will help to present it as a simple code. Coding is used to find out the most appropriate solution for the programming problems. Coding involves drawing diagrams that generate code, scripting a web-based system, or designing and developing a program that needs to be compiled.

The customer is the major driving force in XP. In XP, it is necessary to meet the customer needs as simply as possible. The developers must aim to reduce complexity when they begin the coding. Each code should be refactored frequently to make it simpler.

Continuous practice of simplicity requires developers to invest their time in identifying customer's need. As a developer, first do what you need to do to solve the current problem. Implement the code and make it work. At the final stage, you can refine the code.

In XP, the word 'simplest' is left vague. The developers should decide the appropriate choice in each situation. The simplest may be the use of a library or reuse of code present elsewhere in the system. It can also be refactoring a portion of the code into a reusable class to use for the current task. Refactoring refers to a group of techniques for identifying unnecessary code. It is a disciplined technique that restructures the code by changing only its internal structure without modifying its external behavior.

Writing a simple code does not imply that you have to code based on the first idea that strikes your mind. Looking out for the simplest solution is difficult. It is fine to begin coding with a simple style. Later, you can refactor it to identify the unnecessary code. You can simplify the solution more when you come up with a better idea.

If you develop the habit of estimating the future needs, writing simple code will be easy for you. Follow the story cards and task cards (discussed in the unit 'Extreme Programming Artifacts'). The developer should have clear idea of the requirements. If there are gaps in the stories, the developer should get it clarified by the customers. A simple code is easier to understand and test. A code of some ten lines is easy to understand than a code of hundred lines.

Test-driven development generates simpler code which is easier to improve. Test-driven development helps to achieve simplicity of implementation. Every line of code must be tested and if the test can be successful without a particular line, that line can be deleted. The test that is supposed to be performed on the code needs to have simple steps and it should test one feature at a time. The code should be simple enough to pass the current test. Refactoring is used to simplify the code.

Consider a queue system. If the queue holds only five items, the items can be hardcoded in get_items(). Add flexibility to contain more items only if a failing test prompts you to do so. A test that checks for more items should be added only when the task card prompts you to do so. You will realise that your code can still be made simpler.

Once the current test passes, check whether you can refactor the code. Check whether you have a duplicated code elsewhere. When all the tests run successfully, the code design can be improved largely.

XP allows you to make design decisions at any time. The design will be clearer with every new story. With every implemented task, you will get more chances to refactor. XP produces systems that are simple enough to be changed. In XP, you can write code that can be modified to meet the user needs as they become known.

A simple code will have the following four subjective qualities:

- **Testable -** You can write unit tests and acceptance tests to test the code.
- **Understandable -** If your team has been working for a system since a long time, your team will not find it difficult to understand the code. In this case, your understanding level will be good than someone who is new and completely baffled.
- **Browsable -** This is the quality of being able to find what you want at the right time. Using good names for functions and other elements will help you find things easily. Polymorphism, delegation, and inheritance makes your work simpler.
- **Explainable -** A team working from a long time can easily understand a code than new people. Hence explaining already existing code to new people is also a quality.

There are some problems with simplicity, mostly to the effect that the simplicity may not hold up and may be difficult to fix later. These problems can be overcome by some facts and XP practices. The facts relate to the characteristics of well-factored objects that can behave according to different functions. When behavior of an object needs to be modified, it is not difficult to do so because you need to modify the object only in one place. There might be problems due to code that is not encapsulated. It happens if you do the simplest thing and leave the unnecessary code. The redundant code can be eliminated by a rule known as 'RefactorMercilessly'.

Many tools are available for refactoring. Some of the features of such tools are:

- The ability to rapidly find the occurrences of fields, methods, and classes. This ability will help you estimate the effects of changing a code.
- The ability to automatically rename fields, methods, classes, and other constructs and update the same in all references.
- The ability to automatically convert a selected piece of code into a method call. This conversion is called as 'extract method' in most of the tools.

Expert programmers are very good at implementing superior solutions using simple code. This is an indication that simplicity is harder than complexity. It takes time to develop the habit of simplicity.

Activity 1:

Assume that you are asked to code an enhancement for a feature that asks for a password for logging into an application. The enhancement must not only accept a password, but also a security key of 16 digits. You need to implement this enhancement by coding in a simple way. What measures will you take to code it?

(Hint: Refer section 21.2 for detailed guidelines)

21.3 IMPLEMENT ONLY THE NEEDED FEATURES

"You Are not Gonna Need It" (YAGNI) is an XP practice that states that we must implement the features only when we actually need them, and not when we think that we may need them. It is risky to do future work because the requirements may change in the future. Spending too much time and resources on one feature results in lesser time and fewer resources for other features. Therefore, it is essential to implement only the required features.

Even if you are sure that you will need a feature in the future, do not implement it now. Usually, that feature may turn into a feature that is not at all required or a feature that is quite different from what you thought of adding in the future. This does not mean that your code should not be flexible to add new features. It means that you should not waste resources by doing tomorrow's work.

There are two advantages of practicing YAGNI. They are:

- It saves time because you avoid writing code for a feature that may not be needed in the future.

- It makes the code simpler because you avoid adding some code with guesses that it may be of no use but still remains in the system.

Building extra flexibility comes from two motivations - fear and desire to work on interesting things. Let's discuss the first motivation that is, fear.

Many software projects are brittle and inflexible and a simple bug may have indirect effects throughout the codebase. Practicing XP with discipline can help to overcome the fear of bugs. Testing the code will allow you to modify it according to the requirements and refactoring makes it flexible. Coding in a simplest way will produce understandable and changeable code.

The second motivation is the desire to work on interesting things. Exploring the latest and greatest library or coding a complicated new algorithm can be exciting. However, writing code for an unrequested and unscheduled feature undermines the customer's business authority.

Anticipating future needs may result in a loss of time twice. First, time that is spent on development for creating a general feature takes more time. Time will also be lost when a foreseen feature is unused. The customer's requirement may change unexpectedly and the feature that was very important may be rendered completely unnecessary.

As unnecessary features make the code complicated, it is good to delete them. Most of the time, the unnecessary code will remain entrenched and requires time to work on it. The code becomes complex if a new feature gets added. A complex code needs more tests, refactoring, and maintenance.

Trust the customer to determine the important features when they are required. Solve any coding issues then and there and give importance to testing, coding, and refactoring features that benefit now. Simple and well factored code makes it easy to make any changes in the future. Add features when you need and refactor them as if they would always be there.

Customers specify the required features and programmers work on those features first. Once a new feature is implemented, the work is delivered to customers and they will provide an immediate feedback. In this customer-centric approach, there will be short time for design and analysis. The schedule cannot afford to develop complex code to include every required feature. If any of these two things happens during a project, the customer may not get the correct working code on time.

Customer's immediate feedback on the developed feature is very important. If there is a delay in getting the feedback, there will be more chances of developing wrong features. The best developers will not worry much about developing framework; instead they will be worried more about what needs to be done currently along with the extensive tests. The developed code may not be required at all but it can be resolved later using refactoring.

When you complete developing a feature and move on to next, do additional design work for the next feature only if necessary. As the code can change over time, the original design documents may not be useful. The next thing you need to do is to perform unit tests on developed code.

XP cannot be complete without unit tests. The unit tests check the code for correct functionality. Tests also enable programmers to confidently make changes to any piece of code. Modifying code written by someone takes courage because you may not be familiar with the code.

21.4 ELIMINATE REPETITION

Every piece of code within the system should be represented in a single well-known place. It is essential to avoid repetitions in XP. Many programming concerts like loops can be used to avoid repetitions.

In software engineering, 'Once and Only Once' is the rule for achieving refactoring. This rule applies to code and design concepts. Andy Hunt and Dave in their book 'Pragmatic Programmer' suggest a different rule known as 'Do not Repeat Yourself (DRY)'. This rule applies to code, design, and other concepts of project. Eliminating duplication will avoid maintenance problems, poor factoring, and logical contradictions. Thus it is strongly suggested to avoid duplication and repetition which is also stated in the DRY (Don't Repeat Yourself) rule. The DRY rule states that "Every piece of knowledge must have a single, unambiguous, authoritative representation within a system." Duplication may occur in design, analysis, code, or documentation. Duplication leads to bad code.

The DRY software design rule is one of the coding standards defined in the book "Extreme Programming on rethinking programming practices for managers, customers and programmers." The DRY rule came into existence with the idea that 'the standard should lead to minimum work possible and be consistent with avoiding duplication.'

XP clearly brings up the picture of extreme sports and repetition can also be considered as a physical exercise because coding is a physically exhausting work. Repetition is the main cause of software problems for most of the programmers.

When the DRY rule is applied successfully, a modification of any piece of code in the system can be done without affecting other logically unrelated elements. Some of the reasons for code duplication or repetition are:

- Writing different methods or classes that are the same except that they operate on different data types.
- Writing same methods in different classes.

Code duplication is unnecessary and can cause major maintenance problems. Some of the problems of code duplication are:

- **Comprehension difficulty** - *Code duplication results in long repetitive sections of code that differ in few lines or characters. The length of such code makes it difficult to understand the code easily.*
- **Purpose masking** - *The duplication of largely identical code that varies only in a few parameters can hide the purpose of different sections of the code.*
- **Update anomalies** - *Code duplication contradicts a basic principle of database theory - avoids repetition. Code duplication adds on to anomalies which increase maintenance costs.*
- **File size** - *Code duplication results in lengthy code and the file occupies more space on the computer.*

Code repetition and duplication result in inertia. It takes longer to make changes that require modifying different pieces of code. It becomes more complex if the logical flow is scattered throughout the code. Comprehensive tests may fail to help you identify whatever changes you want to update in the code.

The practice 'Once and Only Once' suggests identifying and eliminating complexity. The code becomes robust and easily extensible when concepts are expressed only once. The performance of the code becomes better when we avoid unnecessary duplication. The phrase 'You Are not Gonna Need It' recommends against adding complexity. It is not possible to identify all complexities and duplications in advance, so refactor it when you identify them.

It is wise to know when to reduce duplication. The first time you write some code, leave it as simple as possible. Second time, if you are writing the same code, refactor it just to eliminate the duplication. If you are writing the same code for the third time, you will probably know how to generalize the code for different conditions.

The phrase 'Once and Only Once' applies not only to code but also to every process. If a process is worth automating, do it. If you have to perform a task repetitively, script it. Scripting can be anything from creating header files to logging integration failures. The phrase is also applicable to documentation and other written artifacts. The tests and code represent the business knowledge of the project. The tests help you identify what the code should do and the code describes how it should be done. Any further documentation should complement this knowledge and not duplicate this.

XP appreciates code that is easy to modify and maintain. Rigorous testing and simplicity generates small, loosely coupled units of code. Refactoring brings cohesion. In spite of changes in the code structure, adjustments can be done to achieve project design. Eliminating duplications and repetitions makes this process faster.

Code repetition can also be an opportunity for refactoring. It indicates that your code can still be simpler and generalized.

Any programming language which does not provide good facilities to reduce duplication should be considered harmful. In the 80s, the keyword 'Subclassing' was used to remove duplication but today it is considered a performance killer. Now the software designers follow constructs called 'patterns'.

The weakness of XP is that there is no master plan for a whole team to follow. Each pair of programmers implements features according to their user stories. There is no communication with the other pairs. Hence, they are not aware of the user stories of the other pairs. It is essential to remove repetition in all parts of the code as soon as they are discovered.

21.5 SUMMARY

Let us recapitulate the important concepts discussed in this unit:
- Making any changes to the code over the lifetime of a project is very expensive. This is even more expensive in the design phase.
- Making any changes in the coding phase is difficult because you need to modify the code.
- Ideally, coding is done as simple as possible along with all the tests. Subsequent tests ensure that the code works as per necessary requirements.

- Writing a simple code will be easy if you follow story cards and task cards.
- Most software designers consider simplicity of design as a basic software principle.
- The four subjective qualities of simplicity are:
  o Testable
  o Understandable
  o Browsable
  o Explainable
- A simple code is easier to understand. Test and test-driven development generates simpler code.
- Avoid implementing features that may be needed in the future. It will save and make the code simpler.
- A flexible code can be developed from two motivations - fear and desire to work on interesting things.
- Anticipating future needs may result in effort being wasted and loss of time.
- Unnecessary features make the code complex, it is good to eliminate them.
- Customer's immediate feedback on the developed feature reduces the chances of developing wrong features.
- Code repetitions or duplications can be avoided by using other programming structure like loops.
- The 'Do not Repeat Yourself' (DRY) rule states that "Every piece of knowledge must have a single, unambiguous, authoritative representation within a system."
- The application of DRY rule helps to modify any piece of code in the system without affecting other logically unrelated elements.
- Some of the problems of code duplication are:
  o Comprehension difficulty
  o Purpose masking
  o Update anomalies
  o File size
- XP recommends code that is easy to modify and maintain.
- A harmless programming language will provide good facilities to reduce duplication.

21.6 GLOSSARY

Encapsulation: The inclusion of a piece of code within another code so that the included code is not apparent.

Story cards: The cards which are used by the customers to write the details of the user story or of a feature.

Task cards: The cards created for the individual programmers for smaller units of a story.

22   Adopting XP

Structure

22.1   INTRODUCTION

In the previous unit, you were given an overview of coding in the Extreme Programming (XP) style. You also studied how functionality is balanced with simplicity. You learnt the importance of implementing only required features and eliminating repetitions.

Adopting XP means using practices that help the team improve its productivity in all possible ways. As the name suggests, it is a programmer-centric methodology that emphasizes on technical practices for promoting efficient development by frequently delivering working software. Many projects adopt XP in stages. Introducing XP gradually requires careful planning and thought. Some practices are risky and require the assistance and support of others. Organizations must look at the realistic results before committing to it completely. Before adopting XP completely, an organization must consider the strengths and weaknesses of the methodology.

This unit will familiarize you with the fundamentals and recommendations for adopting XP. You will learn the various practices in XP practices like eliminating fear and working together, starting feedback and including managers and customers.

Objectives

After studying this unit, you should be able to:

- provide an overview of adopting XP
- explain how XP helps to eliminate fear and work together
- describe the role of feedback in steering development
- explain the importance of including managers and customers in the team

---

22.2 BEFORE COMMENCING XP

As you already know, XP defines a set of values, principles and practices for quickly developing high-quality software that satisfies the customer in the shortest duration possible. Before adopting XP, it is always a good idea to discuss working agreements. You must discuss the practices the team will pursue and how the practice of XP will differ from the current practice. Before adopting XP, you must discuss your roles and what is expected from each team member. It is best to carry out these discussions as a collaborative team discussion.

There are some prerequisites and recommendations which must be met before you adopt XP. Meeting the prerequisites is more effective than working around limitations.

22.2.1 XP PREREQUISITES

The following are the prerequisites for adopting XP:

- Team agreement
- A collocated team
- On-site customers
- The right team size
- Use all XP practices

Let us now discuss these prerequisites.

Team agreement

The team's agreement to use XP is as important as management support. If team members do not want to use XP, it's not likely to work. XP assumes that each team member's willingness to adopt it. It is not a good practice to force the process on somebody who is resisting it.

A collocated team

XP relies on high-frequency and high-speed communication for most of its practices. To achieve that communication, the team members must sit together in the same room. The figure 22.1 represents the seating arrangement of a collocated team.

The seating arrangement of a collocated team is based on a 'caves and commons' approach. The objective of this approach is to provide people access to 'commons' where they can interact together, and 'caves' where they can work alone.

On-site customers

On-site customers are essential to the success of an XP team. They, led by the product manager, decide which features the team will develop. These decisions impact the value of the software. Therefore, the customer is part of the development environment. Having an on-site customer is the best way to get immediate feedback. When the customers are on-site they can answer queries immediately. When both customer and developers are guided by a reflective mode of thinking, they can improve their understanding of the software or application being developed. For example, when after some problem is corrected, the customer and the developers can reflect on their current understanding of the software or application and compare it with the understanding that preceded it.

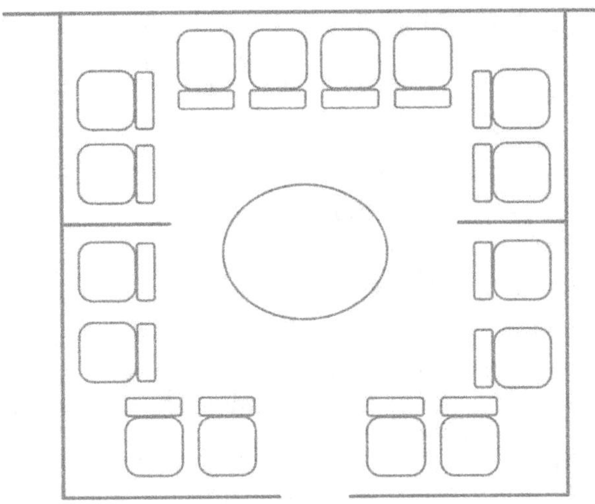

Figure 22.1 A Collocated Team

XP encourages short release cycles. Consider the problems when the customer only sees new releases of the software every few months. If there is considerable time in between feature releases, the customers cannot give real-time feedback to the programming team. Months of hard work may go waste if customers change their minds, or if the programmers do not deliver what is expected by the customer.

The Right Team Size

According to the proponents of XP, certain factors make some projects well suited for this methodology. The first major issue is the size of the team. In general, XP is most effective in cases where small teams, of usually two to 12 programmers, are involved. Small teams are more flexible, and better able to adapt to changes than 50 or 100-person programming giant teams.

An XP team cannot just have one member. It needs an even number of programmers due to the XP concept of pair programming. To use this approach, pair the team. Each pair must share a single computer and each person in the pair must focus on a different angle of the problem. While one developer types and actually applies and implements the code, the second developer must check for syntax and spelling errors. The other developer must understand how the current module that is being developed fits into the whole work. The two developers in the pair alternate their roles as required and brainstorm on the best approach to a particular problem.

Teams with less than four programmers may not have the intellectual diversity needed. They will also have difficulty using pair programming, which is a significant support mechanism in XP. However, large teams face challenges of coordination. Although experienced teams can handle those challenges efficiently, a new XP team may experience difficulties in the beginning.

Use all XP practices

XP utilizes all the resources of the project efficiently. It also ensures that every practice directly contributes to the development of valuable software.

The recommended practices of XP are as follows:

- A brand-new codebase
- Strong design skills
- A language that is easy to refactor
- An experienced programmer-coach
- A friendly and cohesive team

Let us now discuss these practices in brief.

A brand-new codebase

XP teams try to keep the code clean, straightforward and easy to change. This is easy to do if you have a new codebase. If a team has to work with an existing code, it can still practice XP, even though it may be difficult.

Strong design skills

Simple, upfront and easily changed design is XP's main enabler. This implies that at least one person from the team -- preferably the leader of the team -- must have good and strong design skills.

A language that is easy to refactor

XP relies on refactoring to constantly improve existing designs. Any language that makes refactoring difficult will make XP difficult.

An experienced programmer-coach

An XP team needs a coach. The finest coaches are natural leaders- they are the people who make others in the team do the right thing by virtue of who they are rather than due to the orders they give. The coach must be an experienced programmer to assist the team with the technical practices of XP.

A friendly and cohesive team

XP necessitates that everybody must work together to meet the team goals. There is no provision for someone to work in isolation. Therefore, a friendly atmosphere is necessary for team members to enjoy working together.

22.2.2 APPLYING XP IN A PHASE-BASED ORGANIZATION

The exact approach of XP to use depends on the organization. Phase-based organizations must adopt the following practices in the different phases:

- *Planning phase* - Organizations may have a planning phase that anticipates delivering a detailed plan. Organizations must allocate sufficient time for the planning phase and use it to run for actual iterations. This will enable the team to formulate a good plan and produce efficient software.
- *Design phase* - XP adopts the use of incremental design and architecture that is coupled with programming with test-driven development. Therefore, a design phase in the beginning stages of the project adds little value to an XP approach.
- *Coding phase* - Coding phase is where XP fits very well. To conduct XP as usual, organizations must break the coding phase into one-week iterations.
- *Testing phase* - XP performs a lot of testing in each iteration. A phase-based organization that considers XP to be the coding phase and expects a long testing phase may allot too little time for coding and more time for the testing process. However, testing is an important part of XP and must continue to be incorporated.
- *Deployment phase* - With a good build, a developer must be ready to deploy at the end of any iteration. An organization can schedule the wrap-up activities of XP for the deployment phase.

In this way, XP can be used in all phases of the Software Development Life Cycle (SDLC).

> **Activity 1:**
>
> Assume that you are an XP practitioner. Your manager has asked you to prepare a report on the prerequisites and recommendations that you must have before you begin a new project. What are the important points that you will mention in your report? Give reasons to support your answer.

22.3 ELIMINATING FEAR AND WORKING TOGETHER

You have learnt that the four values of XP are simplicity, feedback, communication, and courage. Being with customers to get immediate feedback and talking to the programmers to get an idea about the software or application is essential in XP. It is also necessary to use simple design and programming practices, and simple methods of planning, tracking, and reporting. The XP team must test programs and practices and use the feedback to decide how to steer the project. Working together in this way gives the team confidence. It has been found that many practices in software projects are due to the fear of the unknown. That fear is reduced or eliminated by the high level of communication in XP. It has also been found that many practices in software projects are based on the fear of losing. XP prefers to focus on winning, by delivering what the customer wants, when the customer wants it, in the context of solid software engineering.

XP can be successful only when developers want to produce good quality software as a team. Team members must trust each other's ability and work. It is easier to do the right thing when all the co-workers are also doing the same. It is common knowledge that trust and honesty will dispel many fears and uncertainty that would otherwise slow down or sink the project.

When teams sit together, they can eliminate delays. This can greatly improve productivity. A field study of six collocated teams, found that sitting together doubled productivity and reduced the time to market to almost one third of the company's baseline. Although programming is the descriptive activity of software development, communication is the real key to software success. When team members sit close enough to each other, they can easily have quick discussions. Osmotic communication, which relies on team members overhearing conversations, is also encouraged.

Developing coding standards can actually bring developers together. A strong team will produce a small and functional set of community standards for all new codes which include refactoring. These standards serve as common vocabulary for developers to communicate. Well-defined standards make adopting the other XP coding practices easier.

Adopt a common vocabulary with the coding standards. XP relies heavily on communication. Design patterns use metaphors to communicate designs and design strategies. Similarly, features and stories are communicated through common names and ideas.

Coding standards and common vocabulary will develop with time. The team may start small but it must implement the common standards and vocabulary quickly. It is essential that the whole team is involved. The team members must agree on a few ground rules and decide on changes if necessary.

22.4   STARTING FEEDBACK

Any team can work efficiently if an effective feedback system exists within the team. Continuous feedback is one of the values that govern XP.

XP is extremely well-designed. All changes requested by the customer are reflected in the software. Adjustments are perceptible right away. The customer can give feedback and steer the development as needed. The customers can see their requirements or corrections implemented within weeks.

Programmers incorporate the changes requested by the customers every few hours, and receive code reviews and test results every few minutes. Users see revised versions every month or two.

Feedback also includes tracking and measuring the development life cycle to control the project. This helps to take corrective actions to prevent situations where the code complexity is high or time spent on a particular task has increased. Unlike the traditional system development method contact with the customer occurs in more frequent iterations.

Feedback helps to keep the team on the right track. Therefore, it is essential to ensure that feedback is obtained regularly. XP considers feedback to be more useful if it is given quickly. The time between an action and its feedback is an essential factor for learning and making changes.

Unit tests also help to contribute to the quick feedback principle. While coding, unit tests provide direct feedback about how the system reacts to the changes one has made. If the changes affect a part of the system that is not in the scope of the programmer who made them, that programmer will not notice the error. The probability that this error will appear when the system is in production is greater.

Feedback relates to the following dimensions of system development:

- *Feedback from the system* - By writing unit tests, or running periodic integration tests, programmers can obtain direct feedback from the state of the system after implementing changes.

- *Feedback from the customer* - The customer and the testers write the functional tests (also known as acceptance tests). This helps in getting concrete feedback about the current state of the system. To enable the customer to easily steer the development, the customer review is planned once in every two or three weeks.

- *Feedback from the team* - When customers come up with new requirements in the planning phase, the team directly gives an estimation of the time that it will take to implement the changes.

The significance of immediate, real world feedback should not be taken lightly. The project risk is reduced by taking iterative development to the extreme. The involvement of customers does not end at the planning phase so requirements errors are reconciled almost immediately. The programmers working in pairs strive for simplicity yet, they maintain the system's internal quality. The automated testing gives the feedback on how well the system is meeting its expectations.

Feedback is used by XP to have an integrated approach to obtain a solution, instead of trying to obtain the solution through a discontinuous process.

22.5 INCLUDING MANAGERS AND CUSTOMERS

It is very difficult to use XP in the face of opposition from management. XP requires the active support of the management. Managers must communicate regularly with those implementing XP in the organisation.

To practice XP as described, you will need the following:

- Pairing stations in a common workspace
- Exclusive allotment of the team members in the XP project
- A product manager, on-site customers, and integrated testers

Management help is required to meet all these requirements. The management also must ensure the following:

- The team must have authority over the entire development process, including builds, database schema, and version control.
- Compensation and review practices must correspond with team-based effort.
- New ways of demonstrating the progress and showing results must be accepted.
- There must be patience when the productivity is decreased while the team is still learning the techniques or practices.

The success of an XP team depends to a great extent on the presence of on-site customers. They, led by the product manager, decide which features the team will adopt and develop. In other words, the customer's decisions determine the value of the software.

In XP it is essential to get regular, direct customer involvement. This meets the XP values of sincerity and communication. It is a good idea to include the customer from the beginning of the project. If not, you can still improve your development process. Though some teams may use a customer proxy, there can be no substitute for an actual on-site customer. The manager may represent a customer, or find a customer representative who can sit through the project regularly. Without a real customer, it can be difficult to manage development and business concerns. However, the customer must keep business interests in mind and must have the final authority on business matters.

Including a customer helps everyone adjust to the idea of divided roles and responsibilities. The earlier this is done, the more effective it will be. Blurring business and technical responsibilities, especially story scheduling, can weaken the customer's investment. It is better to be clear about who makes which decisions.

With an on-site customer, the planning game is made more effective. Internally, the team can write its own stories and plan its own iterations within a larger milestone schedule. But, according to XP, the team must adjust to the customer's needs as quickly and flexibly as possible. The customers communicate their needs throughout the planning game.

Regular releases are also possible with an on-site customer. You can perform the planning game completely with on-site customers. The code is well-tested and is integrated regularly. You must start working in iterations and plan small and regular migrations. XP will be more effective and efficient this way.

22.6 SUMMARY

Let us recapitulate the important concepts discussed in this unit:

- For adopting XP there are some prerequisites and recommendations which must satisfied. They are:
  - Team agreement
  - A collocated team
  - On-site customers
  - Right team size
  - Use all the practices
- XP can be successful only when developers want to produce good quality software as a team.
- When the team works together, it eliminates the delays caused and improves productivity. Although programming is the descriptive activity of software development, *communication* is the real key to software success.

- A team can work efficiently if an effective feedback system exists within the team. Continuous feedback is one of the values that govern XP.
- Feedback helps to keep the team on the right track.
- It is very challenging to use XP if there is opposition from the management. XP requires the active support of the management.
- On-site customers are essential to the success of an XP team. On-site customers led by the product manager, decide which features the team will develop.

22.7 GLOSSARY

Iteration: The process of repeating a set of instructions a specified number of times or until a specific result is achieved.

Osmotic communication: Information flows into the background hearing of members of the team so that they pick up relevant information.

Prerequisites: Something required as a prior condition.

Refactoring: A disciplined technique for restructuring an existing body of code, altering its internal structure without changing its external behavior.

22.8 CASE STUDY

Adoption of XP by Infora Corporation

Infora Corporation, based in Cupertino, California, is a software retailer known for its security, utility and remote management technologies.

Internally, Infora used its solution centered process to manage software development. Infora acquired another security firm, Axent Technologies. Axent was already experimenting with XP at their laboratory based in American Fork, Utah. This made Infora also to decide to adopt XP.

The development team, which was working on a new Java-based security product code-named Orca, preferred to adopt XP over other heavy substitutes such as PSP (Personal Software Process). A level of support for XP at both management and developer levels had already been obtained, which simplified the selection of XP.

One of the XP practices was to have an on-site customer. This was clearly was a challenge when writing a commercial software product. The problem of the missing customer was resolved by an internal product manager who acted as a pseudo-customer for the team. Another Infora XP project had problems when the product manager was not collocated with the team. The team lacked clear direction though the issues were not technical in nature. The team struggled without clarity on what exactly the customer wanted.

Contd...

QA (Quality Assurance) was essential to the process at Infora. The role of QA in the XP project was predominantly two-fold: to provide user-centered feedback and to write acceptance tests. In keeping with XP values, the development team worked with QA to automate their tests into a complete suite.

Developers worked with their automated test tools, such as JUnit, and were intent on code-level tests. However, these programmer-friendly tests did not always satisfy QA. Hence, the team produced detail defect reports in XML. These were then translated into graphs and summary form. Whenever possible, QA began to specify tests to ease part of this tension between test results produced by developers and to ensure useful output.

Result

XP seemed appropriate to the software-engineering culture at Infora with its explicit development practices and lightweight process requirements. Senior management buy-in and support was a key factor in the adoption rate and success of XP at Infora. Against all odds, the team completed the project successfully.

Lessons Learned

Infora learnt the following lessons after adopting XP:

- The team will lack direction and focus without an on-site customer.
- QA must be tightly coupled with the development team.
- Grass-roots support will smooth the transition to XP.
- For XP to be successful, management buy-in is crucial.
- Expect compromise between existing methodologies and XP.

Discussion Questions:

1. What were the problems faced by Infora Corporation while adopting XP?

2. What were the lessons learned by Infora Corporation after adopting XP?

Agile Modeling with XP

Structure

23.1 INTRODUCTION

In the previous unit, you were provided an overview of adopting Extreme Programming (XP). You studied how to eliminate fear and work together in an XP environment. You learnt how continual feedback from the customer helps to make the team more effective. You also learnt the importance of including managers and customers in the XP team.

Agile Modeling (AM) is a practices-based software process developed to explain how to model and document in an effective and agile manner. One of the major goals of AM is to address the issue of how to implement modeling techniques on software projects by adopting an agile approach such as Dynamic Systems Development Method (DSDM), extreme Programming (XP), and Scrum.

XP covers the complete development lifecycle because the scope of XP is much greater than that of AM. XP is considered to be a candidate 'base process' into which the methods of AM can be tailored. Moreover, even though XP clearly includes modeling as a part of its process, it does not clearly state how to do so.

In this unit, you will learn AM and its principles. You will become familiar with the differences between XP and AM. You will also be provided an overview of Scrum methodology.

Objectives

After studying this unit, you should be able to:

- explain Agile Modeling and its principles
- compare the performance of XP with Agile Modeling
- provide an overview of Scrum methodology

23.2 AGILE MODELING - PRINCIPLES

This section describes the principles of AM. AM describes a collection of core and supplementary principles that when implemented on a software development project set the stage for a collection of modeling practices. Some of the principles are adopted from XP. The AM principles are categorized into two types. They are:

- *Core principles -* These are the principles that you must adopt to be ready to implement the Agile Model Driven Development (AMDD) approach.

- *Supplementary principles -* These are the principles that you must consider fitting into your software process to meet the exact requirements of your environment.

Table 23.1 lists some core and supplementary principles of AM.

Table 23.1 Some Core and Supplementary Principles of AM

Core Principles	Supplementary Principles
Assume simplicity	Content is more important than representation
Embrace change	Open and honest communication
Enabling the next effort is your secondary goal	Everyone can learn from everyone else
Incremental change	Know your models
Maximize stakeholder ROI (Return on Investment)	Local adaptation
Model with a purpose	Work with people's instincts
Multiple models	
Quality work	
Rapid feedback	
Working software is your primary goal	
Travel light	

Let us now discuss the core principles first.

23.2.1 CORE PRINCIPLES OF AM

As shown in table 23.1, there are 11 core principles that an organization must completely adopt to claim that it is following agile modeling.

Assume simplicity

As development occurs, you must assume that the simplest solution is the best solution. You must not overbuild your software. Do not describe additional features in your models that are not currently required. You must have the confidence not to over-model your system and that you can model depending on your current requirements and refactor your system in the future according to the changes in the requirements. You must maintain your model as simple as possible.

Embrace change

Requirements eventually change and the understanding of the requirements also changes. As the project advances, project stakeholders may change, new resources may be added, and the existing ones may leave. Project stakeholders may also change their opinions which in turn, can potentially change the goals and success criteria of your efforts. As your efforts progress, the environment of your project changes and consequently your approach to development must reflect this change.

Enabling the next effort is your secondary goal

The project can still be considered a failure even when you deliver a working system to your users. One reason for meeting the requirements of project stakeholders is to ensure that your system is robust enough to extend gradually. Your next effort may include development of the next important release of your system, or it may be the operations and support of the current version being developed. To enable it, you need to develop quality software, adequate documentation, and supporting materials so that the next phase is more efficient. You must consider the following factors:

- The possibility of the members of your current team to be involved in the next phase.
- The nature of the next effort.
- The importance of the next phase to your organization.

Therefore in AM, even when you are currently working on your system you must also consider future requirements.

Incremental change

You must understand that in modeling you may not be perfect the first time. You do not have to capture every detail of your model. Instead of attempting to build an encompassing model at the beginning, develop a small model or a high-level model and then develop it over time in an incremental way.

Maximize stakeholder Return on Investment (ROI)

Project stakeholders invest resources such as money, time, and facilities to enable the team to develop software that meets their requirements. Hence, it is the responsibility of the team not to waste the resources and ensure that the project benefits stakeholders.

Model with a purpose

Most of the developers are concerned if their artifacts including source code, models, or documents are sufficiently detailed, too detailed, or accurate. These concerns arise because they have not taken a step back to analyze the purpose for creating the artifact and their audience. With regard to modeling, you must:

- Understand the aspects of your software in a better way.
- Convey your approach to the senior management to defend your project.
- Develop documentation that explains your system to those who will be operating, maintaining, or developing it in phases.

Your initial step must be to recognize a valid purpose for developing a model and the audience for that model. Based on the purpose and audience, you must develop it so that it is detailed and accurate. After the model has met its goals, you must start writing code to prove that the model works. This principle is also applicable when you make a change to an existing model.

Multiple models

Since every model explains a single aspect of the software, you must employ multiple models to develop the software. The complexity of modern software makes it necessary to have an extensive range of techniques for a modeling toolkit to be effective. You need not develop all the agile models for any given system. However, based on the exact nature of the software you are developing you may need at least a subset of the models.

Quality work

No one likes careless work. It becomes difficult for the resources to understand and update the work while refactoring. Similarly, the end users do not like such work because it is not robust and cannot meet their expectations.

Rapid feedback

The time period between an action and the feedback on that action is important. By working with other people on a model, particularly with a shared modeling technology (including white board, Class Responsibility Collaboration (CRC) cards, or necessary modeling substances like Sticky Notes), you may receive immediate feedback on your ideas. Opportunities for rapid feedback are provided when you work closely with your customer to understand the requirements, to analyze those requirements, or to develop a user interface that fulfills their requirements.

Working software is your primary goal

Generating high-quality working software that fulfills the requirements of your project stakeholders efficiently is the primary aim of software development. The primary goal is not to create irrelevant documentation, irrelevant management artifacts and models. Any action that does not directly contribute to this goal must be questioned and avoided if it cannot be justified appropriately.

Travel light

All the artifacts that you create and then decide to keep must be maintained eventually. If you decide to keep six models, then whenever there is a change (regarding updating of requirement, or adoption of a new approach or new technology by a team) you must consider the impact of that change on all six models and then act accordingly.

If you decide to keep only four models then it is obvious that you have less work to do to implement the same change. This makes your work more agile because you are traveling lighter.

The individual model is 'heavier' and is hence more of a burden to maintain. Therefore, if your models are more complicated or detailed, it is likely that any given change will be difficult to implement.

23.2.2 SUPPLEMENTARY PRINCIPLES OF AM

Sometimes, an organization may not be ready to adopt the core principles. If an organization is non-agile, then adopting the core principles at once may be difficult. Such organization may prefer a gradual adoption of AM.

As shown in table 23.1, AM has six supplementary principles that you can adopt to formulate an AM version that meets your requirements.

Let us now discuss the supplementary principles of AM.

Content is more important than representation

Any given model can have numerous ways to represent it. For example, a User Interface (UI) specification can be developed as:

- Post-It notes on a large sheet of paper (an important or low-fidelity prototype).
- Sketch on paper or a whiteboard.
- 'Traditional' prototype developed using a prototyping tool or programming language.
- Formal document with both visual representation and a textual description of the UI.

A model is not necessarily a document. Even a complex set of diagrams, drawn using a CASE (Computer-Aided Software Engineering) tool, need not be part of a document. You can instead apply them as inputs for other artifacts or source code. But these are not formalized as official documentation. Therefore, you can take the benefits of modeling without incurring the expenses of creation and maintenance of documentation.

Open and honest communication

Your resources must feel to offer suggestions. Their communication can include:

- Ideas relating to one or more models. A suggestion may be a new method to approach a portion of the design or have a new thought regarding a requirement.
- Delivery of bad news of being behind schedule.
- Current status of the work.

Open and honest communication also helps people to make proper decisions.

Everyone can learn from everyone else

Agile modelers realize they can never really master something. They recognize that there is always a chance to learn more and to increase their knowledge level. They make use of opportunities to work with and learn from others. They try doing things in new ways, and analyze what works and what does not.

Know your models

Since several models are available for agile modelers, it is essential that they know their strengths and weaknesses to successfully use them. A person need not be an expert in all modeling techniques. However, it is essential that they are aware about these techniques and be eventually prepared to learn more.

Local adaptation

It is very uncertain that an individual can 'use AM out of the box'. It may be necessary to alter AM to reflect the nature of the organization, the project stakeholders, and the project itself.

Work with people's instincts

The instincts of a resource become sharper with more experience in developing software. An individual's instincts guide a resource subconsciously and may often lead to a significant input to the modeling efforts.

23.3 COMPARING XP AND AGILE MODELING

You have learnt in the earlier units about XP. We have also discussed AM in the previous section. Let us now compare these programming practices.

XP is a group of practices that agree with the values and principles of Agile. XP is a discrete technique, while Agile is a classification. There are several agile techniques and XP is one of them. None of the agile techniques are as well defined or as wide in scope as XP. For example, Scrum is almost equivalent to XP's planning game practice, with components of Whole Team. Although there are discrepancies seen in the details, Scrum is still considered as a subset of XP. Most of the Scrum teams include many XP practices such as pair programming, acceptance testing, continuous integration, and test driven development to enhance their process. Of all the agile techniques, XP is the only technique that provides a structured discipline for the way developers perform their daily tasks. Test driven development practice of XP is the discipline that has great impact on the development process.

AM must be adapted into an existing, complete lifecycle methodology to enhance its strategy of modeling. Since modeling is a part of XP, AM can add value to an XP project. XP's practices of refactoring and test-first development help to achieve two important goals – promoting clean design and thinking through your design before developing code - that are usually associated with traditional modeling processes.

A major problem that needs to be addressed is how well AM correlates with XP. Table 23.2 lists the practices of AM. It either maps the AM practices to available principles or practices of XP or discusses the potential fit of an AM practice when it is not clearly a part of XP. Most of the practices map straight to XP because XP was employed as a foundation for AM.

Table 23.2 Cross-referencing AM and XP Practices

AM Practice	Correlation with XP
Active stakeholder participation.	This practice is equivalent to the XP practice of having an on-site customer.
Apply modeling standards.	This practice is similar to XP's 'coding standards' practice.
Apply patterns gently.	This practice is in conformance to XP's 'simple design' practice.
Apply the right artifact(s).	This practice does not directly relate to any XP practice.
Collective ownership.	AM has employed XP's 'collective ownership' practice.
Consider testability.	This practice is related to the XP testing practice.
Create several models in parallel.	This practice is not directly related to any XP practice.
Create simple content.	This practice is complementary to XP's 'simple design' practice that recommends the simple maintenance of project models.
Depict models simply.	This practice is complementary to XP's 'simple design' practice which advises that a model need not be elaborate to be effective, For example, user stories.
Discard temporary models.	This practice matches XP's 'travel light' principle.
Display models publicly.	This practice matches XP's value of communication and principle of 'open and honest communication'. It also relates to XP's 'collective ownership' practice.
Formalize contract models.	This practice is not directly related to any XP practice.
Iterate to another artifact.	This practice is not directly related to any XP practice. However, it reflects the way in which practitioners of XP iterate between functioning with user stories, tasks, CRC cards, tests, and codes.
Model in small increments.	This practice promotes XP's iterative and increment approach to development. Both AM and XP have an evolving approach to development and not a Big Design Up Front (BDUF) approach.
Model to communicate.	This practice is modelling-specific. It reflects XP's and AM's 'open and honest communication' Principle.

Table 23.2 Contd...

AM Practice	Correlation with XP
Model to understand.	This practice is modelling-specific. This practice is consistent with XP's existing application of CRC cards to determine design issues.
Model with others.	This practice is the AM version of the 'pair programming' practice of XP.
Prove it with code.	This practice is the AM version of the 'concrete experiments' principle of XP.
Reuse existing resources.	This practice is not directly related to any XP practice.
Update only when it hurts.	This practice reflects the 'travel light' principle of AM and XP. It suggests that you must update an artifact only when required.
Use the simplest tools.	This practice reflects the 'assume simplicity' principle AM and XP. It is consistent with XP's choice of low-tech tools like index cards for modeling.

From table 23.2, it is evident that we have a good alignment of value, principle, and practice between XP and AM.

23.4 SCRUM METHODOLOGY

Let us now discuss another subset of Agile Methodology – the Scrum methodology.

Scrum methodology is a popular project or program management strategy. Scrum methodology is iterative (manufacturing of product takes place during the small cycles known as iterations) and incremental (product's functionality increases in each iteration by addition of new properties). The Scrum process is divided into three phases -- pre-game, game and post-game.

Scrum is a process template regularly used to supervise projects and manage difficult tasks. Agile software development normally complements Scrum, thereby promoting teamwork and self-organization.

History of Scrum Methodology

In 1986, Hirotaka Takeuchi and Ikujiro Nonaka explained a new approach to product development where all the stages of the processes overlap and the team work together across different stages.

In 1991, DeGrace and Stahl in 'Wicked Problems, Righteous Solutions' named this approach as Scrum (which is a term in rugby).

Ken Schwaber introduced the Scrum methodology into some companies in the early 1990s. For the first time, Jeff Sutherland, John Scumniotales and Jeff McKenna termed it as Scrum. Jeff Sutherland and Ken Schwaber explained Scrum in 1995 and presented the results at OOPSLA (Object-Oriented Programming, Systems, Languages and Applications) in Austin. Ken Schwaber and Mike Beedle composed the book 'Agile Software Development with Scrum' in 2001.

In the software industry, the Agile Methodology is not new for most of the developers. They know that Agile was a direct response to the Waterfall Project

Management model. Agile borrows several principles from the Lean Manufacturing technique.

In 2001, the agile project management model eventually started to gain momentum and was made official when 17 pioneers met at the Snowbird Ski Resort in Utah and issued the Agile Manifesto. Their manifesto is now regarded as the fundamental text for agile practices and principles. The manifesto significantly explained the philosophy behind Agile, which emphasizes on communication and collaboration, working software, and the flexibility to adapt to evolving business realities. However, the Agile Manifesto failed to provide the concrete methods that development teams depend on when deadlines and stakeholders start to pressurize. Hence, when it comes to the process of running a team with Agile regularly, organizations opt for particular subsets of the agile methodology. Some of the subsets of agile methodology include XP, Crystal Clear, Dynamic Systems Development Method (DSDM), Feature Driven Development (FDD), Scrum, etc. Among all these subsets, Scrum is considered an extremely effective management methodology for all the people involved in the project management, along with developers and stakeholders.

Scrum is a unique methodology when compared to all the other Agile methodologies because it brings the concept of 'empirical process control'. In Scrum, projects are divided into concise work cadences, termed as sprints, which normally have duration of one to three weeks. Towards the end of each sprint, the team members and stakeholders meet to evaluate the progress of a project and also plan the next steps. This helps to adapt or re-orient a project's direction based on the completed work, and not on assumption or predictions. The importance given to an ongoing evaluation of completed work is mainly responsible for its popularity with managers and developers alike. The functioning of Scrum methodology takes place with the help of set of roles, responsibilities and meetings that do not vary. If Scrum's ability for adjustment and flexibility makes it an appealing option, then the stability of its practices provides teams something to lean on when progress gets disorganized.

23.4.1 THE ROLES OF SCRUM

There are three major roles in Scrum as illustrated in figure 23.1. They are:

- Product owner
- ScrumMaster
- Team member

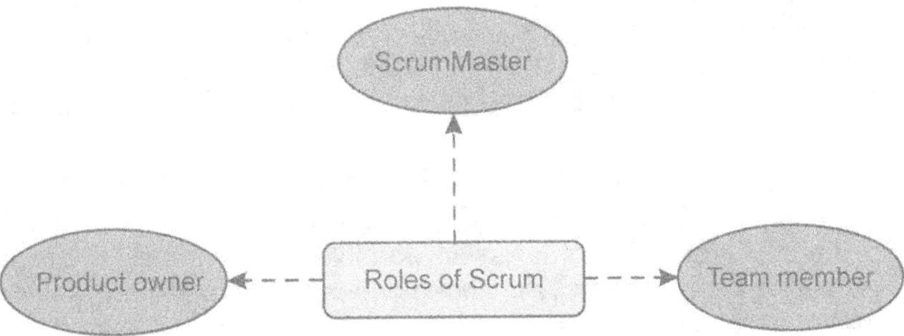

Figure 23.1 Roles of Scrum

Let us now discuss these roles in brief.

Product owner

The product owner in Scrum helps to communicate the vision of the product to the development team. The product owner also indicates the customer's interests through requirements and prioritization. The product owner's role is the role with the most responsibility. The product owner is the individual who must face the consequences if the project is not successful. The issues existing between authority and responsibility indicate that it is difficult for product owners to have the correct balance of involvement. A product owner must avoid micro-managing as Scrum emphasizes on self-organization in teams. However, product owners must be available to answer questions from the team.

ScrumMaster

The ScrumMaster is as a link between the product owner and the team. The ScrumMaster does not handle the team, but works to eliminate any barriers or hurdles that are obstructing the team from accomplishing its sprint goals. The role of the ScrumMaster enables the team to remain creative and productive, while ensuring its successes are visible to the product owner. The ScrumMaster also advises the product owner on gaining the maximum ROI for the team.

Team member

In Scrum, the team is responsible for completing the assigned work and preferably, teams comprise seven cross-functional members. In software projects, a typical team includes a combination of architects, analysts, programmers, Quality Analysts (QA), software engineers, testers, and User Interface (UI) designers. In each sprint, the team determines how it will accomplish the work that needs to be completed. This provides teams with autonomy to a great extent. However, like the product owner's situation, that freedom is accompanied by the role of meeting the goals of the sprint.

Let us now discuss the advantages the Scrum methodology offers project teams.

23.4.2 ADVANTAGES OF SCRUM

In any form of methodology, there are always positive and negative aspects of allocating a task or project to a set workflow. The precise nature of Scrum template varies from more conventional development methodologies, as the latter are only developed to consider and anticipate unpredictability of the external and development environments at the beginning of the enhancement cycle. There also exist innovative methodologies, like Spiral Boehm model. But, its variants are still limited because they are quite inflexible in their ability to respond to varying needs once a project has started.

Flexibility and adaptiveness as work requirements vary is one of the major advantages of Scrum methodology. It has control mechanisms for the planning phase of a product release and deals with variables as the project is executed. It implies that although the project can be changed and modified based on the varying requirements, yet it manages to establish and deliver the most appropriate release. This is due to the ability of Scrum to adjust work to varying expectations once the project is in progress.

Since the Scrum process also provides a great scope for individual tasks and contributions, developers are free to develop ideas and solutions. These ideas are normally pioneering and innovative as the team depends on the best possible formula to finish their task, and to complete the project as appropriately and effectively as possible. The Scrum model uses professionals to work effectively unsupervised within their own divisions. The influence of professionals also reveals tactic knowledge in the development process. Consequently, innovative work techniques may be less risky due to prior experience of the team members.

The Object Oriented approach to methodology is another major benefit of the Scrum model which recommends a discrete, dependable and manageable environment. Procedural code is not applicable to Scrum project management because the Scrum model is an extremely adaptive and flexible form of project management. Set approaches and intertwined interfaces are in variance with the nature of the Scrum model. Increased control over the variables does not conform with the purpose of the model. Scrum is a useful and exceptional approach to project management and efficient workflow due to its lack of external policy and procedure. It ensures work competency and is strongly based on the experience and dependability of the people involved. Scrum improves the efficiency of team members and provides greater scope for improvement of individual work ethics and innovation. Scrum obtains its basis from personal experience and strives towards future improvements in project management. Through this process, Scrum methodology may develop procedural systems within itself. Scrum continues to render a clean interface even if it is assigned as a procedural system. It is mainly based on data orientation and does not obstruct any methodological developments that may appear during successive projects.

Activity 1:

Assume that you are a project manager and you have decided to adopt Scrum methodology for your project. You must choose a resource to be the ScrumMaster. List the qualities you will expect in the ScrumMaster.

23.5 SUMMARY

Let us recapitulate the important concepts discussed in this unit:

- Agile Modeling (AM) addresses the issue of implementing modeling techniques on software projects by employing an agile approach.
- The AM principles are divided into two types -- core and supplementary principles. Core principles are the principles that you must adopt to be able to claim that you are prepared to implement Agile Model Driven Development (AMDD) approach. Supplementary principles must fit into the software process to meet the exact requirements of your environment.
- Core principles include simplicity, adaptation to change, incremental change, multiple models, etc. Supplementary principles include open and honest communication, recognition of your models, local adaptation, work with people's instincts, etc.

- Extreme programming (XP) is a group of practices that agree with the values and principles of Agile. XP is a discrete technique, whereas Agile is a classification.
- AM must be adapted into an existing and complete lifecycle methodology to enhance its modeling approach.
- There is a good alignment of value, principle, and practice between XP and AM.
- Scrum methodology is considered the most popular project or program management strategy. The three major roles of Scrum are: product owner, ScrumMaster, and team member.
- The Agile manifesto explains the philosophy behind Agile. It focuses mainly on communication and collaboration, working software, and the flexibility to adapt to evolving business realities.
- Flexibility and adaptiveness as work requirements vary is one of the major benefits of Scrum methodology.

23.6 GLOSSARY

Big Design Up Front (BDUF): A software development approach wherein the program's design is to be completed and perfected before that program's implementation is started.

CASE (Computer-Aided Software Engineering): A scientific application of a set of tools and methods to a software system which is used to produce high-quality, defect-free, and maintainable software products.

Class-Responsibility-Collaboration (CRC) card: An index card that specifies the responsibilities and collaborators of classes.

Lean manufacturing: A unified, comprehensive set of philosophies, rules, guidelines, tools, and techniques for improving and optimizing discrete processes.

Micromanage: To manage mainly with excessive control or attention to details.

Post-It note: A small colored piece of paper for short messages which can be stuck temporarily to something else.

Spiral Boehm model: A spiral model, also termed as the spiral lifecycle model, is a systems development lifecycle (SDLC) model used in information technology (IT) which combines the features of prototyping model and waterfall model.

Sprint: A set period of time during which specific work has to be completed and made ready for review.

Stakeholder: A person, group or organization that has direct or indirect stake in an organization and can affect or be affected by the organization's actions, objectives and policies.

Waterfall model: A sequential software development model wherein development is observed as flowing steadily downwards (like a waterfall) through several phases.

24 Dynamic Systems Development Methodology (DSDM)

Structure

24.1 INTRODUCTION

In the previous unit, you learnt Agile Modeling and its principles. You also compared the performance of XP with Agile Modeling. You were also given an overview of Scrum methodology.

Dynamic System Development Method (DSDM) is an approach to system development. As the name suggests, it develops the system dynamically. It is originally based on the Rapid Application Development (RAD) methodology. It is an iterative and incremental approach that clinches constant user involvement. It seems preferably suited for software development that consign a high importance on the user interface or usability aspects of products. Its goal is to deliver software systems on time and budget while adjusting for changing requirements along the development process. DSDM is one of the agile methods for developing software, and it forms a part of the Agile Alliance.

This unit familiarizes you with the concept of DSDM. You will analyze the various principles of DSDM. You will also learn the different phases of DSDM.

Objectives

After studying this unit, you should be able to:

- provide an overview of DSDM
- explain the principles of DSDM
- list the different phases of DSDM
- describe the core techniques used in DSDM

24.2 OVERVIEW OF DSDM

Dynamic Systems Development Method (DSDM) is a planned, well-organized, and realistic process aimed at delivering business solutions quickly and effectively. It is similar to SCRUM and XP in many ways, but it can be effectively used only in circumstances where the time requirement is fixed. DSDM focuses on delivery of the business solution, rather than just team activity. It ensures the feasibility and business sense of a project before it is created.

DSDM is based on Rapid Application Development (RAD). It concentrates on information systems projects that are characterized by tight schedules and financial plans or budgets. It tackles the most common breakdowns of information systems projects, including exceeding budgets, lack of user involvement, missing deadlines, and high-level-management obligation. Cooperation and collaboration between all interested parties are highlighted. DSDM makes extreme use of prototyping to make sure that the interested parties have a clear picture of all aspects of the system.

DSDM Roles

DSDM identifies the following basic roles that should be filled by members of the team:

- **Ambassador -** This refers to the person who acts as a mediator between the customer(s) and the development team. The ambassador directs the development team. Hence, the ambassador needs to have a good overall understanding of how the system works.
- **Visionary -** This refers to the person who keeps the project moving towards its goals and acts as a driving force behind the project. In general, the visionary is the one who has started the project or the one who conceived the project.
- **Advisers -** This refers to the people who are experienced in the area(s) of the business that has to be automated, and/or in the technologies that are required for automation of these areas.

The other roles that are defined by DSDM are:

- **Technical coordinator -** This refers to the person who coordinates the various technical features of the system and makes sure that all features interact smoothly and accurately.
- **Executive sponsor -** This refers to the person who can contribute the funds and resources to the project.
- **Project manager -** This refers to the person who supervises the progress of the project and is responsible for the creation of the prototypes.
- **Team manager -** This refers to the person who manages the people aspects of the team and ensures that the team functions smoothly as a unit.
- **Senior developer -** This refers to the person who has the knowledge and proficiency to convert the plans and requirements into deliverable code.

- **Facilitator -** This refers to the person who facilitates the smooth functioning of the functional areas of the team's work.
- **Scribe -** This refers to the person who documents the decisions, discussions, and plans made by the team.

Benefits of DSDM

DSDM offers the following advantages:

- Outcomes of development are directly and quickly visible.
- Users are able to have an effect on the project's direction.
- As the users are on-site and are actively involved during the development of the system, they are more likely to accept it.
- Basic functionality is delivered quickly and enhanced functionality is delivered at regular intervals.
- It eradicates bureaucracy and helps to overcome the communication barriers between the stakeholders.
- The system being developed is more likely to meet the need it was designed for because of constant feedback from the users.
- It gives early indications of whether the project will work or not.
- It ensures the delivery of system on time and within the estimated budget.

DSDM is very useful for the systems to be developed in a short time span and where the requirements cannot be stationary at the start of the application building. Whatever requirements are known at a time, the design for them is prepared and the design is developed and incorporated into the system.

24.3 THE PRINCIPLES OF DSDM

DSDM consists of nine basic principles. These principles form the cornerstones of development using DSDM and direct how development progresses. Ignoring any one of them will break with the frameworks philosophy and significantly increases project risks. The principles are as follows:

- Active user involvement is imperative.
- Teams must be authorized to make decisions.
- Focus on frequent delivery.
- Fitness for business objective is the key criterion for acceptance of deliverables.
- Iterative and incremental development is mandatory.
- Ability to reverse all the changes made during development.
- Baseline high-level requirements.
- Integrate testing throughout the life-cycle.
- Collaborative and cooperative approach.

Let us now discuss these principles.

Active user involvement is imperative

User involvement is the main key in running a well-organized and successful project. Both users and developers share a common workplace, so that the decisions are made collaboratively and quickly.

Teams must be authorized to make decisions

Ensure that the members of the team are authorized to take decisions that are important for the progress of the project, on behalf of those they represent without waiting for sophisticated approval.

Focus on frequent delivery

DSDM focuses on frequent delivery with the assumption that to deliver something 'satisfactory', earlier is better than to deliver everything 'perfectly' in the end. The product is rested and reviewed if the product is delivered frequently from an early stage of the project. The test record and review document is then taken into account at the next iteration or phase.

Fitness for business objective is the key criterion for acceptance of deliverables

The main criterion for acceptance of deliverables in DSDM is on delivering a system that deals with the current business needs. It is not so greatly focused at delivering a perfect system addressing all possible business needs, but focuses its efforts on critical functionality.

Iterative and incremental development is mandatory

DSDM allows systems to expand incrementally. The development is iterative and incremental, driven by users' feedback to run an effective business solution.

Ability to reverse all the changes made during development

To control the evolution of all products, everything must be in a known situation at all times. This is exclusive within the Agile approaches and necessitates a strong source control system.

Baseline high-level requirements

Ensures control and allows flexibility. This provides the DSDM team a better idea about the requirements and scope of the system at each level.

Integrate testing throughout the life-cycle

Integrated testing is crucial for the success and quality of the project. As the development proceeds incrementally, users and developers incrementally do the testing to check that the development is going in the right business and is technically correct.

Collaborative and cooperative approach

There must be a collaborative and cooperative approach between all the stakeholders.

Activity 1:

Assume that you are a DSDM practitioner. Your manager has asked to prepare a report on the principles that you have to follow and possess in a new project. What are the principles that you will mention in your report and why?

24.4 PHASES OF DSDM

The DSDM consists of three chronological phases namely the pre-project, project life-cycle, and post-project phases.

The project life-cycle phase of DSDM is the most sophisticated of the three phases. The project life-cycle phase consists of five stages. They are:

1. Feasibility study
2. Business study
3. Functional model iteration
4. Design and build iteration
5. Implementation

These five stages form an iterative step-by-step approach in developing an information system. The three phases and subsequent stages are extensively described in the following section.

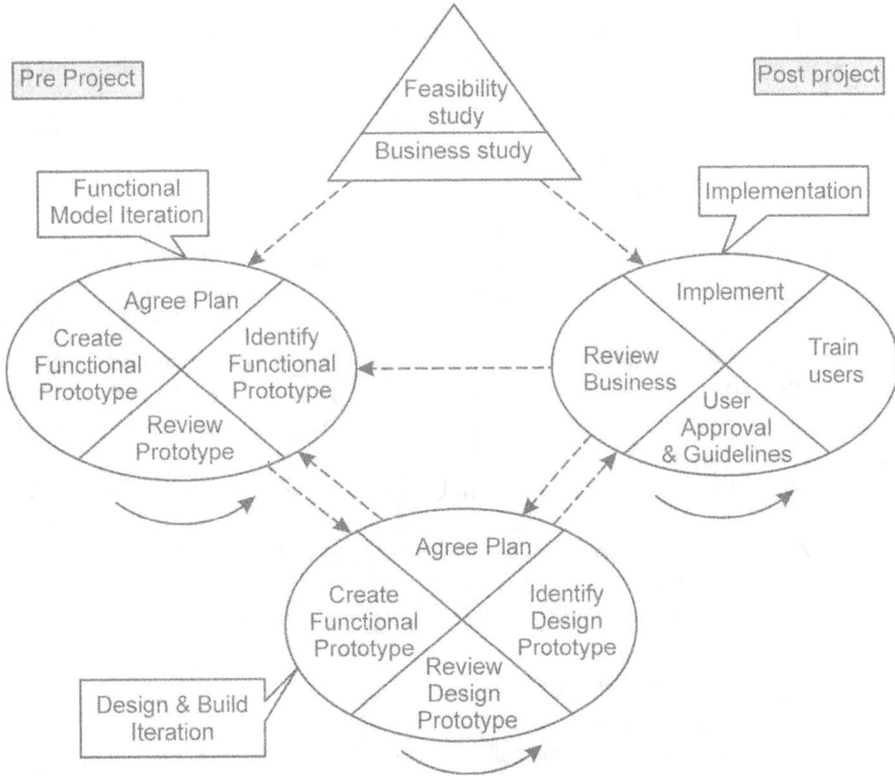

Figure 24.1 DSDM Life-cycle

Pre-project

Project suggestion and selection of a proposed project candidate are included in the pre-project phase. It ensures project commitment. The problems are handled at an early stage of the project to avoid issues at later stages.

Project life-cycle

The actual project occurs in this phase. This phase is divided into five stages. A project must go through all the five stages to create an operational system. The feasibility study and business study are the first two chronological phases that complement to each other. After these phases are achieved, the system is developed iteratively and incrementally in the functional model iteration, design and build iteration, and implementation stages. Figure 24.1 depicts the DSDM life-cycle.

- *Feasibility study* - In this phase, the initial project suitability is assessed, the problem is defined, and the feasibility of the desired application is verified. Apart from these routine tasks, it is also checked if the application is suitable for RAD approach or not. The development continues only if the RAD is found as an acceptable approach for the desired system. Feasibility reports, prototypes, high-level plans, and risk logs result from this phase. The feasibility report is a high-level report that enables the project routing group to decide on the project's potential, and any need for further feasibility study. Feasibility prototyping is a methodology of developing a prototype as a proof of concept.

- *Business study* - The business study stretches the feasibility study. After the project is accepted as feasible for the use of DSDM, this stage examines the influenced business processes, user groups involved, and their needs. The business study provides a base for all the subsequent work. This phase leads to a detailed outline of business processes affected and their information needs.

- *Functional model iteration* - This phase is incremental and iterative in nature. A functional model which consists of both working software prototype and static models are delivered in this phase. A high-level processing of information obtained in business study is the outcome of this phase.

- *Design and build iteration* - This phase refines the functional prototype developed in the functional model iteration phase to meet the functional requirements. This phase primarily develops a system to satisfy the user requirements. The major outcome of this phase is a tested product. Design and build iteration consists of the following four activities:

  o Find out the requirements of the module.
  o Plan and commit the requirements.
  o Develop the module.
  o Validate the functionality of the module.

  Design and build iteration phase results in a time box plan, design prototype, tested system, and test records. The technical issues are dealt with the design prototype. This does not include functional module activities. The final system which can be moved for operational use is a tested system. The test records have the statistics about product quality.

- ***Implementation*** - The last and final development stage in this methodology is implementation. The users are trained and the system is actually put into operational environment in this phase. The future development requirements are also framed. An incremental review document is used for illustrating planning activities for the subsequent increments.

Post-project

This phase ensures that the system operates effectively and efficiently. This is understood by maintenance, enhancements, and fixes according to DSDM principles. The maintenance is considered as continuing development based on the incremental and iterative nature of DSDM. Instead of completing the project in just one cycle, the project can return to the previous phases so that the previous step and the deliverable products can be improved.

According to this approach, time is taken as a constraint, that is, the time and resources are fixed while the requirements are allowed to change. This does not follow the basic assumption of making a perfect system the first time, but provides a usable and useful 80 percent of the desired system in 20 percent of the total development time. This approach has proved to be very useful under time constraints and varying requirements.

Activity 2:

Assume that you are a DSDM practitioner. Your project manager has asked to prepare a report on the different phases of DSDM and mention the objectives of each phase giving a small explanation.

24.5　CORE TECHNIQUES USED IN DSDM

The techniques featured within the DSDM framework are explained in terms of what is important and considerable when applying them in DSDM's business-centered development tactic in addition to providing practical assistance as to how and when they should be used in projects. The techniques of DSDM are as follows:

- Timeboxing
- Moscow
- Prototyping
- Testing
- Workshop
- Modeling
- Configuration management

Timeboxing

Timeboxing is used to support the key goals of DSDM to understand the development of an information system on time, within the budget, and with the preferred quality. The core idea behind Timeboxing is to divide the project into parts, each with a preset budget and delivery date. For each part, a number of requirements are chosen that are prioritized according to the MoSCoW principle. This is because, time and budget are presets and the only remaining variable is the requirements. That is, if a project is running short of time or money, the requirements with the lowest priority are discarded. This does not mean that an incomplete product is given away because of the Pareto principle (80–20 rule) that 80% of the project comes from 20% of the system requirements, so provided that those most important 20 percent of requirements are employed into the system, the system thus encounters the business needs.

Moscow rules

Prioritizing requirements are served in MoSCoW technique. It is an acronym that stands for:

- *MUST have* - All features classified in this group must be implemented and if they are not delivered, the system will not work.
- *SHOULD have* - Important but the project's success does not rely on this.
- *COULD have* - This requirement can be easily left out. It will not have any impact on the project.
- *WOULD have* - This requirement can be left out this time and done on a later date.

Prototyping

Prototyping technique refers to the formation of prototypes of the system under development at an early phase of the project. It allows future users to test the system by enabling the early sighting of faults in the system. Hence, a good user involvement is accomplished, which is one of the keys for the success of DSDM.

Testing

An important feature of DSDM is the establishment of an information system with high-quality. In order to achieve a solution of high-quality, DSDM supports testing in iterations. Since DSDM is a technique and a tool-independent method, the project team has the freedom to choose the test management methods on its own.

Workshop

Workshop is a fundamental technique used in DSDM. It is used to ensure that high-quality, team-based decisions are made quickly and efficiently within the expected small timelines. It also brings the stakeholders of the project together to discuss the requirements, functionalities, and mutual understanding of the project.

Modeling

Modeling technique is a means by which a pictorial representation of a particular feature of the system is developed. Modeling helps the DSDM development teams to gain a good comprehension of the system domain.

Configuration management

The implementation of configuration management technique is essential for the dynamic nature of DSDM. Since, there is more than one thing being handled at once during the development process of the system, and the products are being delivered frequently at a very fast rate, the products therefore, need to be controlled strictly as they achieve (partial) completion.

24.6 SUMMARY

Let us recapitulate the important concepts discussed in this unit:

- Dynamic System Development Method (DSDM) is an approach to system development. It develops the system dynamically.
- DSDM focuses on delivery of the business solution, rather than just team activity.
- It ensures the feasibility and business sense of a project before it is created.
- DSDM is based on the Rapid Application Development (RAD) methodology.
- The nine principles of DSDM are:
  - Active user involvement is imperative.
  - Teams must be authorized to make decisions.
  - Focus on frequent delivery.
  - Fitness for business objective is the key criterion for acceptance of deliverables.
  - Iterative and incremental development is mandatory.
  - Ability to reverse all the changes made during development.
  - Baseline high-level requirements.
  - Integrate testing throughout the life-cycle.
  - Collaborative and cooperative approach.
- The DSDM consists of three chronological phases, namely pre-project, project life-cycle, and post-project phases.
- The project life-cycle phase of DSDM is the most sophisticated of the three phases.
- The project life-cycle phase consists of five stages. They are:
  - Feasibility study
  - Business study
  - Functional model iteration
  - Design and build iteration
  - Implementation
- The post-project phase ensures that the system operates effectively and efficiently. This is understood by maintenance, enhancements, and fixes according to DSDM principles.
- The techniques of DSDM are as follows:
  - Time boxing
  - Moscow
  - Prototyping
  - Testing
  - Workshop
  - Modeling
  - Configuration management

24.7 GLOSSARY

Design prototype: It is a temporary protocol that deals with the technical issues.

Functional prototyping review document: It collects the users' comments about the current increment, working as input for subsequent iterations .This review document is used to update the risk log and prioritized requirements list.

Prototyping plan: The activities planned within the prototyping process that will be performed in the available time slots according to the schedule.

Test record: Record set of testing where the test script, test procedure, and test result are included. This test record is used to develop the functional prototyping review document and is also used indirectly to update the prioritized requirements list.

Timebox: A technique that allots a fixed period of time for an activity. Timeboxing plans an activity by allocating Timeboxes and is a distinctive feature of several unorthodox project management approaches.

24.8 CASE STUDY

Implementing DSDM by Southern Trust Investment Management

Background

Southern Trust Investment Management is one of the largest self-governing finance managers in the U.K. They wanted to further develop the finance management segment of its business. Hence, Southern Trust decided to develop the necessary processes, which would provide quick, detailed, and accurate information about individual client portfolios.

The challenge

Southern Trust had six months to implement the new processes, and they knew that user involvement is very indispensable. Active user involvement in the development process is one of the principles of DSDM. Similarly, Southern Trust turned to DSDM to ensure that it designed and delivered the right application. The overall intention was to develop a system whereby individual client portfolios are reviewed in a standard, professional manner.

The solution

The result was the Asset Manager project. An in-house development team was created, because it was felt this would better ensure the application fitted the business purpose. User involvement and prototyping were two of the most critical factors in the development process. The first release had to go through five prototype cycles during which it changed extensively in the process, which became more acceptable to users. Focus on iterative and incremental development is one of the principles of DSDM. This facilitates both the developers and the users to see how the system will work and to ascertain if the system meets the project requirements. The first release was up and running within 6 months.

Contd...

As the project moved forward, discussion with a lead user replaced the full-scale involvement with all the users in order to diminish the risk of overloading the feature set. However, the lead user consulted with the wider user community in order to ensure continuity of user involvement. Six months later, the second release went through three iterations before it was released. The accomplished project enabled the information to be extracted from the database that allowed the finance managers to supervise the key aspects of individual client portfolios, particularly allocation of assets and performance relative to the relevant standard. In addition, models could be applied in individual cases to determine the best possible investment combination according to the specific objectives set by the client.

Update

This update of how Southern Trust is continuing to use DSDM was provided by John Bennett (IT Services Director).

Southern Trust are now delivering Version 6 of the Asset Manager product, having incorporated many new functions and improved and extended the original components drastically. The system is currently used on a daily basis throughout the company and is an essential tool for the business in applying finance management process. The continuing development has reinforced the value of the DSDM approach and also highlighted some areas where extensions or modifications to the principles are necessary in this situation.

The nine principles of DSDM appear to be simply common sense at the first sight, but experience has revealed how important these are, and where the idea has had to be negotiated in the real world. How Southern Trust Investment Management has managed in implementing some of the principles is summarized below.

Active user involvement

This principle has been applied in two levels, neither of which conforms to the classic facilitated workshop approach. Mainstream strategic and infrastructure development has been determined by a compassionate dictatorship of one key business representative on each functional development. At the lower level, every single user is canvassed regularly for their opinions on the systems, and their requirements have been integrated, along the way to the extent that is possible, leading to a high level of perceived ownership by the users.

DSDM teams must be empowered to make decisions

This principle has been followed with no genuine problems, and it has contributed to a large extent for successful delivery.

Frequent delivery of products

Settled on a planning and delivery timescale based on periods, which is a refreshing modification from the nanoseconds that computing activity is normally measured in. This provides four very important deliveries per year, each one with an important functionality.

Fitness for business purpose

This has been a challenging cultural issue which we are still struggling to do better. IT and business sides both have this problem. IT Developers want to develop features, most of which will never be used in the lifetime of the system. The expectation is that anything less than a must have will never be delivered on the user side, so prioritization becomes difficult. Involvement with just one DSDM project gives the impression to overcome this issue splendidly.

Iterative and incremental development

Iterative and incremental development is necessary to the types of development that are suited to DSDM. The most valuable developments are in the new areas where the business prerequisite is not known in detail. It is also very important to allow for the world changing, as usually happens during the lifetime of any important development.

Testing is integrated throughout the process

Testing helps especially in ensuring fitness for purpose, but there is still no replacement for the traditional approach before a software release of system testing (to make sure all developments still work together), regression testing (to make sure that existing functions are not compromised by new developments), and stress testing (coping with transaction and data volumes).

Result

DSDM is an extremely feasible and beneficial methodology which achieves results and makes the process more agreeable for the participants. It is not easy and is not applicable to all projects. If it is applied positively and is applicable and involved by all, then DSDM works extremely well.

Discussion Questions:

1. What were the problems faced by Southern Trust Investment Management?

2. Briefly describe the background of Southern Trust Investment Management?

3. How did Implementing DSDM help Southern Trust Investment Management?

25 XP Tools

Structure

25.1 INTRODUCTION

In the previous unit, you were provided an overview of Dynamic Systems Development Methodology (DSDM). DSDM is an approach to system development that develops the system dynamically. You learnt the principles of DSDM and different phases of DSDM. You also analyzed some case studies on DSDM usage.

Java is an object-oriented programming language which handles graphics and user interface and can be used for creating applications. XP works well with Java because of the speed with which it compiles and its suitability for test-first approach. Recent Java open source tools will help developers during the difficult part of XP process-testing, integration, and deployment. XP tools optimize the performance of your computer and help you to customize your system.

In this unit, you will learn some XP tools. You will also learn different tools and philosophies. You will become familiar with Java tools and open source tools for XP.

Objectives

After studying this unit, you should be able to:

- explain why Java is a good choice for XP development
- analyze different tools and philosophies of XP
- describe open source tools for XP

25.2 JAVA AND XP

XP includes a set of principles and practices that guide software development. It is a language-independent software development approach. It mainly focuses on coding. It is an agile process, in that it makes every effort to eliminate unnecessary work. It focuses on tasks that deliver value to the customer.

Although XP can be used with any programming language, it works well with Java for specific reasons. One of the important reasons is the speed with which Java compiles. XP depends on test-first development. In this, the programmers write tests for code before they write the code. For each new feature you add, you should write a code, compile, and run the tests frequently. Java is well-suited for test-first approach because it compiles quickly.

Java is a good choice for XP development because Java has a number of tools that support unit testing and continuous integration. A lightweight framework for writing automated unit tests is provided by JUnit. Ant, a premier build tool for Java, enables continuous integration when working with large development teams. Testing tools such as Cactus and HttpUnit are also available for server-side testing.

The power and simplicity of Java make it a good language for writing codes using XP. The features of the tools such as Ant and JUnit are built based on the reflection capability of Java. Java's relatively easy syntax makes it easier to maintain code written by other team members, which is important for XP's concepts of pair programming, refactoring, and collective code ownership.

Another XP practice that is benefited by the use of good software tools is continuous integration. Continuous integration means the complete copy of the system is built several times in a day. This ensures that the system is ready to move out at any moment. We can also detect and fix defects early in continuous integration. The reasons for spending time and energy to achieve continuous integration are:

- **Visible progress** - Continuous integration affirms the unity of the team development effort. The entire development effort is concentrated on the built and tested system which acts as the center of gravity. As you know that once your code is checked into the repository, it is pulled into the main development stream. The state of working system is visible to everyone at anytime.
- **Reduced integration pain** - Continuous integration ensures that the incompatible partners meet within hours or minutes. The defects introduced by incompatible changes are solved. Continuous integration also forces the developers to examine why the defect has occurred in the first place.
- **Tests run frequently** - The integral part of a continuously integrated system is unit testing. The build is complete only when the unit tests pass the entire functional and integration test successfully. The test should be run frequently to provide a constant update of the system performance.

You need to automate the build, distribution, and deploy processes in order to facilitate continuous integration. Ant will help you to integrate with source control, Java compilation, creating deployment files, and automated testing. Ant sends mails groups to inform them about the tests that did not conform to the build and the tests that did not execute successfully.

Continuous integration performed using Ant will change the development blueprint of the project. It reduces the problem related with time spent for fixing integration bugs. Continuous integration implemented using Ant and JUnit often identifies bugs immediately once they enter into the system. It is easy to eradicate this bug as the code responsible for this bug is fresh in the mind of developers. The tasks which can be automated using Ant are:

- Obtaining source from configuration management system
- Compiling the Java code
- Creating binary deployment files
- Automating testing

25.3 TOOLS AND PHILOSOPHIES

In the previous section we discussed how Java tools works well with XP. Now you will learn different tools and philosophies. Creating software is an art. If you ask programmers to solve a particular problem, you will get different solutions from each programmer. The programmers use different sets of tools to solve the problem.

The difference in opinion occurs at the team and company level. Some companies feel comfortable with enterprise class commercial tools, while others use a variety of open source tools. XP works with any tools provided that the tool supports continuous integration and automated unit testing.

IDE philosophy

Commercial Integrated Development Environment (IDE) focuses on graphical wizards that help us to automatically generate the code. If you use such tools, make sure that it allows command-line operations so that it can support continuous integration and automated unit testing. If you are using graphical wizards you will be unable to automate your processes. XDoclet is an alternative to wizard based code generation that does not lock you into a particular vendor's product.

You can use free tools to build your own development environment and support XP practices. The commercial development environments provide support for the open source tool. IDEs such as Eclipse and Netbeans that are growing in popularity and functionality are available free of cost.

Tool requirements

XP works efficiently when your tool selection supports continuous integration and automated unit testing. Let us now discuss the three concepts–automation, regression testing and consistency among developers.

Automation

XP requires automation. In an XP project, programmers work on code from any given part of the application and constantly pair with one another. The system is coded in small steps, with many builds occurring each day. The programmers cannot be successful if they need to remember the series of steps to compile, deploy and test different parts of the application.

The "one-button testing" in XP means that you compile, deploy and run all the tests when you click a single button or type a single command. Automation is applied to repetitive coding tasks. It reduces the chances of human error and makes coding more enjoyable.

Regression testing

Automated testing is the building block that makes XP possible. The automated build process is coupled with unit testing. Each new feature in XP is implemented along with complementary unit test. When a bug is identified, a test is written to depict the bug before the bug is fixed. The test passes after the bug is fixed.

Tools make it easy for the programmers to write and run tests. You can make use of JUnit to write basic unit tests and more specialized testing for Web applications and other types of codes. IDEs make it easy to run JUnit tests by clicking on a menu and selecting "run tests".

Consistency among developers

In XP environment, developers always make some changes and work with new programming partners and make changes to the code throughout the system. The tools enable the developers to build their personal environment identical to other team member's environment. For example, if someone types 'ant junit' and all tests run successfully, then the others also expect the same when they type the command on their system.

Many IDEs do not support consistent configuration across a team of developers. The developers have to build their own personal project file. It is difficult to ensure that two persons in a team use the same version of the files for a project. One may use the older version while the other may use the newer version.

There are a few tools you need to implement XP. There is always a bit of learning curve. But, only a few tools are needed in the beginning. To make your software efficient, you need to implement document authoring and design tools. Working with XP is very simple and it applies to design, code, process, and tools.

Simple tools offer lots of power and capability in exchange for non-trivial learning curve. Assume that you want to work with Java language. The tools you use for your projects are:

- Eclipse for team-friendly development environment
- Source code control tool
- JUnit for customer tests and programmer tests
- HttpUnit for testing Web applications
- Ant for building everyday applications
- Shams for stubbing unbuilt components

> **Activity 1:**
>
> Assume that you are working in a software project and you are using XP. The project is related to updating the cash flow financial systems in use by your organization. The project has a tight budget and critical deadlines. The project involves the addition of a new set of features to two modules. You also have to fix the problems with the existing codebase. What are the tools you would suggest for the development using XP methodology?

25.4 OPEN SOURCE TOOLKIT

Although open source tools have been available for some time, they did not always enjoy wide-spread acceptance within the corporate environment. Now many new tools are becoming increasingly powerful and popular. By using open source tools, you can achieve the same end result without investing more money in tools. Let us now discuss some of the tools of open source toolkit.

Version control

Version control tools are essential building blocks of any software development projects. Concurrent Version System (CVS) is the most popular version control system. CVS keeps a master copy of each file on a server known as repository. The repository has a history of all the files. You can view history of changes, recover previous revisions of files and mark particular revisions with tag names. The files can be maintained in a predictable and repeatable way by using tools like CVS.

The copy of the entire code is available for the programmers on their computer and they can make changes without affecting other programmers. The programmers commit the modified files to the CVS repository after the current task is completed. The revised files are visible to other programmers and they can choose to update to the new versions when they are ready.

Working in small steps is a necessity because XP requires pair programming. If you work on a task that takes several days to complete, then you cannot switch your programming partners several times. A key to XP success is completing a task within a few hours by breaking the project into smaller tasks. Working in small steps also helps when using CVS because your personal workspace is always synchronized with the repository.

Multiple programmers may work on a team on the same files concurrently with CVS. So you have to merge changes and resolve conflicts before committing your modified code to repository. The conflicts can be minimized by performing frequent updates. The likelihood of conflict increases with work done by other team members if the programmer does not get the code for days and weeks at a time.

CVS allows concurrent edits to the same files but other version control programs force programmers to lock files before making changes. While exclusive locking seems safer than concurrent editing, it can impede development if other team members are unable to make changes. When working with locking version control tools, working in small steps is the best way to avoid problems. The likelihood of lock connection is reduced if each programmer locks only few files at a time.

Ant

Ant uses an XML build file named 'build.xml'. Ant controls all aspects of the software build process and guarantees that all developers have a common baseline environment.

All programmers in the team share a code in the XP model. Programmers constantly shuffle and work in pairs. In order to finish the task, the programmer is allowed to work on any piece of the code in the application. Shared code makes people to swap programming partners and spreads knowledge.

Ant is important to XP because you cannot afford to have each developer compiling different parts of the system using different system configurations. The code compiles for one team member, but fails to compile for others in individual classpath settings. This problem is eliminated by Ant as it defines a consistent build environment for all developers.

Ant buildfiles consist of targets and tasks. The target defines how developers use the buildfile and the tasks define how the actual work is performed. Table 25.1 describes the Ant buildfile targets and description.

Table 25.1 Ant Buildfile Targets

Targets	Description
Prepare	Creates the output directories which will contain the generated .class files.
Compile	Compiles all Java source codes into executable.
Clean	Removes the build directory and all generated files.
JUnit	Searches for all unit tests in the directory structure and runs them.

The Ant buildfile should define its own classpath internally. The Ant buildfile should be added to the version control tool and you have to write few simple classes to confirm that it runs successfully. The other developers make use of the Ant buildfile from the version control repository.

JUnit

The most important facet of XP is automated testing. JUnit tests are designed to test individual modules and are written by programmers. They must be designed to execute without human interaction. JUnit is not well suited for all types of testing. It is used for writing unit tests in Java. The TestCase base class is extended by the programmers and they write individual unit tests following a simple naming convention. These tests are organized into test suites and executed using a text or graphical test runner.

JUnit can be easily extended and is a simple framework for writing tests. For a number of testing tools, JUnit is the starting point. The tools are more powerful when everyone in the team use them consistently. There are some steps for adding new features to your application. They are:

- Update the PC with the latest source files from CVS repository. This reduces the chance of conflict.
- JUnit is used to write unit test. Write a test to expose the bug you are trying to fix.
- Run the test using JUnit and Ant typing 'ant junit'. The JUnit Ant target is defined on the compile target, so all code is automatically combined.
- If the test fails, write some code to make the test pass.
- Type 'ant junit' to run the test again. Repeat steps 2-5 until the entire test is successful.
- CVS update is performed to ensure that you are updated with all recent changes.
- In order to perform a full build, run ant clean junit.
- Commit changes to CVS and move to next task if all code is complied and all test passes.

Every developer must follow these steps because they use XP and practice pair programming. Each of the team members is allowed to make changes to any part of the code. Developers rely on automated unit tests along with a consistent build environment to immediately find errors because they are constantly updating shared code base.

HttpUnit and Cactus

HttpUnit is a tool used for testing Web applications. HttpUnit tests execute only on a client machine and send HTTP requests to access the Web server. In this way HttpUnit simulates a Web browser hitting a Website. You use JUnit when working with HttpUnit, but the tests you write are considered as functional tests. The reason is HttpUnit can only test Web applications, instead of unit testing individual classes and methods.

Cactus is closely related to HttpUnit. Cactus is built on top of JUnit and it is more complicated than HttpUnit. True unit testing for Web applications is performed by Cactus tests. Cactus tests simultaneously execute on both client and server. The client portion of the test issues requests to the server portion. The client portion acts like a Web browser and the server portion acts like a unit test. The client interprets the result received from the server. For parsing the HTML output from Web applications, Cactus can make use of the HttpUnit library.

JUnitPerf

A performance testing tool built on top of JUnit is the JUnitPerf. JUnitPerf ensures that the tests run within predefined performance limits. It does not help you to find performance problems. JUnitPerf is used to complement commercial profiling tools. A profiling tool is used to isolate performance bottlenecks in your code. JUnit test is written to ensure that the code runs within acceptable time limits after fixing the bottlenecks. If someone changes the code, the JUnitPerf test will fail. You have to go back to the profiling tool to find out the cause of the problem.

Application servers

The two open source server tools are JBoss and Tomcat. JBoss is a free application server and Tomcat is a servlet. JBoss and Tomcat are configured to support automated testing and continuous integration. When working with an application server, a command like ant junit will perform the following:

- Compile all codes
- Build a Web Archive (WAR) file
- Start Tomcat if it is not running
- Deploy new WAR file
- Run all unit tests
- Display summary of test results

Setting up a build server

You will probably create a build server at some point. It is a shared machine that performs a clean build of the software on a continuous basis. The build server checks that your application compiles and runs the entire test. If you are using CVS and Ant, it is very easy to set up the build server. The build server operates like a developer's Personal Computer (PC) most of the time. The build server gets a copy of the code, builds the application, and runs the test suite at regular intervals throughout the day.

Overtime, you may want to make the build server more sophisticated. For instance, the build server is used to monitor the changes in the CVS repository. The build should wait for a short period of inactivity and it can start after some files have been changed. During the inactive period, the server can get copy of sources using timestamp. While the programmers are committing changes to the repository the build servers will not get any code.

Whenever the build succeeds or fails, you must maintain a change log to notify the correct developers. The change log is used to notify people who actually made changes.

25.5 SUMMARY

Let us recapitulate the important concepts discussed in this unit:

- XP tools optimize the performance of your computer and help you to customize your system.
- XP includes a set of principles and practices that guide software development. It is a language-independent software development approach. It mainly focuses on coding.
- Java is a good choice for XP development because Java's wealth of tools that support unit testing and continuous integration. A lightweight framework for writing automated unit tests is provided by JUnit.
- Continuous integration means the complete copy of the system is built several times in a day. This ensures that the system is ready to move out at any moment.
- The integral part of a continuously integrated system is unit testing. The build is complete only when the unit tests pass the entire functional and integration tests successfully.
- Commercial Integrated Development Environment (IDE) focuses on graphical wizards that help us to generate codes automatically. If you use such a tool, make

sure that it allows command-line operations so that it can support continuous integration and automated unit testing.

- Tools make it easy for the programmers to write and run tests. You can make use of JUnit to write basic unit tests and more specialized tests for Web applications and other types of codes.
- Version control tools are essential building blocks of any software development project. Concurrent Version System (CVS) is the most popular version control system.
- CVS allows concurrent edits to the same files but other version control tools force programmers to lock files before making changes. While exclusive locking seems safer than concurrent editing, it can impede development if other team members are unable to make changes.
- Ant uses XML buildfile named build.xml. Ant controls all aspects of the software build process and guarantees that all developers have a common baseline environment.
- HttpUnit is a tool used for testing Web applications. HttpUnit tests execute only on client machine and send HTTP requests to access Web server.
- A performance testing tool built on top of JUnit is the JUnitPerf. JUnitPerf ensures that tests run within predefined performance limits. It does not help you to find performance problems.
- The two open source server tools are JBoss and Tomcat. JBoss is a free application server and Tomcat is a servlet. JBoss and Tomcat are configured to support automated testing and continuous integration.

25.6 GLOSSARY

Graphical test runner: It is typically a desktop application or part of an IDE.

Servlet: A Java programming language class used to extend the capabilities of servers that host application access through a request-response programming model.

Web application: An application that is accessed over a network such as Internet or intranet.

Web browser: A software application for retrieving, presenting, and traversing information resources on the World Wide Web.